DOUBLE ENTENDRE

The Parallel Lives of Mae West and Rae Bourbon

Patrick C. Byrne
Edited by David W. Jackson

Double Entendre: The Parallel Lives of Mae West and Rae Bourbon

Double Entendre: The Parallel Lives of Mae West and Rae Bourbon
Copyright © 2017 Patrick C. Byrne.

All rights reserved. No part of this book may be reproduced in any form or by any electronic or mechanical means including information storage and retrieval systems without permission in writing from the author, except by a reviewer who may quote brief passages in review. All images courtesy the author's private collection, which is intended to be donated to the Gay and Lesbian Archive of Mid-America (GLAMA). For details, visit glama.us.

Byrne, Patrick C. (1942-); and Jackson, David W. (1969-)
Double Entendre: The Parallel Lives of Mae West and Rae Bourbon
Includes bibliographic references, illustrations and index.

Published in the USA by:
BearManor Media
P O Box 71426
Albany, Georgia 31708
www.bearmanormedia.com

ISBN: 978-1-62933-157-7
BearManor Media, Albany, Georgia
Printed in the United States of America
Book design by Robbie Adkins, www.adkinsconsult.com

1. West, Mae. 2. Bourbon, Rae. 3. Motion picture actors and actresses--United States--Biography. 4. Entertainers--United States--Biography. 5. Vaudeville--United States--20th century. 6. Motion picture actors and actresses--United States--Biography. 7. Humorous songs. 8. Female impersonators--Songs and music. 9. Gay wit and humor. 10. Bawdy songs--United States. 11. Gender identity. I. Byrne, Patrick C. (1942-). II. Jackson, David W. (1969-). III. Title.

Table of Contents

Dedication..v
Acknowledgments vii
What's in a Name? ix
Introduction xi
1 Out of the Mouths of Babes 1
2 A Dame of Drag..7
3 The Queen of Sex..13
4 Rehearsal..19
5 Blurring the Boundary.................................25
6 Very Loud, Very Fast, and All Together.......37
7 Making Explicit What Used to be Implied... 45
8 Lights, Camera..53
9 Touring the Sticks 67
10 Up the Ladder, Wrong by Wrong 73
11 Only Pansies Know How............................79
12 Grab a Dyke, It's a Raid: The Law, the Latin Lover, La-La Land . 83
13 East is East, West is West........................125
Gallery of Photographs...............................147
14 Cut, Don't Print That!...............................187
15 Command Performance, Controversy, Cabaret 227
16 I've Been Famous Wicked Women Before; I Can Be 259
    the Woman I've Always Wanted to Be
17 Taking *IT* on Tour 303
18 I Damn Well Need the Dough!..................315
19 You've Gotta Hold on to Fame 343
Appendix A: Rae and Mae Comment on Longevity, ...353
    Show Business, and Life
Appendix B: Films and Plays of Mae West 355
Appendix C: Films of Ray/Rae Bourbon 357
Appendix D: Sound Recordings of Ray/Rae Bourbon........359
Appendix E: Cookin' With Mae and Rae.......367
Bibliography..371
About the Author...373
About the Editor..373
Index..374

Dedication

This is dedicated to Ray Bourbon, the "Dame of Drag," whose uncouth music hall dame, brash and blowsy, delivered truth and reality couched in crude comedy. The "Queen of Sex," Mae West, was an important muse to Ray. Her brazen, self-assured sexuality, closer to comedy than lust, became both script and pattern for a host of impersonators, including the inimitable Ray Bourbon.

Acknowledgments

My deepest gratitude to everyone involved in the creation of this book: David W. Jackson, always there with an idea for improvement and an unfailing eye for detail; the unique Randy Riddle library of Ray/Rae Bourbon material; Steve Puckett and Steve Harris, owners of Steves' Market and Deli in Brownwood, Texas, for keeping Rae's memory alive... and on their menu; David Menefee, who knows how to crack the whip of correction without inflicting damage; and Ray himself, who awakened me to that most ancient theatrical art, female impersonation.

What's in a Name?

The spelling of Ray Bourbon's first name is a conundrum "wrapped in a mystery inside an enigma," to paraphrase a quotation of Winston Churchill. "But perhaps there is a key."

He vacillated between Ray and Rae for the better part of his adult life. The media, the acting craft, and the impersonation community spelled his name both ways. It is impossible to ascertain a distinct timeline when one spelling was used over another. He used both interchangeably.

He was asked repeatedly about his alleged and well-publicized sex reassignment. Once, he answered, "Some background to the stories circulating about my 'change' may be in order. When asked by friends about my new existence, I hardly know where to begin . . . ." His answer had nothing to do with his gender identity, gender expression, or sex.

When asked about the difference between the spellings, he said in one interview, "They are both simply names . . . Ray was my given name and one I used for many years . . . Rae is really my stage name." Still, there is evidence that both he and the industry applied either without any steadfast rule.

To clarify, he was asked, "Do you mean the Rae character, or the person Ray?"

"It is complex, the Ray is the person you are interviewing now, the Rae is the name that makes my living. Rae doesn't really exist . . . if so I might be committed to a mental hospital . . . What I do onstage, to make people laugh, is not the person you would see in private life. My stage persona is a joke. So many critics cannot seem to get past the gowns, wigs, and makeup."

Our hope is that readers, too, may "get past the gowns, wigs, and makeup."

We also invite you to be open-minded and compassionate as you follow the lifelong struggle for success, acceptance, and accolade, of two long-time friends, who also happen, as it turns out, to be two of our nation's treasures. One, iconic the world over, Mae West; the other, in and out of fame and popular in a certain era and in selected markets like Kansas City, the performer and renowned female impersonator sometimes known as Rae Bourbon.

Don't be confused or fooled by a name, or how it "mae" be spelled.

David W. Jackson
May 2017

Introduction

"Mae West is a man!" This was something I often heard in the early 1960s. Some still hold to that bizarre notion. The autopsy of the octogenarian film and stage icon in 1980 seemed to dispel the rumor, at least at that time.

From an early age, I was totally in the thrall of this contradictory comedienne, as was my Irish immigrant father. My father's mother, Mary Morgan, had danced in the music hall in Dublin before World War I. His tales of the discord that Grandma's theatrical career spread among his conservative relatives piqued my curiosity about women on the stage.

When he later described to me the impact Mae West had made on him during the Great Depression, I wanted to see for myself just what all the excitement was about. Unfortunately, there was no way for me in the very early 1950s to experience Mae on a movie screen. She had not appeared in a film since the ill-fated, *The Heat's On* (1943), one year after I was born. Television was in its infancy. Needless to say, there were no VHS, DVD, or DVR players.

The best examples I remember of the magic of Mae were my dad's stories. My father was a superb mimic, easily recreating the voices of Mae and W. C. Fields. While my friends were daffy over cartoon ducks and mice, I wanted more than anything to see this woman who invited men to "Come on up."

Television finally gave me the opportunity to witness the sensation that was Mae West. As the numbers of channels expanded, late night movies began to fill the hours after midnight. Mae could be frequently seen in glorious black-and-white, sashaying across the screen, seductively tossing out delicious dialogue tidbits like, "When I am good, I am very good; but, when I am bad, I'm better."

Playing up her image as a sexual predator, she would run her eyes up and down a man's body, sampling his bulging biceps as she purred, "A thrill a day keeps the chill away."

Her often garish style, honking Brooklyn accent, and self-written dialogue titillated millions of moviegoers and horrified the pious across the country. In fact, her films were so successful during the Great Depression of the 1930s, she is credited with saving the failing fortunes of Paramount Publix Corporation.

Unfortunately, her ribald humor and casual treatment of the male sex often fell victim to the onerous Motion Picture Producers and Distributors of America (MPPDA) and their Production Code, headed by their President, Will B. Hays. Despite their best efforts, Mae frequently got around their strict film standards with cleverly-written double entendres.

During my late teen years in the 1960s, when I was first captured by Mae West, I was just beginning my education as a cosmetologist. The idea of me following this profession upset my father. Having come to America with $50 in his only pair of pants, and the vague promise of job in a bakery, he placed great value on higher education and the opportunities that the resultant parchment promised. Sheer sweat and gritty determination were his only tools, along with a glib personality and an eye on the prize. Ultimately, he became master of his destiny. A place in business—any business—was what he was sure I must have.

Nothing could have interested me less. I had a vague idea of my life's role, something that involved art, glamour, and the opportunity to meet a cross-section of humanity. Cosmetology school seemed to promise all of this, at least in their glitzy brochures I collected in the search for my niche.

To me, it seemed the logical answer for a newly "out" gay man, who had tried the traditional venues of private school and Catholic college, with their narrow outlooks. This certainly included the gay lifestyle, and all that it encompassed.

In close proximity to my family home in Kansas City, Missouri, was a certain hair academy, attractive for a pay-as-you-go plan, excellent facilities, and instructors, and a loose attendance code for those who had to work nights or Saturdays. There was also the knowledge that many of the male students were of my same persuasion, which would allow me to relax and be myself, rather than pretending I was an eternal altar boy.

I quickly gained several fine friends, who would remain such for a good period of my life. My new circle of "hair fairies" soon introduced me to a district of our city that housed several gay bars and night clubs. Troost Avenue was the perfect entertainment strip. Like a faded, jaded old hooker, it promised an exciting and affordable night on the town.

Kansas City's notorious Troost Avenue, running between 31st Street and Armour Boulevard, was breathing a last gasp in the 1960s. These five blocks contained a diverse and colorful collection of businesses and clubs. On the South end was a rundown movie house, a faded relic of the Art Deco period. Across the street was a complex of apartments that contained a dimly lit strip joint. Its main feature was a revolving bar, where the inebriated could ogle the dubious charms of a chorus of small-time strippers.

Daytime along the Avenue was filled with ordinary citizens going about their business. As the day dimmed and the street lamps came on, another sort of citizenry stepped out of the shadows. This was a seedy mix of streetwalkers, pimps, and junkies. The most colorful component of those that plied their trade on the corners and dark alleyways were the "street queens," or transvestites. These tough and tacky cross-dressers often competed with prostitutes for a "John." The dangers involved in this profession often ended in violence, or worse.

Running to the North along Troost Avenue was a hodgepodge of greasy diners, barbeque vendors, and several gay bars.

Interspersed were a few straight watering holes. Outstanding among these was the Golden Horseshoe. This was a stylish jazz club, which managed to attract an equally stylish clientele. Their regular roster of famous jazz artists included the legendary Betty and Milt Abel. They were world-class artists with a devoted following. The Horseshoe also managed to keep out the less desirable denizens of the street with a hefty cover charge. Weekends at the Golden Horseshoe were very popular with the sheltered suburbanites, who imagined they were being more than a little daring by even patronizing such a risqué neighborhood. This certainly wasn't a place they would talk about at the church social.

Emboldened by a parade of cocktails during the two-hour Golden Horseshoe show, a large portion of the patrons would pay their bill and head out the door. Rather than seeking the safety of their giant Continentals and Cadillacs parked along the Avenue, they would turn right, nervously quickening their steps in the direction of another entertainment venue. Their destination was a notorious night club where, "Anything goes," or, so they had heard.

Their destination was the notorious Jewel Box Lounge, housed in an unremarkable two-story brick building. The bland façade had been altered over the decades. The once businesslike structure now featured a giant marquee flashing the club name in neon lights. The outside walls had been inlaid with 1940-style glass bricks. On either side of the entrance were large black-and-white photographs of the club's entertainers, opulently gowned singers and dancers posing coquettishly and swathed in feathers and furs.

As the parade of the Golden Horseshoe patrons passed through the red, leather-padded, double doors of the Jewel Box, they entered a totally alien world. On the right of the show room ran a long, curving bar lined with ornate mirrors. Dimly reflected in these were the images of what appeared to be a number of dramatically coiffed, over made-up women. To the left of the bar were twenty round tables grouped together facing a large stage that was surmounted by a gold proscenium. In the orchestra pit sat a battered upright piano that proudly wore the scars of decades of cigarette burns and spilled cocktails, and a nondescript drum set.

A rotund man in a shiny sharkskin suit effusively greeted the customers and guided them to their seats. This was the last show of the night, the "red hot" midnight show. The match books on each table promised "K.C.'s Most Unusual Show." At a given signal—an arpeggio on the slightly out-of-tune piano—the glamorous group that lined the south wall slid off the battered bar stools and filed to the dressing rooms behind the stage.

One mid-week evening, my fellow schoolmates decided we should take in this famous drag club, a place known more as a "straight" club, where the heterosexuals could safely jeer and cheer the drag queens from a comfortable distance. We combined our meager tips for the day with what our perpetually empty pockets held and boarded the bus for the thirty-minute trip down Troost Avenue.

As always, we were hungry, and, as always, we were broke. With an hour remaining before the show began, we decided to split an order of soggy fries and a large scorched burger from the barbeque joint, Bob's Meat Market, opposite the Jewel Box. Everyone dug deep in their pockets to scrape up the tab. Our remaining funds were combined on the faded Formica table, with just enough left over to buy one drink each at the club. It was a week night, and the cover charge rule applied only to the weekend shows.

We nursed our soft drinks until it was almost time for the drag revue to begin, ignoring the brusque remarks from the frazzled haired waitress, who kept returning to our table in an effort to empty our booth.

Fifteen minutes before show time, we crossed the busy Avenue, dodging the traffic and giving the finger in response to an insult hurled from a passing car. Apparently we looked like what we were, a gaggle of giddy queens hell-bent for an evening of fun. For us, it was the, "Swinging 60s," and life could not have been better. We burst through the doors as if we owned the place, enjoying the startled stares of the mostly heterosexual crowd.

A member of our group, Jaimie F., had a romantic connection with one of the bartenders and inveigled a table in front for our party; but, not before making a noisy scene for the benefit of the gaping tourists. Always vying for attention, this very vocal flamer relished any chance for a confrontation. When it looked like Jaimie might incite an ugly response from one of the men seated at a nearby table, we managed to quickly drag him away.

The watered down drinks arrived and the house lights dimmed. What I was about to see that evening would forever transform my thinking about the art of female impersonation.

The clattery piano accompanied by a long drum roll momentarily hushed the audience. A short, stocky, red head parted the curtains. A voice somewhere between a frog and a tenor welcomed, "All you mothers to the world famous Jewel Box."

Many years later, I would have my memory jolted, when I recognized this same dizzy drag, Mr. Butch Ellis, in the Academy Award nominated film, *The Rose* (1979). His appearance in this Bette Midler movie was brief. Butch played the greeter at a colorful drag bar; but, his personality came across as strongly as I had remembered him from years before. Butch was aptly named, as he possessed the compact and muscular frame of a wrestler. His manner was abrupt, and his walk left little doubt as to his gender.

A well-oiled heckler greeted Butch's entrance with a slurred insult, only to be shot down with, "Honey, I'm twice the man you'll ever be, and more woman than you could hope to handle." As the thoroughly embarrassed heckler slid lower in his seat, Butch flipped the hem of his sparkly, red cocktail dress, kicked-up his six-inch-heel, and invited everyone to enjoy the show.

First to step from behind the slightly tattered gold curtain was a tiny Oriental. This petit drag appeared to be a mini turquoise tornado, swirling in endless yards of chiffon. At first, all that was visible were two very gracefully jeweled hands. A credible striptease followed, as layers of fabric floated to the floor. Underneath was a wasp waist and shapely legs. The kicker was a glittering g-string that showed no signs of male genitals beneath. Finally, the dancer turned defiantly toward the rear of the stage, dropping the g-string, as the drummer pounded out a staccato beat. As the last veil dropped, the dancer revealed a tight female bottom. Turning quickly around, with a hand deftly covering the pubic area, the stripper took a deep bow.

Conversations overheard from the surrounding tables hotly debated the performer's gender. The program listed a "Mr. Salome."

As the night progressed, so did the intensity of the crowd's reaction, particularly that of the men. They were unbelieving at first that any member of their own sex could appear so sexy and desirable. The removal of a wig, or the discovery of a hairy chest, when just before there had been what appeared to be a bountiful bosom, quickly deflated their fantasy of a luscious woman. It also presented a threat to a less than secure male.

Act followed act. Some were beautiful and only slighted talented, some marginally attractive but gifted. There was the stunning brunette, Mr. Terry Lee, a dead ringer for the then popular film siren, Gina Lollobrigida.

Just prior to the star of the show was a remarkable operatic voice, Mr. Carrie Davis, who sang in a shimmering falsetto soprano. The applause for Carrie was interrupted with a loud drum-roll and a sweeping piano arpeggio accompanying the voice of the mistress of ceremonies: "Ladies and gentlemen, the Jewel Box proudly announces the world-renowned Mr. Rae Bourbon."

From the wings swayed a tall, buxom, and somewhat elderly vision in a long, silver gown, dragging a rather moth-eaten white fox stole in one hand and a bar stool in the other. Clamped in what were obviously ill-fitting and impossibly white false teeth, was a long rhinestone cigarette holder. Large droopy ear lobes were adorned with the longest chandelier earrings I had ever seen. Framing a pleasant but well-worn face was a carefully waved and curled silver wig that matched the color of the gown. I suddenly realized that the hair was a dead ringer for the style that Mae West favored in so many of her films, a retro "do" from the 1930s.

The makeup, too, resembled something from a bygone era: a gash of Chinese red lipstick fully outlining pendulous lips; carefully drawn eyebrows that bore no resemblance to anything human; and, eyelashes that were so long they touched the upper reaches of the penciled brows. All of this maquillage spoke of a vision of feminine glamour that was now only a faded memory.

Nothing prepared me for the voice, a startling baritone at the bottom, a nasal buzz in the middle, and a flapping soprano at the top. All of this was punctuated with a laugh best described as a chicken's cackle. I can't help but think that Phyllis Diller must have seen Ray Bourbon at some point in her career.

This unique vision carefully sat on the high stool, crossed a somewhat shapely leg, and launched into a non-stop dialogue. The audience was soon eating out of the palms of those long, silver, satin evening gloves, the kind designed to camouflage a flabby arm.

Ray regaled the audience for half-an-hour with tales of arrest by the vice squad in Chicago for impersonating a woman; hiding inside a church organ during a gay wedding; and, hilarious vignettes of the time he entertained the Duke and the Duchess of Windsor at Fort Belvedere, Surrey, England.

Barely bolstered by the watery gin martini I had nursed through the hour-long show, I finally summoned the courage to approach Ray as he returned to the club's smoky bar following his well-received act. The room was now nearly empty, as I nervously straddled the bar stool next to him.

I began the conversation by asking for his autograph on a cocktail napkin, and then lapsed into silence. I could tell he was wondering what this skinny young queen was up to. The one thought in my slightly gin-flavored brain was how much he reminded me of Mae West. Thoughts became words, as I spilled out my fascination for this legend from another era. To my utter surprise, he informed me he knew Mae, had worked with her, and they were, indeed, very good friends. That was all I needed.

During the months that followed, I returned many times to the Jewel Box, always making sure the bartender sent Ray a drink onstage. If none were forthcoming, he'd signal for the pianist to stop.

"Send mother another teeny one," he'd growl in the direction of the bar. The libation would quickly arrive with the tiny flame-haired waitress, who would stand on tip toe as Bourbon reached down from the stage's edge. He'd stir it with a well-manicured finger and hammer it back in one silent slurp. Licking his digit, he would hand back the glass and continue, "God, I needed that! What a bitch of a day I had," and he'd spin out another hilarious tale of his misadventures at the then chic cocktail lounge of Kansas City's Hotel Muehlebach. Much of it was raunchy fantasy, such as bending over to straighten his garter, which resulted in his Tampax® shooting a patron in the eye. Some of it was truth-based, such as his brief incarceration for propositioning the wrong man, an undercover vice cop. He had moments during his monologue when he veered very close to self-awareness.

"I suppose I have always been rather odd to look at, from a beauty expert's point of view, but, then, cosmetic queen, Helena Rubenstein, was no prize. I have a sort of untidy elegance like a tall thin bird. Helena, on the other hand, looks like an old squaw that was left in the sun too long."

If Ray was really in his cups, he might coyly confess to cruising around the bus station in his ancient convertible. The story always ended with a graphic and boisterous description of a tryst with some hustler, told so cleverly that it hid the inherent danger of this behavior. At the time, I could not have guessed the catastrophic consequences that this foolhardy habit would bring to the aged and defenseless entertainer.

All I knew then was I was hooked on the strange and outrageous pictures Ray painted of his long career as a comedian, chorus boy, drag artist, movie extra, and finally, a stage actor. In particular, I never tired of the tales of his work with Mae West. None of this came in any sort of order, and at times seemed to contradict a previous story. No doubt, the doubles of straight vodka fueled some of the mix.

What follows are my memories of these tales, and my efforts to fill-in the sometimes-glaring gaps with as much research as possible.

Ray, I later learned, was renowned for his colorful depictions of his life as he wanted everyone to see it. The picture I hope to convey is painted with recollections, both personal and re-counted, from many sources within the wonderful world of impersonators, those unique artists who take on the difficult challenge of portraying the opposite sex.

Patrick Byrne
May 2016

Out of the Mouths of Babes

August 17, 1893, dawned as a sultry morning in what had already been a sweltering week in Bushwick, New York. This residential section of the North Brooklyn borough was an average middle-class neighborhood. The avenues were wide, lined with neat tree shaded homes. Children played in the streets, dodging the occasional horse-drawn rig. The automobile was still a bit of a rarity. The sidewalks were swept daily, and small gardens blossomed with the care of work worn hands. Most of the residents embodied the strict German work ethic, tidy and tireless, carried from the old country.

Inside one of these modest but well-tended two-story brick homes, there was an unusual amount of activity. Already the temperature inside was rapidly climbing. By mid-morning, all the windows and doors had been thrown open in an attempt to bring some relief to a stifling upstairs bedroom. Up and down the narrow staircase was a steady stream of women in long dresses and starched aprons. They carried basins of cold water and muslin cloths to soothe the sweaty brow of the occupant of the first room at the top of the landing. In addition there were icy pitchers of water and tea offered, but the object of this care was having none of it.

Propped up on mounds of snow-white pillows was a very pregnant and very nervous Matilda West. "Tillie," as she was known to most of her friends, was the center of all this attention.

The midwife clucked and nodded, hustling the room full of neighbors and family out to allow the mother to-be a moment of rest. This portly, pleasant woman with a visage like a Hummel figurine was convinced the blessed arrival was due at any moment.

Matilda West was a handsome and full-figured young woman of twenty-three. She had abundant honey-colored hair, blue eyes, and that bisque complexion peculiar to those from Bavaria, her birthplace.

At sixteen, she had made the long and arduous voyage to America, along with her parents, three sisters, and two brothers. Her family had settled in Brooklyn. Brooklyn was the home of her cousin, Peter Doegler, a prosperous brewery owner, who opened the doors of opportunity to Matilda's father. In a short time, Matilda's family, too, enjoyed the comforts of the middle-class.

Matilda thought of those earlier years, as she waited for the arrival of her child. She had been very pretty and popular, and quite headstrong—so headstrong that she had defied her conservative parents and chosen to love and marry a man they felt was beneath her.

Jack West had easily won romantic Tillie's heart. He was a muscular and ruggedly handsome fellow. His father was from Newfoundland and his mother an Irish immigrant. His tough roots gave him a chip on the shoulder and a lightning-fast temper. Bouts of heavy drinking inevitably led to wild scraps in the local pubs, ending with triumphant Jack standing over his recumbent challenger.

In those days, boxing was an extremely popular sport, and none were better at it than "Battling Jack West." He never turned down a wager to test his pugilistic skills, and frequently returned home with a wad of cash in his pockets. All this came to an end after Tillie agreed to become Mrs. Jack West. He would have to settle down and provide a steady income. No more fighting, for he was soon to become a father. He agreed, hoping he would have a boy to teach the art of boxing.

Jack's hoped for son turned out to be a beautiful daughter. Tragedy struck soon after, carrying away the infant during an influenza epidemic. Tillie sadly remembered that Jack quickly returned to his old habits.

His dreams of success in business took him from one scheme to another: a stable of horses for hire, real estate, and finally a detective agency. All of this was made more difficult by Jack's return to drinking. Still mourning the death of that tiny daughter, Tillie was particularly anxious about her present condition. Perhaps another child could tame some of Jack's demons.

Late that night, the temperature outside began to drop. Through the fluttering lace curtains, Tillie could see the street lamps down the avenue come on one by one. Within hours, she would deliver a tow-headed and decidedly vocal baby girl.

The parents had decided, if the child was female, to name her Mary Jane West. Somehow this girl child would not answer to Mary Jane as she grew from childhood. Mae was an appellation that was to stick to her early on.

Mary Jane brings to mind sweetness, curls, and patent leather shoes, something that Mae West was never accused of, not even as a child.

Exactly one year earlier, on another hot August morning in Hudspeth County, Texas, a chubby baby boy had entered the world.

This was a far less safe and gentle world than Bushwick, New York. Hudspeth was a desolate and hard place, where homesteaders fought dust, drought, and debilitating heat.

This was a place through which travelers quickly passed on the way to another destination. That isn't to say there wasn't a rugged sort of beauty to the region. Mountains on the horizon and stands of Yucca could make a memorable impression on the occasional visitor. Locals liked to brag that they had a "forest of Yucca" nearby. It was a standing joke in those parts of West Texas that five or more trees-per-acre qualified as a forest. Visitors seldom lingered very long.

One visitor did linger that year for a few months. This was a mysterious and beautiful visitor, a dark-skinned young woman with black eyes, and an equally dark past. She was rumored to be of Mediterranean descent, possibly a Spaniard. Her sudden appearance in the tiny town of Sierra Blanca sparked a flurry of rumors.

Wizened old gossips whispered through toothless mouths about the past of this obviously pregnant new resident. She had come without a spouse. It was tattled that she was a recent widow who had fled from France. Others repeated a tale of an innocent convent girl from Paris, seduced by an older man who held a royal title. In the years that followed, a bizarre tale of lineage to the royal House of Bourbon spread among the locals.

What was repeated as certain truth was the tale of a pregnant young girl from of a French convent, cast into the street by the goodly and Christian nuns. They may have fancied themselves "the brides of Christ," but there was certainly no room at the inn for an unmarried girl heavy with child. Without mother or father to turn to for succor, she desperately sought the help of one of her convent mates, a wealthy young nun who had relatives in Texas.

This angel of mercy, defying the strict dictates of the merciless Mother Superior, contacted her distant American cousins. Paying from her own resources, the friend saw to it that her hapless friend, in her final month, could cross the ocean. From there, she would make her way to the home of Mr. and Mrs. Frank Waddell in Sierra Blanca, Hudspeth County, Texas.

The first part of the journey involved a lengthy sea voyage in the belly of a rusty old ocean liner, in steerage class. This was assigned to those with the most meager of resources. Cramped quarters, poor food, and the violent rolling of the ship quickly drained the strength of the mother to be.

The second part of the travel was a three-day train journey across the United States. Sleep was impossible in the hard wooden coach seats. The lack of ventilation turned the train coaches into an oven, and there was little offered in the way of food or drink.

As she stepped off the train, weak and unsteady, it was obvious to the family who had come for her that she was a very sick young woman. Her strength never returned during the remainder of her difficult pregnancy. The intense heat of West Texas and her fragile condition led to her death soon after the successful delivery of her baby.

The concerned and kindly Waddell's were suddenly confronted with a situation that required a decision. The deceased mother had absolutely no relatives or friends that they knew of. The nun who had sent her was not a candidate to accept a bastard child. The plan had been for the Waddell's to take the mother into their employ, possibly as a housekeeper, and they would allow her to raise her child in their household.

Frank Waddell quickly decided to assume the responsibility for the poor orphaned baby boy. Adoption would be the Christian thing to do, and the assumption of the family name would give the child a fresh start in life.

At the baptism, the minister doused the head of the screaming baby clutched in Mr. Waddell's strong arms. Little Ray Waddell had found a home.

Frank Waddell had made something of his life, and was looked up to by many of the locals. By sheer grit, he had managed to forge a comfortable life from the difficult landscape. Cattle and horses had brought him a good living, and he was proud of the large comfortable ranch home he had helped to build with his own hands. It quickly occurred to him that a son would be a great help, extra hands to work and lift, and muscles to swing a rope.

Frank Waddell, rancher, cowboy, and all-around Texas he-man, could not have possibly imagined that the pudgy hands of his new son gripping his sun-burned fingers would one day be used to lift nothing heavier than a mascara wand, or a lipstick tube. Rather than swinging a cattle rope from the back of a galloping steed, Ray Waddell would swing a rope of pearls on stages across the world. He would become known on stage as Rae Bourbon, one of the best-known female impersonators of the twentieth century.

2
A Dame of Drag

Ray's first years as a citizen of Texas remain somewhat clouded, much like the dust storms that bedeviled this part of the Lone Star State.

Sierra Blanca sprang up from the dry Texas soil as a result of the arrival of the Southern Pacific and Texas and Pacific railroads in 1881. Many homesteaders moved to the area around Sierra Blanca only to fight the lack of water, endless dust, and several scarlet fever epidemics. Many were defeated and fled. This was not to be the way of Ray's adoptive father, Frank Waddell. By the time Ray was born, the Waddell's resided in a fine, two-story ranch home, with adjacent cattle acreage, and an impressive herd of horses.

Ray learned from a very early age to ride a horse, and how to care for the animals on the farm. In particular, he lavished attention on a pair of lop-eared hound dogs that stood guard on the porch of the Waddell house. It was here that his lifelong love of all animals was fostered.

He attended the local school, but preferred the freedom of the ranch while galloping across the plains at breakneck speed on a handsome steed. What he didn't like was the work that was part of this lifestyle. Lifting and laboring seemed pointless to him. That was the job of the strong hired hands that slept in the top of the barn and the tiny bunk house.

He was fascinated by these men who drifted in and out of the Waddell's employ. At the end of the day, he sat crossed legged, listening raptly as they spun yarns far too adult for young ears. He never entertained any ideas of being like them, but realized as he got older that he had a strange attraction to their home-spun masculinity.

There were several Mexican workers on the Waddell ranch, who were dark-haired, black-eyed men with compact, muscular bodies.

Ray was captivated with their look and the Spanish language, trying to absorb what he could of the worker's conversations.

Noting the young boy's interest in their language, one of the hands decided to teach Ray a folk song in Spanish. The song was a particularly dirty version of an old bar tune. Ray's parrot-like reproduction of the scurrilous lyrics brought gales of laughter.

In September, the one-room school that Ray attended announced the yearly open house for all the parents. As part of the activities, those children who wished could participate in a school talent program. Ray proudly announced he would perform. His contribution would be a Spanish folk song, accompanied by a dance.

On the day of the event, Ray went hand-in-hand with his parents to the school, carrying a brown paper bag with the costume he had created for his number. A makeshift stage had been erected at the back of building. Ray waited his turn, as a parade of tots performed for their proud parents.

At last, his named was called. He went to the adjacent out house and changed into his costume. The good folk of Sierra Blanca were startled to see a gawky figure emerge from the toilet dressed in one of his mother's pink underskirts, an embroidered towel wrapped around his head. A striped tablecloth served as a shawl. As Ray approached the stage, he sensed the silence of the crowd, until he began to sing. Those in the audience who understood Spanish sat with open mouth. The others only heard a child's voice singing in a pretty language. When it was over, there was a round of applause and several very shocked faces. Unfortunately, Ray's father was fluent in Spanish. He would have been even more disturbed had he realized that his son had unwittingly opened a Pandora's Box.

The applause his son had received for his little performance would act like a narcotic on his impressionable mind. Like the little blonde back in Bushwick, Ray would become hooked on performing.

When Ray was eight-years-old, the untroubled security of his life was shattered by the sudden death of his father. Immediately following Mr. Wadell's funeral, his foster mother noticed a marked change in Ray's behavior. He spent less and less time around the house and wandered off for hours alone. Often, he forlornly followed one of the hired men on his daily tasks. He received failing grades in school and became belligerent when chastised for his poor marks.

After a respectable time of mourning, Elizabeth began to receive the attention of several of the local men. She had been a widow for four years with a considerable dowry, and needed another strong man to help in the running of the ranch. Her eventual marriage to a neighboring rancher, Mr. Hughes, isolated Ray even more from his mother. He did not consider this interloper a father.

Unlike Frank Waddell, a practical man of simple tastes, Elizabeth's new husband liked to attend any and all social events within driving distance. He took pleasure in showing off his pretty wife and the things her inheritance now afforded him. It was during these long evenings alone that Ray discovered a new hobby.

His mother had a number of large trunks in the attic. Rummaging through the contents of a dusty box one evening, he came upon a garment that was unlike any he had ever seen Elizabeth wear. A full-length, crimson-colored dress trimmed in shiny black fringe was the sort of garment women in this part of Texas didn't wear, at least none that Ray had ever seen. Holding the gauzy red dress to his shoulders, he walked to a long antique dressing mirror. He carefully draped it against his tall frame and looked at the image reflected in the dirty glass. He liked what he saw. He had watched folks dance to the fiddle players at local barn dances. Imitating these movements, he slowly began to turn about the room, imagining that he was the center of attention. The sheer gown billowed and shimmered as he twirled.

He didn't realize it, but looking into that cracked mirror was a reflection of his future. One day he would step through the looking glass and into a wonderland not even Alice could ever have imagined.

One searing August afternoon, Mr. and Mrs. Hughes went to town to do some shopping. Rather than return to the safety of the attic, which by now was 20° hotter than the broiling outside, Ray looked around the parlor for something he could use to play his wonderful new dress-up games. Over a battered upright piano in the parlor was draped a vibrant Mexican shawl. On top of the shawl were silver-framed tin type pictures of distant family members.

Ray carefully laid the photographs on the piano bench and began to wrap his hips in the silky yards of the shawl. He soon fashioned a long skirt, which had ample fabric to toss and flip, as he danced an imaginary dance such as he had seen done by the local Mexican laborers.

"Spaniiiiish!" Ray wailed in his high, thin, prepubescent tremolo. Already the budding performer was composing songs. He continued:

> "Now talk of your wild senoritas
> Clavitas, papitas, Lolitas
> I make 'em all look quite gentle
> When I grow sentimental
> I can out Spanish the locals
> I'll banish the yokels
> My nature is so damned temperamental
> Oh Spaniiiiish!
> I'm wicked and wiry
> Spanish
> I'm fickle and fiery
> Pin a tamale or rose on me
> Let some toreador shake his dagger at me . . . ."

Oblivious to the fact that the parlor had several long windows with drawn-back curtains, he continued to stamp his feet at an ever faster pace, clicking his fingers in an imitation of the clattery castanets that accompanied the dance.

The tempo increased and Ray whirled ever faster, until he nearly stumbled into the piano. With a start, he realized that there was someone standing in front of one of the windows, staring at this strange exhibition with a wide, toothy grin. It was the foreman, George, a man that Ray greatly respected and admired. Dropping the shawl, he rushed upstairs and slammed his bedroom door.

Would the foreman report this strange behavior to his mother? Would he tell the other hands of this? For days, Ray refused to have any contact with the workers, and often refused to come down to dinner, provoking the anger of his mother and her husband. Finally, he realized that no person on the ranch gave any hint they knew his secret. Perhaps the foreman had not spread the tale of the strange sight in the parlor.

Timidly, Ray approached the foreman one afternoon, offering to help with a minor task he was doing in the stable. Little conversation ensued, but Ray sensed that somehow his secret was safe. As he would soon learn, so many things in life have a price, and keeping his secret carried a heavy one.

Several days later, lulled into the sense that his secret was safe, Ray was again alone with the foreman. This time, he found himself the object of the man's intense stare. He thought he knew what was coming, but what happened caught him completely off guard.

To his shock, he was drug to the back of the stable and roughly thrown to the floor. Within seconds, his trousers were ripped open and pulled to his knees. A large hand was placed across his mouth as the foreman forced him into a pile of hay. He felt a shattering pain as he became aware that he was being raped by the burly cowboy. Ray lay gasping, his faced buried in the scratchy hay.

This scene would be repeated many times, although never with the violence that had occurred at the onset. Ray began to resist less and less, though no words ever passed between them. George had only to give Ray a certain look and they would meet at day's end in an abandoned storage shed near the windmill.

One afternoon, something occurred there that would change everything. A ranch hand came upon the two of them just as the foreman was pulling his clothing together. An ugly argument turned physical. Blows were exchanged and the foreman was temporarily knocked out. His assailant ran toward the house.

That evening at dinner, Ray sensed that the household was aware of what had happened in the stable. Prepared for the worst, he was surprised nothing was discussed for the next several days. Afraid to inquire as to the whereabouts of the now missing foreman, he later learned that George had been found murdered in a nearby town. He was never to learn the circumstances surrounding his death, but he carried an unshakeable guilt for many years.

This tragic chain of events was the impetus for a dramatic change in the direction of Ray's future. He was now almost thirteen. At the supper table one evening, his mother approached him with an offer to send him abroad to further his education. Elizabeth's husband seemed particularly keen to see that Ray continued his life away from their home. Mr. Hughes had a good friend in London, England, who was a headmaster at a boarding school for problem boys. The school had agreed to accept Ray on a one-year trial basis.

Ray immediately accepted the offer with a barely disguised smile. England, so far away, seemed like a perfect answer... a way to gain some independence and perhaps find a new life. He wasn't sure just what he had in mind, but he knew that frontier life would never again be part of it.

3
The Queen of Sex

Back in Bushwick, twelve eventful years in Mary Jane West's young life had passed since her arrival. Mother Tillie had presented Jack with another daughter, Mildred, and a son, John Edwin. From the time of her birth, Tillie had lavished all her attention on the tow-headed May.

Her marriage had entered a rough period, with her husband going on and off the wagon. In addition to his drinking, Jack West had fallen in with a dangerous crowd of thugs and extortionists. This risky game increased the West bank account considerably, but took him away from home most of the time.

Tillie saw in the beautiful girl child a chance to help mold the future she had once wanted for herself. She had dreamt of being on the stage as a singer or actress. Inspired by the theatrics she had seen in the theatre and Vaudeville, she had approached her parents when she was young, with a hope that they might encourage her ambitions. Her rather straight-laced family made it clear that the stage was not a proper place for a well brought up young lady.

By the time May was entering her pre-teen years, Vaudeville had become more of a family entertainment. Tillie took the child as often as possible to this evening of mixed performances.

Vaudeville at that time consisted of acts as varied as contortionists, trapeze artists, jugglers, trained dogs, seals and birds, roller skating, and comedians of every ethnicity.

The two things that captured baby May's attention were the song and dance acts, in particular the single woman act. These ladies were usually attired in eye-catching gowns that sparkled under the spot lights. They sang torchy songs, some about love and heartbreak, or a comedy song. May noticed that comedy garnered the biggest applause.

After one of these theatre evenings, riding home in the family carriage, May informed her mother that she, too, would be a stage star someday. With a dramatic gesture, she pointed to a theatre marquee and said that someday her name, "Mae" West, would be up there in lights. When Tillie corrected her spelling of her Christian name, the bold child turned an angelic face to her mother and said, "E is up and Y is down." Never in her remarkable life would she admit to a downer.

That was all it took to solidify her mother's ambition to see that her little girl find a place in show business. Upon returning home that evening, Tillie announced to Jack that May was going to be enrolled in dancing and theatrical school the very next day.

True to her word, Tillie enrolled her daughter at The Studio of the Dance, run by Professor Watts. Mae took to his directions with gusto, displaying a maturity far beyond her youth.

May quickly absorbed the Professor's entire curriculum and began to demand more. The harried teacher had given May all the classes he felt appropriate for a student her age. Never satisfied to return home when her lessons were finished, she sat on the sidelines and watched the older girls go through their routines.

Emboldened by her mother's constant praise, May informed the Professor she was ready to join the line-up of older chorines. Despite the teacher's protestations, the precocious student was added to the class the next day.

May continued to attend as much live theatre as possible, finding a gesture or bit of stage business at each performance that she would incorporate into her act. Full of confidence, she informed her mother she was now ready to show the world just what she could do. Tillie saw to it that May was entered in the little shows staged by neighborhood churches and her local social clubs.

This was not enough to satisfy the budding thespian. She knew that the Professor worked with the local Elks Club to stage amateur night contests that followed the regular Vaudeville acts at the Royal Theatre. Her constant pestering of her teacher soon paid off. Baby May would be added to the next Elk's amateur night. Despite her protests, she was encouraged to continue with the infantile "Baby May" stage name. She silently swore to rid herself of that mousey moniker as soon as possible.

At home, May constantly performed her song and dance routine for any and all who would listen. This included her sister, Mildred, who, by now, had become increasingly jealous of all the attention lavished on her precocious sibling.

Later in life, Mildred would adopt the name "Beverly," thinking it more glamorous than her birth name. To add to the child's jealousy was the sad fact she had been born with a club foot. May's brother, John, was her favorite. He enjoyed life in much the same manner as May, and constantly delighted her with bright sayings and decidedly off-color stories.

Tillie, who excelled at sewing, quickly concocted a frothy satin frock in floral colors, festooned with sparkling sequins, that was a perfect ensemble to showcase May's creamy complexion. From her own closet, she contributed a very large lace picture hat, to which she attached a veritable garden of tiny rosebuds and flowers.

May rehearsed in her new costume in front of a full-length mirror. She wanted to judge the effect her finery would have, but soon discovered that the adult hat, far too large for her child's head, wobbled about as she gyrated.

Rather than give up the fine chapeau, she created a novel movement: with one tiny hand on her hip, and using the other at the back of her head to secure the headpiece, she undulated suggestively like the vamps she had seen on stage. (This bit of stage business, which at first had grown out of necessity, was later to become an integral part of the Mae West persona. In later years, as her fame grew, most of her costumes would grow increasingly elaborate, topped by outlandish head ornaments. She would frequently clash with costume designers over the amount of embellishments that rose to startling heights from her glossy blonde head. She often appeared to be sporting a virtual aviary; such were the number of exotic feathers attached to her hats and head pieces.)

For the much anticipated debut night, May and Tillie arrived early at the Royal Theatre. They wanted to see the Vaudeville show first and get a feel for the mood of the audience. The theatre was full and the patrons very receptive to the show.

When the professionals finished their performances, they exited to a roll of the drums and a trumpet chord. A dapper mustachioed announcer stepped on stage. With a broad gesture, he bowed and welcomed the audience. In a stentorian voice, he encouraged the audience to give the amateurs a great big hand. There was not only applause but a few cat calls mixed in.

Vaudeville audiences were notorious for openly verbalizing their opinions, and amateurs in particular could be the target of some vociferous booing. This didn't bother May at all. She was confident that when they heard and saw what she had to offer, they'd be screaming for more.

That night at the Elk's show at the Royal Theatre, May had her first taste of a professional stage. The theatre was very large. There were two balconies and ornate boxes lining the walls. What she liked the best was the twelve-piece orchestra. It made her feel like one of those songstresses she admired, a star with an orchestra to place her front and center.

She danced and sang in a style that was adult in manner and innuendo. Her voice had a certain edge to it that suggested emotions usually alien to one so young. Her body, moving sinuously to the beat of the drum, confirmed what the audience suspected... this was a child woman. She basked in the waves of applause, and walked off with the first prize in the contest. May had tasted the forbidden apple, and there was no turning back.

The amateur night was often a starting point for new performers. Some budding artists would go for years before they finally landed a professional spot. Just about anyone with an act, and a lot of nerve, could get onstage on amateur night.

The prizes were usually in the form of cash, ranging from $1 to $10. Almost all contestants received a token payment of about 50¢. Some made a living by going from contest to contest every night, as there were as many amateur contests as there were Vaudeville theatres, and that was a very big number. They could earn as much as $5 a week, the cost of feeding a family in those days.

One of the customs at these contests was to throw coins onstage, if the audience liked the performer. From the beginning, precocious May was showered with these tokens of appreciation. She bowed deeply at the end of the act, and unlike the others who scooped up all the tossed coins, she allowed her father or brother to retrieve the loot.

With her powerful vocal tones, she radiated maturity. She soon learned to give another meaning to the lyrics, however innocent they might appear on the sheet music.

One evening there was a gentlemen in the audience who thought this child prodigy had something unlike anything he had ever seen. After the performance, he approached May's parents with an offer to include her in his touring stock company. He told them his group traveled locally, staging famous plays that frequently included parts for a child.

Both May and Tillie immediately accepted the offer. May would soon sharpen her stage skills playing a variety of characters, but always with a style that was purely her own.

At this time, nature intervened and May began to blossom—literally—into the spectacular hour glass figure that was to become her stock in trade. Her bosom expanded almost overnight, and her hips and bottom filled out in equal measure. She was still not officially a teenager, but what others saw in the eye-catching figure was a mature female form divine.

Unfortunately, this seemed to get in the way of the child roles she was still playing. Despite Tillie's best sartorial efforts to reign in her daughter's assets, May frequently burst forth from her constrictive costumes to the amusement of the audience.

May's services with the touring company were terminated. She returned to her parent's home, where she began to fill her idle time with a new interest . . . boys.

4
Rehearsal

As May took a brief hiatus from her stage career, Ray Waddell had settled into his new life as a pupil in a boy's boarding school on the edge of London. He stood out as an American, particularly with his decidedly Texan drawl. He became the center of attention because of his unique persona, attention that was not always welcome.

A boy's boarding school can be a cruel experience for any boy that does not fit in. Teachers at such institutions seldom have time to take into account the character of a student who is somehow different than the others.

Several of Ray's classmates delighted in tattling on him to the professors with imagined infractions of the school's strict code of conduct. One particular teacher, the athletic director, frequently administered corporal punishment to Ray. Ray had trouble hiding his feminine side and was naturally awkward at any sport. He was alternately teased or ignored by the other boys.

The second half of the school year, Ray struck an unlikely friendship with a new teacher. Sensing that this gawky newcomer was lonely and unhappy, the kind man made it a point to speak to Ray and inquire as to his hobbies and interests. Ray told him he was interested in music and the theatre. He admitted he had never seen a play or stage entertainment, but was fascinated by what he read in newspapers. The teacher suggested they take in some of the local entertainment over the weekend.

Their first outing was to a music hall, a form of entertainment peculiar to England. These were similar to the American Vaudeville, but with a much older history. Music halls represented a decades-long parade of talent and tradition. It began somewhere in the long past *Commedia dell'arte*. It evolved into the anarchy, noise, and hilarity that made it the most popular entertainment in England. The mixture of the bawdy and sentimental endeared it to millions. The specialty acts, the jugglers, comedy pianists, magicians, and impersonators both male and female, were but a small portion of the music hall repertoire.

England had seen the true beginnings of the music hall fifty years prior to the first real American Vaudeville and it outlasted Vaudeville by decades. The English prized traditions in the theatre, and were unwavering in their loyalty to their favorite artists. Age was seldom a factor. In America, you were applauded as long as you were a hit. Take a misstep, and both the impresarios and the public promptly ran mindlessly to the next new thing.

What Ray saw that first night in the music hall was beyond anything he could have imagined. There were singers in outlandish costumes, some beautiful and others purposely ridiculous. Comedians were interspersed with dancers and acrobats. He was amazed at a tiny 4-foot 6-inch fellow named Little Tich. He performed a routine called "Big Boots" (1889). He stood on point, like a grotesque ballerina, on a pair of 28-inch 2x4 boards attached to the sides of his shoes like skis.

It was on that same stage that Ray witnessed for the first time the British tradition of cross-dressing. Unique was the act of Max Walden, a classically-trained ballet dancer. At first, he tripped lightly onstage, in a parody of ballet, all the while yodeling to the music. He changed in minutes to a Spanish dancer, and then to a scantily clad French danseur. His finale was a traditional ballerina doing Swan Lake.

Next came "The Best Boy," a woman dressed neatly in the men's fashion of the time: silk top hat; starched shirt and tie; black tail coat; and gold-headed cane. This manly vision sang in a deep contralto voice of the pleasures of courting pretty young women and imbibing with the lads at the local pub. She even smoked a cigar as she sang "All the Nice Girls Love a Sailor" (from *Ship Ahoy*, 1909) and "She Never Had Her Ticket Punched Before" (Victorian Music Hall ballad).

Ray was astounded that the audience responded positively to this gender-bending performance. What fascinated him even more—and would soon set him on the path he would follow the rest of his life—was "The Dame."

"The Dame" is a classic part of the music hall tradition, a man dressed in drag, a man playing a woman, fully accepted, and even cheered, by a boisterous audience. Ray's companion could see the look of wonder on his student's face as he watched a middle-aged man, elaborately gowned and wigged, prance about the stage in a comic parody of a chorine. He explained that this was something he would see in every music hall across England.

In the following months, Ray attended many music halls around London, usually with his professor. They would meet outside the theatre, the professor with a pair of tickets already in hand. After the performance, Ray was treated to a sandwich and a cider at a local pub. Whether this bond ripened into a more fruitful relationship was never revealed.

It was during one of these delightful evenings on the town that Ray began to form an idea of what he wanted to do for the rest of his life. He loved the songs of the music hall, mixtures of sentiment and comic bawdiness that audiences found so appealing. The whole atmosphere was a sort of mad and lively evening, almost an organized anarchy. He wanted very much to entertain, to be clever, and most of all to be accepted.

The renowned dame, Harry Randall, served as the impetus for Ray to give voice to his ambition. Randall had begun his career at the age of eleven. He modeled himself after a previous impersonator, Dan Leno. They both specialized in patter songs, a sort of sung-spoken comedic routine that did not require professionally trained voices. The night Ray saw Randall, he was in his most famous role, *Old Mother Hubbard* (1893). The audience frequently interrupted the performance with outbursts of applause and laughter.

For Ray, this was an inspiration. At the interval, he broached the subject with his professor of a theatrical future. Rather than the cautionary warning he had expected, Ray was surprised with words of encouragement and an offer to help in any way possible.

After the performance, Ray was taken backstage to meet some of the performers. The professor was on a friendly basis with one of the stage managers, and through him began a life-changing turn of events.

The manager arranged an audition for Ray the next Monday. He was disappointed to learn there was no opening for a cross-dressing part, but he was being auditioned as a member of the chorus. This was a chance to set foot on stage. The audition consisted of a series of simple dance steps demonstrated by the director, which Ray had no trouble repeating. Next was the song. Rather than handing Ray a song sheet to follow, the director told him to pick any song he knew and sing unaccompanied. Without thinking, he blurted out the name of a song that he was very fond, "An Old Man's Darling" (1903). He then realized he had chosen a song written for the opposite sex. Gathering up his courage and his imaginary skirts, he began:

"Some girls when they think of marriage, fancy a nice young man.
But I'm not so inclined, for none of these things I crave,
I'd rather be an old man's darling than be a young man's slave!"

He then sang the second chorus and held his breath in nervous anticipation. The director asked him to sing something else. To drive home the type of role he really wanted to play, he continued in the same vein:

"My mother always said, remember, look under the bed
Before you blow the candle out, to see if there's a man about
And I always do. But you can make a bet,
It's never been my luck to find a man there yet!"

He got the job, but not playing a dame. He'd have to work his way up from the chorus first.

The hall where Ray made his theatrical debut was typical of the suburban bourgeois style that prevailed in the lower-class London neighborhoods. At that time, there were over 300 music halls operating in greater London. Unlike the handful of really fashionable theatres, these halls were generally dingier establishments, decorated in a gaudy manner. There were great bunches of artificial flowers everywhere, with crude plaster statuary holding garishly colored lamps. Gilding and crimson covered the interiors.

The audiences generally were not distinguished-looking, but mostly respectable. One advantage to those in the balcony seats and stalls was that they were seldom exacting in their tastes. The meat and potatoes of a successful performer were hearty and comedic songs, an occasional off-color joke, and the inevitable patriotic song with waving flags and a ringing chorus.

Ray would have to wait his turn to present a solo performance. He perfected his singing and dancing in the chorus, and was soon moved from the back row to a favored spot on either side of the star.

The director noticed Ray had something extra, a turn of the head, a wink of the eye, a bit more flair than was usually found among the ordinary chorus boys.

When one of the residents of Ray's boarding school discovered that he was performing on stage on weekends, the word spread among the student body like wildfire. A plan was hatched among some of the bolder fellows to attend a performance and see just what this was all about. Filling the front row, ready to jeer and hoot, the lads soon realized that this was not something at which to sneer. They saw a professional and entertaining routine. Handsome singers and dancers surrounded a beautiful young woman, gracefully executing choreography and singing in fine harmony. Ray held a place of honor next to the evening's featured performer, doing a waltz with the young woman at the finale.

The next day at the academy, he found himself being treated with a little more respect and a newfound fascination. What they could never have guessed was the direction Ray had planned for his career.

5
BLURRING THE BOUNDARY

May was beginning to experience that hormonal rush that can come a little early to certain girls. She realized at a very young age she was not a woman's woman. She adored being the one female in a room full of the opposite sex. She loved to sing an impromptu song to the boys who gathered in her parlor when her father was away. She stole kisses from her favorites, and she had plenty of those.

Men fascinated her. Her mother seldom attempted to interrupt May's little parties, insisting that no harm would come of it. What her mother didn't realize was that her daughter was as bold as a man. She sat extremely close to a boy and fondled what few girls her age would dare.

This brief hiatus from the stage soon bored the ambitious teenager. May returned to work. The only role she could find was the antithesis of what would become her true persona. She was forced to play a country bumpkin with a silly bonnet and lacy bloomers . . . another child's part . . . but this time, May's womanly charms were obvious and she played it for comic effect. The theatres that booked this tour were in a bad part of lower Manhattan, and the blue collar audiences appreciated the titillating sight of a full-figure in a child's costume. Tillie insisted on accompanying the rapidly maturing prodigy to ward off any unwelcome attention backstage.

Burlesque houses were a staple entertainment when May was touring in this ingénue role. Based on remembrances from fellow performers and an unexplained gap in her memoirs, there is a strong indication that she probably trod the boards at more than one Burlesque house.

She vehemently denied in later life, when she was an established star, that she had ever been part of Burlesque, a form of entertainment that was looked down upon by even the least of the Vaudeville players.

Burlesque was a rough slice of theatre. It required a good display of the undressed female form with a lot of suggestive movement. It was entirely bawdy, with dirty-mouthed, baggy pant comedians, and an audience that was almost completely male. Comic scenes were interspersed among the half-nude female purveyors of the art of the strip tease. The comedy was low and ribald. There was no subtlety. Nothing was left to the imagination.

It has often been said that only a stint in a Burlesque house could have taught May to keep her motor running. The permanently gyrating hips, the swaying shoulders, and the come hither body language all spoke of experience on the stripper's runway.

The same anecdotes followed the platinum siren as her fame grew. Ironically, it was during her early career that a critic from *Variety* wrote: "Unless Miss West can tone down her stage presence in every way she just might as well hop right out of Vaudeville and into Burlesque!"

Old-timers who had worked in New York's seedy Burlesque houses swore they remembered a young May bumping and grinding with the best of them as she struggled to gain a foothold in the dog eat dog world of show business.

Female impersonators were becoming an accepted part of many Vaudeville shows. Their talents ranged from merely being a clothes horse to singing in an operatic falsetto voice.

Around this time, May changed her stage name to "Mae." She loved the bold and often outrageous attitude about sex that these performers could get away with. A woman who expressed the same sentiment would have been quickly removed from the stage.

One of her earliest and strongest influences was the impersonator, Bert Savoy. Boston-born Everett McKenzie began his career in show business as a chorus boy, singing in touring musicals. As a child he had seen several comic drag performers in the old Blackface Minstrel shows. He decided that comedy was his forte, and drag would be his medium. Adopting the stage name "Savoy," he struggled for several years in rough and tumble saloons in the West, perfecting his material. On his return to Boston he met handsome Jay Brennan, a former impersonator, who now did a small solo act in Vaudeville. The two clicked personally and decided to form a duo act. Bert was the drag, and Jay was his "straight" partner.

Savoy, though primarily a comic, dressed in elegant gowns and furs, but behaved in an outrageous manner. He flirted in a sexually-charged body language on stage with Jay shaking his hips like a belly dancer and tossing-off suggestive lines.

Mae incorporated several of Savoy's mannerisms in her act, including his signature phrase, "You must come over." Mae paraphrased in *She Done Him Wrong* (1933), "Why don't you come up sometime and see me?" Later, she used, "Come over and see me some time," or simply, "Come up and see me," her most-quoted witticism.

Savoy was absolutely fastidious about his gowns and accessories. Unlike many of the impersonators, he employed a wardrobe mistress. When asked why he didn't use a male dresser, his answer was, "It takes a woman to understand a woman's clothes. You cannot *ever* depend on a man. Just when you want him to tighten your corset, you find him in the wings making whoopee with some chorus girl. Why put temptation in the poor Devil's way?"

Savoy was frequently criticized by the critics for being crude and vulgar. His reply was, "They are the natural things people say and do." His audiences seemed to agree with him, egging him on with applause and laughter.

Mae's use of the Savoy character, all brassy and bold, caused a different reaction from audiences. Where Savoy was obviously an impersonator, audiences were never quite sure just what Mae was up to. Was she spoofing sex, or was she truly as libidinous as she appeared? This dichotomy would follow Mae for her entire career.

Savoy had married, hoping to hide his true gender orientation. One day, returning from a tour, he found his home deserted and his bank accounts cleaned out. His trophy wife had had enough.

While Savoy was on an east coast tour with Mae, he met a dramatic and darkly comedic end. Savoy and Brennan, now openly a couple, were on a weekend trip to New York's gay Mecca, Fire Island. After supper, they strolled along the beach. The wind picked up. Flashes of lighting lit the evening sky. Their companions suggested stepping in to a bar. Just then, a particularly loud clap of thunder shook the ground. Savoy, never at a loss for a comeback, exclaimed in his campiest manner: "Mercy! Ain't Miss God cuttin' up something awful!" Just then, a bolt of lightning pierced the ominous clouds. Savoy's hair stood straight on end and he was instantly struck dead.

While touring in another small revue, Mae met the man who would decades later claim to be her one and only husband . . . a husband that she would later deny she had ever married. Frank Wallace was a specialty dancer with more personality than talent. His face and demeanor, while not handsome, seemed to strike a chord with the ladies, and with Mae, in particular.

Mae's career was not going in a direction she liked. She approached Frank with a proposition. She felt they would make a terrific song and dance team. Frank had seen Mae on stage and liked her style. He agreed they could build a nice duo around his athletic footwork combined with her insinuating and sultry song styles. Soon, engagements in neighborhood theatres led to a contract. West and Wallace began their own revue, *The Sporting Widow* (1911).

Frank stated years later that they became romantically involved during their tour together, insisting they were partners in and out of bed. This led to a secret wedding in Milwaukee. The honeymoon was one of the briefest on record. Frank claimed that Mae could never focus on one man. When she was sure her unhappy spouse was asleep, she sometimes slipped out. Her appearance, returning at dawn, left no doubt in Frank's mind as to what Mae had been doing. Mae contended decades later that the marriage had never really been consummated.

During the tour of *The Sporting Widow*, the trade papers had finally begun to take notice of this new style Vaudevillian. *Variety* offered: "Miss West is a lively piece of femininity. The girl is certainly the eccentric type."

Mae left Frank and returned to her parents at the end of the tour. When questioned by her mother as to the veracity of the marriage rumors she sidestepped the issue. "Everyone has the right to run his own love life, even if you're heading for a crash. What I'm against is blind flying." She flatly denied any and all rumors of the marriage, and would do so for more than a quarter of a century. Her parents had invested so much emotionally and financially in their daughter's career, she could not bring herself to admit she had made a terrible mistake in her liaison with Frank. Mae also knew that the perception of a sexy single gal on stage added an extra measure to the erotic fantasy that was a constant in a Mae West performance.

Mae was among the most colorful and exciting theatrical women of her time. Her attitude toward sex wasn't entirely unique, but she got her point across in a way that kept her audiences guessing. Was she spoofing it, or ballyhooing it? It was probably both. She soon became known for her attitude toward the stronger sex. She found them, used them, and dropped them. She either grew bored, or soon spotted another more attractive and willing partner.

The split from Frank seemed to be the turning point in Mae's career. Previously, she had been many characters, from an ingénue to a songstress. Now, she would be bawdy, gaudy, and always a reflection of the image she saw in her looking glass.

As her bookings increased, travelling from show to show, she found she needed an assistant . . . a shoulder to lean on, and a constant source of encouragement. The answer was her mother. Not only did Tillie supervise Mae's costumes and the details of her travel, she often intervened when managers and stage hands got the wrong idea about her daughter.

Eventually, Tillie required the services of a lawyer who specialized in theatrical matters. She chose James Timony, an ambitious product of the Brooklyn Law School with a special practice that catered to theatre folk.

When Timony was introduced to Mae, there was an instant chemistry. He was a muscular Irishman, not unlike her father, with a winning charm that soon resulted in a torrid affair. Like Mae, he loved flashy clothes and diamond rings.

At first, he thought he could win her by conventional means: a proposal and perhaps a life together as man and wife. He soon learned this was not Mae's dream. Afraid that he would lose her forever if he pushed too hard, he took another route to keep her by his side.

Gradually, Timony began to use his knowledge of the theatre to handle most of Mae's contracts. Both Mae and her mother noticed he always got better terms for them than they had ever been able to obtain. With each passing year, Mae began to turn over more of her affairs to this rosy-cheeked dynamo. He would be at her side for the decades that followed, always at the ready, despite the steady stream of lovers he saw in and out of Mae's love nest.

As Mae had graduated to more important bookings, Ray had graduated from a music hall chorus boy and been given a few solo spots, consisting of a short song, or a brief dance.

One of the first and certainly the most unusual character Ray created was that of a young child. He dawdled onstage twisting his blonde pigtails. On his tow head was an oversized hair ribbon that matched his gingham short dress with lacy bloomers peeking out from the bottom. He must have been a vision. That he was already tall and gawky only added to the grotesquerie. He skipped on stage with a large basket of vegetables on one arm, took an awkward curtsy, and began in a squeaky falsetto:

> "Then we will make up our big market baskets
> And away to the city we will fly
> For some pigs' heads and cabbage and turnips
> To make us some fine shepherd's pie
> There's mutton to get from the butcher,
> And apples so shiny and bright
> And some sweets for my sister Pneumonia
> From that market they hold every night.
> But we're late don't you see, we must make for that tree
> Where we will eventually have to turnip and pea!"

After a few performances and not many laughs, he dropped this odd character and returned to what would become his specialty, a worldly and witty dame.

He had finished his term at the boarding school with failing academic marks. In light of this, he was told to return to America, as his mother and her husband would not finance any further schooling abroad. They offered to send a steamship ticket for his return, which he gladly accepted, but he tucked it away for a future date. He had no intention of returning just yet. He had spent months perfecting a dame that he could audition to the director. He was promised he could try out the act on an off-night during the middle of the week.

Female impersonation, or, to use the British term, dame, was as old as the music hall. The British music hall was an equal opportunity institution, offering non-heterosexual audiences a little of their own life on stage. Both "The Best Boy," a woman impersonating a man, and "The Dame," the other side of the gender coin, were an integral feature in almost all shows. The sexual layering, double entendres, and comedic mix-ups afforded by the he-she / she-he were endless.

Despite the centuries-long British theatre's tradition of crossdressing, there was very little appetite among audiences for realistic and glamorous female impersonation. Even in the field of classical ballet, British audiences looked unfavorably on male ballet dancers, unless they were playing the role of a grotesque old woman. Two rare exceptions to this attitude were Bert Errol and Billie Manders, both enjoying great success in America, as well as in the United Kingdom.

In contrast to the lack of interest in a pretty drag, English female impersonators who created a grotesque or comedic character enjoyed popularity in both the music hall and the theatre.

In 1892, a play, "Charlie's Aunt," launched a raft of imitators. The title character created by legitimate stage actor W. S. Penley was a thoroughly funny and equally homely impersonation of an old maid aunt. This became a cornerstone of comic impersonation.

There were a number of male and female cross-dressers that Ray had studied, both from the viewpoint of the audience and from his perspective standing in the wings. One of the most famous was a former legitimate actor turned drag, Malcolm Scott. He was comedic and inventive, and befriended ambitious young Ray. Scott specialized in historical women, such as Salome, the Gibson girl, and even one of Henry VIII's wives, Catherine Parr.

Scott, born in the 1870s, was well into middle age when Ray first saw him. Scott had come up the hard way, playing to rough audiences in beer halls and bottom-row theatres. By the time Ray saw him, he was a headliner in the music halls. Ray always remembered how Scott addressed his audience as he came on stage: "When I was just a little unimportant act, they'd say I was a, 'Nancy boy.' Now, it's 'Malcolm is so delightfully eccentric!'"

Malcolm gave Ray a thorough grounding in the history of the dame and of the female impersonator. At first, he explained, everything was strictly a gag with very little attempt at reality. That was still the style that the working class preferred. Over time, the style changed, as cross-dressers hoped to play to a more sophisticated audience.

As women's fashions became more exaggerated, so did their impersonators in the theatre. Female attire took on a much more exhibitionistic quality: bosoms were padded and bottoms were built-up with bouncing bustles. Hairstyles began to reach impossible heights with the addition of fake puffs and curls. Women became much more artificial, thus blurring the line between the true female and her theatrical impersonator.

Malcolm Scott not only gave Ray a thorough understanding of the evolution of impersonation, he gave him his expert advice drawn from a long career as an actor and impersonator. He taught Ray how to hold his arms and hands, to work with a fan or a prop, how to manipulate the long train of a gown so it became an extension of his person. Brusquely kicked aside by a stylish high heel, it could be used to emphasize a feeling, like the exclamation point at the end of a sentence.

A term that would gain greater use over the years was "drag." This name for impersonation seems to have come from the action of a woman's long dress with a train. The train would "drag" as the woman walked. At first the term pertained to a dress or garment that an actor wore when impersonating a woman. Later, it became the name applied to those that practiced the art of female impersonation.

Ray combined his own irrepressible personality with the clever stage business he absorbed from these seasoned artists to create a delightful mélange of eccentrics. One of his first was a fast-talking, slightly dizzy matron of uncertain age, who, for no reason, would launch into a naughty song in a quavering soprano voice:

"If only I could be just a girl
I'd set the Johnnies' hearts in such a whirl
If only I could be just a girl
I'd run upon a Lord or Earl
He would marry me, of course
And then we'd have, you know, divorce
I'd appear before the gay footlights
In silver shoes and silky tights
If only I could be just a girl!"

He suddenly ended the song, turned his back on the audience for a moment, and then turn back slowly, his face transformed from a demure expression to a sly smile. Next, he offered a dirty story punctuated by an edgy cackle. A signature performance style that would evolve from this was an almost non-stop stream of consciousness. It became his trademark for years to come. His banter came fast and furious, built along a script line that allowed him to interject at will an anecdote or bit of scurrilous gossip. In this way, he could recycle a much used monologue by adding the most topical tidbits laced with innuendo and double entendre.

He costumed himself in slightly shop-worn glamour, as if his character had seen better days, giving the whole presentation a slightly jaded but touching effect. It was hard not to love a whore with a heart of gold.

From the first night he paraded this character onto the stage, he felt an immediate connection with the audience. They rewarded him with hearty laughter and a round of applause. The routine became a regular. As his schedule increased, he learned invaluable stage skills from the seasoned performers he worked with. He found himself billed as a "character vocalist," a flexible appellation that allowed him to work both as a dame and a comic in male attire.

There was one particularly memorable evening when he was ready to go on stage, this time as a dapper man about town. Waiting for the first chords of his introduction music, he stood nervously in the wings, fussing with his ruby-colored silk coat that was tailored in the body hugging fashion of the era. His trousers were defined with a knife-sharp crease above pointed-toe, patent slippers. On his head was a shiny black top hat with a long ribbon hanging down the back. He was obviously rouged and powdered, his eyes outlined in kohl, thick mascara, and false lashes. Just as his entrance music began, he was startled to hear one of the burly stage hands behind him whisper in his ear, "Miss, you seem to have forgotten your brassiere!"

Ray found the work rewarding but very hard. He never turned down any offer to perform, sometimes doing performances at three different theatres in one evening. He finished one show and rushed to the next venue in full costume and makeup. His friend, the professor, often had a coach waiting for him. He took great pleasure in his former pupil's success and was glad to be a part of it.

The disparity between the matronly looks of Ray's dame and the type of songs he used added to his character's humor. He borrowed a popular music hall song, "When I Take My Morning Promenade," from the star, Marie Lloyd:

> "As I take my morning promenade
> Quite a fashion card, on the promenade
> Now I don't mind nice boys staring hard
> It satisfies their desire
> Do you think my dress is a little bit
> Just a little bit, not too much of it?
> It shows my shape just a little bit,
> That's the little bit the boys admire."

Another favorite song of the era was added to Ray's growing repertoire. This slightly suggestive ditty was a big hit in London's West End:

> "You can do a lot of things at the seaside
> That you cannot do in town.
> Fancy seeing mother with her legs all bare,
> Paddling in the fountain in Trafalgar Square.
> But bobbing up and down in the ocean with fat old Doctor Brown,
> You can do a lot of things at the seaside,
> That you cannot do in town."

Part of the inspiration for Ray's matronly character stemmed from an artist that he openly copied. Herbert Clayton was a famous music hall impersonator, with a style that was both comedic and musically skillful. He was no beauty; short and plump, with a child-like visage. His billing read "The Male Soprano." Clayton's voice was a true high soprano, not the falsetto used by most impersonators when doing operatic parodies. The unique range of his voice allowed him to do such difficult numbers as "One Fine Day" from Puccini's Madame Butterfly. In addition to his dizzy diva, there was his satirical take on an overweight Burlesque dancer. His elephantine legs, stuffed into tights, and a figure like a tree trunk, convulsed audiences as he shook and shimmied like a pachyderm in heat.

Clayton closed his act with the character that became one of Ray's favorite borrowed creations, the old scrub woman. Dressed in a shop-worn dress and a rag around his head, he shuffled on stage as if he was the cleaning lady mopping the floor after the show closed. He would delight the audience with a mixture of bawdy humor and sentimental vignettes.

Many decades later, Ray would close his own act with this same character, one that was always a hit with his audience. A modern counterpart is Carol Burnett's scrub woman, replete with mop and bucket. She, too, used this classic character to close her show.

From the many performers and acquaintances he met during his London career, he heard constant stories of a place where another form of entertainment was blossoming. This was a style not unlike the music hall, but with a decidedly Yankee flavor. It was Vaudeville.

Malcolm Scott said he was taking his act to American Vaudeville and urged Ray to do the same. The big difference was that Scott was an established star and already had a number of bookings. All Ray had was a one-way steamship ticket, a few second-hand costumes, and very little money in his pocket. Youth and yearning eventually won out. Within the year, he boarded an ocean liner bound for a new and uncertain future.

6
Very Loud, Very Fast, and All Together

Ray endured several days of a rough Atlantic winter crossing. His ticket only afforded him the lowest of the cabin classes, steerage. This was the same cramped and uncomfortable passage endured by his mother years ago on her fateful journey to America.

Unlike that poor soul, Ray was filled with hope. He was leaving an exciting and vibrant theatrical city behind, seeking an even more promising future in a bold, brassy, new metropolis.

Days later, he descended the gangplank, shading his eyes from the brilliant sun of a bright, cold New York morning.

He found New York both exciting and a little daunting. His first priority was to secure a place to stay. He had been given the locations of several neighborhoods, supplied by gay acquaintances from London, who had either been to New York or had friends there.

What was immediately apparent was the steep price of lodging. After a full day's inquiries into rooms for rent in Harlem, the Village, and the Bowery, he was forced to accept the latter.

His home for the immediate future was a tiny furnished room. It was part of what had been a row house, formerly occupied by a single family. It was cheap, sparsely furnished, and had one luxury—the use of a shared kitchen that allowed the tenants to avoid the cost of eating out.

Ray's culinary talents soon became apparent to his fellow lodgers. In exchange for his stovetop skills, the other tenants supplied a steady stream of ingredients. Refrigeration was a rarity, so perishables had to be purchased on a daily basis. Keeping any leftovers seldom proved a problem. At the end of each repast, there was scarcely enough left to feed the hungry mongrels that gathered in the alley behind the kitchen. Ray, always a soft touch for any animal, made sure he put back a little for his furry friends.

This crowded lifestyle was nothing new to Ray. He had occupied similar digs in London. What was new was his discovery of the frequency with which lodgers in the house visited each other's rooms at night, not only men and women, but men and men, as well.

Gay life in New York was much more open than in London, but you had to know the ropes. Gay men created a variety of strategies that helped them disguise their double life and to deal with the hostile straight world. Ray didn't know it, but a good deal of the gay slang that he quickly picked up had derivatives in the language of straight prostitutes.

To "cruise" was a term used by streetwalkers to describe their ritual of looking on the street for a customer. A "trick" was a whore's customer. Double entendre allowed gay men to recognize each other from their speech. Seldom did a member of the straight world catch on to what was actually meant. Ray learned the safe approach to exploring a city rife with gay opportunities. At an early age, he developed a definite proclivity for those men who were willing to set aside their "straight" facade for a stolen moment of pleasure.

The culture of gay men in the United States in the early years of the twentieth century seemed to be markedly different than what he had experienced in the U.K. He noticed the general publics' image of a gay man was almost always that of an impersonator or flamboyant fairy. A limp-wristed fairy that walked with an exaggerated swivel of the hips, or a "swish," was an integral part of the world of Vaudeville. This was an immediate marker in the eyes of the least sophisticated in the audience, and always drew an easy laugh. This clearly defined adoption of effeminate mannerisms was more prominent during this era than it is today.

Ray learned to manipulate his image, depending on the situation. He wore masculine attire when in public and carried himself with a strong self-assured demeanor. When introduced to an exclusively gay environment, his facade suddenly dropped like a whore's bloomers. It was often difficult to decide which face to wear, depending on the type of gay crowd. There was a decidedly negative reaction from conservative gay men to their screaming sisters.

Ray's taste definitely ran to more traditional and masculine men. He quickly toned down his feminine side when cruising for a partner. This was made easy by his natural acting ability. For years, he had performed in male chorus lines in music halls. He was taught to butch it up for the audience. The public did not expect to see a limp-wristed partner propelling a lovely woman in a romantic dance.

One advantage for gay culture at this time was the gullibility of the American public. Since most of the population thought only feminine men were engaging in "the love that dare not speak its name," the majority of straight-appearing gays went about their business unmolested, even by the police.

Ray almost never revealed his partly feminine character when persuading a prospective paramour. As he became more famous, and his stage persona assumed a more glamorous, feminine look, he often found backstage Johnnies who wished to bed him as a woman. When, on a very rare occasion he tumbled, the Johnnie got a shock when he found Ray's big member lodged in a reluctant receptacle. Despite Ray's lifelong fame as a female impersonator, his bedroom theme could best be summed up by the Village People's song, "Macho Man."

Ray had a theory about sex. He felt that the super wealthy and those at the other end of the money spectrum, the very poor, held the same views on good sex. Money bought anything—even sex—but sometimes that sex wasn't the best. Poor people, and Ray counted himself in that group, really appreciated a good roll in the hay. It was often the only thing of joy they had. The group he thought had the least fun in the bedroom was the so-called middle class, those that spent all their lives and energy following that old work ethic and living by the rules of the Good Book.

The Bowery, the site of Ray's new dwelling, contained an area called the Tenderloin. This notorious neighborhood ran up Broadway and Sixth Avenue, from Twenty-Third Street to Fortieth. Here could be found a complete stew of entertainments, from dance halls and booze parlors to any form of sexual satisfaction. Prostitutes, both male and female, could be chosen from the many who wandered the streets and alleys, hocking their wares. These walkers of the street boldly advertised their assets by graphic hand gestures, pointing out their size of their family jewels or some special talent that a few dollars could buy.

Several "resorts," as these drinking dens were called, offered a show that consisted of gay men outrageously dressed as women. They danced and sang, mingling with the male clientele, who, for a certain sum, could join these performers in private booths where they would service their customer's sexual desires. Ray once found himself offered a job to perform as a gay prostitute. Despite his sometimes desperate financial situation, he instinctively knew this would lead to a sad end.

Vaudeville was Ray's consuming ambition. How to break in was even more challenging than the music hall had been in London. There, he had the support of his old friend, the professor.

At this time in New York, Vaudeville was an opiate for the masses, who could afford to seek escape from the hum-drum of daily life. Over half of all theatre audiences could be found nightly in Vaudeville halls. Here, they found as many as twenty different performers in a single evening. If an act was not to their liking, another would follow in a few minutes. These included everything from juggling midgets, bicyclists, trapeze artists, dancers of every description, snake charmers, and magicians. Female impersonators were becoming increasingly popular. Nearly every theatre billboard featured at least one image of these glamorous drag divas.

For the 25,000 vaudevillians performing up to four shows a day, it was simply "the business," a business, a job, and a way of life. To the vast middle class of America, it was one of their prime sources of entertainment. Every night across the country, audiences filled the seats of nearly 2,500 theatres. These Vaudeville houses ranged from grand to grim, and everything in between. Some were as small as 400 seats, while others quadrupled that number.

The average American worker took home about $25.00. The lucky Vaudevillian, if he became a featured act and signed with a major agency for an extended tour, could expect as much as $450.00 in his pay envelope.

To be a featured performer in Vaudeville, you had to learn everything from experience, by yourself. No artist, and Vaudevillians were all referred to as artists, went to school or took a course on how to be a Vaudevillian. Performers learned to talk to the audience, walk on stage in a manner that immediately caught their attention, wear the right costumes, all by trial and error.

An error could be very painful, for audiences were not shy about voicing their displeasure. They heckled and whistled, or worst of all, remained silent and sat on their hands. There was very little time for the actor to create his or her character; a minute or so. Audiences became restless unless their attention was caught and held soon after an artist walked into that spotlight.

Often, Ray tried too hard to grab his audience, and it didn't go over. He learned more was less. By truly becoming the character he was doing, matron or scrub woman, the audience believed him and laughed or clapped. There was always the pressure to succeed, to please an audience. No one had to tell the stage manager if you were not a success. They only had to listen to the reaction of the audience. If you flopped when you opened on Monday night you could find yourself looking for work the next day.

The daily routine of any prospective Vaudevillian was knocking on stage doors, inquiring if there was any work, and a great deal more rejection than acceptance. Ray was growing increasingly concerned as his pockets grew empty. He was not a known quantity, and his work as a dame in English music halls meant little to Vaudeville directors.

His circle of gay friends had increased far more rapidly than his theatre prospects. One evening, he was a guest of one of these buddies for a night on the town. A hard drinking evening ended in a notorious gay night spot that featured a corpulent lesbian vocalist, Gladys Bentley.

Bentley tipped the scales at 250 pounds. She appeared even bigger in her men's full dress, with suit of tails. This most masculine of male impersonators sported a white silk top hat and an elegant ebony and gold cane.

The corpulent chanteuse overwhelmed the piano bench as she beat out time with her size 12 shoe. Her booming voice grated the lyrics of popular songs, transforming them into noxious bastardizations. The lily-white lyrics of "Alice Blue Gown" became an ode to anal intercourse as Gladys shouted, "My dear, won't you please turn around, and he shoved his big thing up my brown!"

Bentley urged the audience to join her in a second chorus of the bowdlerized music. A bleary-eyed Ray and his equally soused companion obliged.

Recognizing Ray's friend, Bentley joined his table at the end of her show. Over a series of cocktails, the songstress explained that she was moving to the Ubangi Club. Her plans included an expanded show, featuring a revue, backed up by a "pansy" chorus line.

Ray quickly tried to focus through his alcohol haze and in a slightly slurred voice began to enumerate his drag credentials. Most of his resume was made up of theatres he had played in London, none of which rang Bentley's bell. Pressing his point, he was told to relax. Bentley promised him a job in the chorus. A few more libations and a firm masculine handshake with this "bull dagger" sealed the deal.

The opportunity to work on a stage, even as a generic chorus member, meant a chance to survive. He could pursue bigger opportunities in his off time.

Six nights a week, Ray joined a chorus of decidedly homely drag queens in a repetitious and rather trite routine, consisting of stock dance numbers and unharmonious singing. The main attraction for the audience was the absurd appearance and costumes of the line-up. Ray loved laughter, but he wanted the response to be in recognition of his humor, not directed at his appearance.

Growing bored with this nightly grind, he began to add his own unique theatricality to the same old steps and songs. This was the same ploy he had first used in the English music halls, a not so subtle attempt to point the spotlight in his direction. He altered the ridiculous dress he and the other cast members wore by removing the tacky streamers and fringe. He showed the chorines how to comb their wigs in a more flattering fashion and gave everyone tips on makeup.

The chorus performed a campy musical number just before the end of the first part of the show, a corny old chestnut called "She Is More to be Pitied:"

> "Do not scorn her with words harsh and bitter,
> Do not laugh at her shame and downfall,"

At this point, the band played a repeat of the melody. Ray took advantage of the brief musical interlude to step out of the line. Before anyone could stop him, he sang:

> "When I started in shows I was thin don't you know
> By a wind through the keyholes I'd blow
> Now it's not like before
> Cannot get through the door
> I'm not pretty, I'm the butt of your jokes
> I'm not pretty, but I'm good to my folks!"

The chorus was drowned out with laughter as they attempted to finish their inane song. Their vocal efforts went unaccompanied as the stunned band leader had forgotten to take up the ending.

Ray didn't know what to expect as he came off stage. He needn't have worried. Bentley was standing in the wings with a huge toothy grin. Before he could say a word, he was given a slap on the back and told to keep his impromptu bit in the show.

One night, this little solo paid off. Ray had a visitor backstage, a manager from a neighboring Vaudeville house. He explained his establishment was small and did not have much of a budget. If Ray was willing to start out on a small salary, he would guarantee him an increase if he could draw an audience.

The next day, an audition was arranged, a contract was signed, and Ray spent the rest of the afternoon combing flea markets and second-hand stores piecing together costumes for this chance at fame.

7
Making Explicit What Used to be Implied

Another more successful New York Vaudevillian was continuing the slow climb up the ladder of fame, "wrong by wrong" as she was often quoted.

Mae was doing a one-night only concert at a theatre she claimed she would normally have shunned, the Columbia. This was a Burlesque house, though decidedly several steps above the average. Mae's part in the performance, though small, offered her an opportunity to display her own brand of humor, liberally laced with sex and innuendo.

In the audience that night was a producer, who was having a night on the town and hoping to enjoy the female charms that Burlesque always offered. What he got was an eye and earful of libidinous Mae, who stood out even among an evening full of more beautiful but less intriguing women. The producer's theatrical sense told him that she was something far different than the usual Burlesque queen.

He joined a crowd of admirers in Mae's dressing room after the performance. When the hopefuls and well-wishers had cleared, he gave Mae his card. Thinking he was just another fan with mischief on his mind, Mae casually dropped the card onto her dressing table along with several others. Her new admirer suggested she take a closer look at his credentials. When Mae realized this was an important connection, she turned on the charm.

In the morning, Mae was in the impressive offices of William Le Baron, a powerful producer with a new play, "A La Broadway." The meeting ended with Mae's signature on a contract that guaranteed her two solo numbers and a second lead role in the production.

Mae arrived at the first rehearsal fully prepared. She knew the numbers and the script by heart. After the first run through, she stunned the director. Why not change the lyrics to both songs. She found them too ordinary and felt they added nothing to the show. More importantly, she boldly offered, they did little to enhance her individual style of delivery.

She demonstrated the revised material, which she had written the previous evening. To the new and more suggestive lyrics she added an insinuating delivery, a wiggle in the walk, and a message that left nothing to the imagination. The producer and director enthusiastically agreed to the changes.

This was to be a constant for her in the future. She would customize both songs and script to suit her own personality. This was a risky stance for an artist to take, even for an established star, and Mae was far from being a true star at this point.

A La Broadway produced excellent reviews for Mae's part in the show. Unfortunately the show itself was not a hit, and closed after a one-week run.

The next important opportunity for Mae would be to work in a venue that was part of Broadway's legend, the Winter Garden Theatre. This time, Mae would be working alongside really big stars. The legendary Al Jolson was included in the cast, as well as the French singer, Mme. Gaby Deslys.

As soon as rehearsals began, trouble developed. Mae, never one to stand in the shadows, noted that a good part of Mme. Deslys' attraction consisted of extravagant costumes, flashy head pieces, and little else.

Mae's wardrobe already contained a number of similar ensembles. These costumes were soon augmented with the help of her mother's considerable dress-making skills. The already glamorous Mae decided to steal the star's thunder.

When it came time for Mae's first song, she slithered onstage to the thumping of a honky-tonk piano, her hips and shoulders grinding with every sexual innuendo in her considerable arsenal. A delighted audience saw her dripping in fake diamonds and dragging the train of a heavily beaded gown as she began her suggestive song.

Her reward was a prolonged ovation. Coming offstage, her ears still ringing from applause, Mae found herself face to face with the show's fiery French chanteuse. Words were exchanged, as the contretemps escalated into a nasty confrontation. Despite the audience's obvious approval, Mae found herself out of the show.

Competition for good Vaudeville bookings was ferocious. At this point, there were less than some 8,000 positions offered with over 20,000 hopefuls waiting in the wings. What was necessary was to stand apart from the other performers. Mae possessed an extra helping of daring. This, combined with her uniquely raunchy humor, was to be her formula for success.

Women, at the time that Mae was breaking into show business, were expected to be demure, modest, pretty in a soft way, and always attentive to the male. For a female artist to be self-interested, assertive, and even willing to walk out was no small matter. There were rules of femininity that were not to be broken.

Mae probably wasn't actually aware of the path she was treading, but she seemed to be on the road to laying the ground rules for early feminists. Mae was liberated, in a sense, at a time when the movement was in the delivery room, not yet fully born.

There was one artist that both Mae and Tillie admired, Eva Tanguay. What was immediately apparent to them was Tanguay's lack of beauty. Her face was not traditionally pretty, and her head sported an explosion of hair not unlike a pile of hay.

What she did have was tremendous verve and nerve, to the point that her performances were described as "maniacal."

Her most famous song was "I Don't Care," an exact description of her attitude. Bounding across the stage in what could only be loosely described as dancing, she shouted rather than sang to the audience, "When I put on my tights, my name went up in lights."

Her best asset was a firm figure and excellent legs displayed to great advantage in shimmering tights. She kicked wildly over her head, turning cartwheels and leaping about in a manner that audiences had never seen before, and they went mad for it.

There was a dance craze in Vaudeville at this time called the "Salome dance." This originated via grand opera, from the Strauss opera of the same name. Every female Vaudevillian with the slightest sex appeal felt it necessary to perform this dance which had shocked audiences everywhere. It required a sultry interpretation that involved a costume made up of seven veils. After dropping six of these translucent panels, every previous Salome had coyly retained the seventh veil until the stage went black.

Eva Tanguay in her inimitable fashion busted things wide open for any Salome dancer who dared to discard all seven veils. Mae incorporated some of this in her act, shimmying behind a transparent veil that cleverly hid just enough to keep the vice squad away.

At the same time Eva and Mae were doing their versions of the infamous veiled princess, Ray's friend from London, Malcolm Scott, was doing a hilarious parody of Salome on his Vaudeville tour of the United States.

Mae envied the enormous success Tanguay was experiencing, but she also heard the many rumors of Eva Tanguay's darker side. She was being hailed as the reigning queen of Vaudeville, and as royalty often does, she thought her wish was a command.

Known for her erratic movements on and off the stage, a serious incident occurred after a performance. In a mad rush to reach her dressing room, the eccentric star crashed headlong into a young stagehand, sending him down a steep flight of stairs. Somehow before his precipitous descent, Tanguay had also managed to insert a long hatpin into the abdomen of the terrified young man.

Several co-workers witnessed the incident and rushed forward to restrain the hysterical diva who was about to inflict further injury. After an ill-advised attempt to pay off the police, screaming Eva was dragged in handcuffs to the local precinct.

A review from *The New York Dramatic Mirror* the year Mae first saw Eva gives some idea of the impact this performer had on an audience. "We can't imagine anyone sitting back in his theatre chair and placidly observing Eva Tanguay. There is no passive way of watching the Cyclonic One. When the spotlight centers on the corner of the stage and the trombones blare, as the Tanguay moment comes, you have a tingling sensation of electrical expectancy...."

Mae, who was very much a sponge when observing other artists, knew that Tanguay's assault and battery approach to performance was something she, too, could use, but in a much less athletic way. The two women shared an attitude about men and sex. Tanguay flaunted her sexual image onstage, as did Mae. They both had more than healthy sexual appetites, and were not shy about satisfying them with anyone who tickled their fancy.

Where Mae would "Love 'em and leave 'em," as she would say, Eva felt the need to marry them, repeatedly. Shock was a valuable tool for Tanguay, just as blatant sexuality and allure were important tools in Mae's formidable stock pile. Mae loved men far too much to just stun them; seduction was her ultimate goal.

Still experimenting with new ideas for her audience Mae decided to appear in masculine attire. She had seen several English women cross-dressers don a man's top hat and formal tails. They sang clever risqué songs about courting a woman or downing a pint with the boys in the pub. Audiences seemed to love this.

Mae's attempt at a drag king fell flat. She didn't seem to understand that less was sometimes more. She put a particularly bawdy slant on her song, and rather than come across as clever she appeared simply crude. *Variety* gave her a strongly critical review: "Mae West will have to clean up her act—she has a way of putting dirty meanings in her innocent lyrics, and she isn't funny."

Baltimore, usually a favorite town for Mae, gave her a particularly hard time while she was struggling to find new material. Normally, Mae drew a bigger percentage of men for her show, but for some reason the "society" ladies had decided to fill the theatre one night.

The front row of the audience was entirely women, chattering away while the act that preceded Mae struggled to gain their attention. As the performers, a handsome pair of song and dance men, exited, Mae could hear them cursing and mumbling. She stood in the wings trying to decide if it was even worthwhile to go on.

Rather than have her musical introduction played while she waited in the wings, she instructed the conductor to play it while she stood center stage. She then came forward, stopping just short of the footlights.

The noisy clutch of hens continued to cackle all through the introduction, so Mae signaled the conductor to play it again, and again. On the fourth attempt they seemed to quiet down.

Taking her time, Mae continued to stare at the front row, until they all squirmed uncomfortably in their seats. With hand on hip, she blew a theatrical kiss in their direction and said, "Now, we can go on!" She had their attention and they responded with hearty laughter.

Mae, despite the rough road that being an independent artist presented, preferred to have the last word on theatre contracts. She would go for months with no work if she felt offers she received would not be a step up in her career.

She was a frequent performer on The Keith-Albee-Orpheum Corporation circuit, an agency that allowed her the freedom to pick and choose a booking. The most powerful Vaudeville agency at that time was The Shubert Organization, run by the Shubert brothers, Lee, Jacob, and Samuel.

They had achieved a near monopoly through schemes, scams, and blatantly illegal maneuvers. They took advantage of their performers, writers, employees, and even the Tax Department. Mae was well-aware of their reputation, but was also aware that any artist who sought stardom would eventually come up against these three theatrical thugs.

They always insisted on long-term contracts with any artist they thought to be a potential money maker for a Shubert Theatre. It will never be known exactly how Mae finagled the freedom to work for this organization at her own choosing, but then she usually got her way. Her charms were not for nothing.

Mae was offered a Shubert production to open in Boston. Her name would be top billed on the marquee. The show was *Spices*, and her co-stars were George Price and Jim Hussey. The contract called for Mae to do the entire run of the show. At first, she hesitated, not wanting to be tied down for an indefinite period. Extended negotiations followed for several days. The offer of a higher salary eventually won her over.

She was particularly glad to be working with George Price, a successful Vaudevillian she had shared the stage with many times on The Keith-Albee-Orpheum Corporation circuit. He was also a top-selling recording artist, the phonograph record no longer a novelty but a staple in every middle class home.

What Mae didn't know was that the Shuberts had stolen Price away from his Keith contract with promises of top billing and more money. When it came time to honor those promises, the Schuberts did a fast song and dance and reneged on them. Price refused to continue, and the Shuberts sued him. With their powerful lawyers, they brow beat the frightened actor into appearing in *Spices* or face financial ruin.

Mae was unaware of all this when George arrived barely a week prior to the play's opening night. She and the other cast members had been rehearsing for three weeks and were wondering how Price would catch up on his role. She need not have worried, as his part consisted of absolutely nothing. The Shubert's forced the embarrassed star to wear blackface makeup in the first act, switching him to white for the second act, and back into blackface for the third act.

When he asked what his numbers would be, he was informed that he had no numbers. "*No numbers?*" he asked incredulously. To his embarrassment he was told, "Numbers? You do nothing, just stand there!"

Mae was astounded to learn from George that he was being paid $1,000 a week for this humiliating experience. He told her this was the Shubert way of punishing him for his defiance. This cruel farce continued for six months, as the show toured the country. There was his name on every marquee, right next to Mae's. Newspaper ads taken out by the Shubert's made sure that audiences would expect to see this star in *Spices*.

As Mae joined in the curtain calls, she watched the humbled Price holding hands with the cast for the final bow. He remained anonymous and completely unrecognizable to the audience.

Mae breathed a sigh of relief as *Spices* eventually ran out of bookings. She vowed to never sign a binding contract with the Shubert's again.

A series of start-and-stop adventures filled Mae's game plan for the next few months. Initially off to a good start with the dancing duo, Bobby O'Neill and Harry Laughlin, Mae experienced one of those incidents that plague every entertainer.

Mae and her partners opened their engagement at Poli's Palace Theatre in Connecticut on a Saturday night. The first number featured the dancing trio in an energetic opening for Mae's featured song. Bobby and Harry dipped and twirled Mae about the stage until she was front and center. They boys exited with an exuberant buck and wing, leaving Mae in the solo spotlight. The orchestra played the opening chords to "Cuddle Up And Cling To Me," gradually building up the percussion as Mae began to sway and grind to the drum beat.

By the second chorus, the undulations and the uncontrolled shimmy of Mae's body created a serious "wardrobe malfunction." The silky straps of her gown finally snapped from the pressure and her renowned bosom burst forth.

The blue-nosed manager was watching from the wings. He ran on stage and ordered the curtain lowered. Despite the trio's protestations that the whole thing was an accident, they found themselves fired on the spot.

The morning headlines read, "Her Wriggles Cost Mae West Her Job." The audience, composed mainly of testosterone-inflamed Yale men, expressed their frustration by nearly destroying the theatre. The law intervened, barely preventing a full-scale riot.

Mae, never one to miss any opportunity to appear in the media, turned the entire well-publicized incident into a reporter's dream. She gave several interviews proclaiming her innocence and praising the fine young students for taking her part in this whole unfortunate misunderstanding.

8
Lights, Camera....

Ray, like Mae, was struggling to perfect his image. Each night, he tried to spice up his performance, often borrowing a bit from another act he had worked with. Like a gourmet dessert, it takes patience and exact measurements to achieve perfection, and Ray was still an apprentice, not a master chef. More often than not, the soufflé failed to rise.

The rage of New York was the impersonator, Julian Eltinge, called simply Eltinge. His gimmick was his seemingly natural beauty. He relied on authenticity and understatement, rather than shock and ribald humor. He dressed in the latest Paris gowns and hats. His mostly female audience came to see and to emulate the high fashion look that was his trademark. Eltinge also had a fairly passable falsetto singing voice.

His prim demeanor was something Ray found just a little too pretentious. He attempted briefly to satirize this strictly highbrow drag, but the inside humor was lost on most of his audience. He quickly dropped his imitation of this famous imitator.

Lestra LaMonte was another female impersonator that was enjoying a successful career, due in no small part to a highly unusual costume feature.

Like Ray, he had begun very young in Vaudeville, working with his mother, who was a singer. In 1917, just about the time Ray was struggling to make it in New York, Lestra began to work as an impersonator. He made all of his own costumes, not a skill necessarily unique in the world of drag, but his were entirely constructed of crepe paper.

He first learned how to work with the product when he was moonlighting at a local department store doing promotions. He was taught to make an infinite number of objects just using crepe paper. With this unique knowledge, he decided to fashion a gown. By using pleated muslin and wrapping layers of the flexible paper over it, he was able to create an evening dress identical to any fashioned from fabric.

He adopted the stage name, "The Crepe Paper Fashion Plate." Later, he formed a company of six drags, all clad in crepe fashions. They toured the country for years with the title "The Paper Creations." A review from The *Cincinnati Courier*, when Ray was sharing the billing with this creative impersonator, describes the act in detail: "Lestra La Monte offers something that is both original and unique. The pictorial value is exceptional, the scenery and costumes are gorgeous . . . everything is made of paper-paper scenery, paper gowns, paper fur and feathers, paper shoes, paper everything!"

Ray realized that he, too, needed a gimmick, but something entirely his own. Vaudeville, like any part of the entertainment industry, was full of copycat performers. In those days, without the immediacy of today's television, movies, and Internet, a performer could get away with lifting material from another artist. With the thousands of venues around the country, there was a strong possibility that local audiences would never see the original and the plagiarizer on the same stage.

He decided to eliminate his monologues and off-color jokes. There was no shortage of musical material, and few artists bothered to pay for song usage. Ray helped himself to several obscure folders of sheet music and set about altering the lyrics to suit his style.

His singing voice was far from terrible, and a few of the songs were mildly amusing, but from the first performance he realized he had made a mistake. The reception he was receiving each night made it difficult to convince theatre owners to retain him for more than one night.

Realizing that comedy was truly his forte, Ray quickly patched together a routine that consisted of jokes, old and new, borrowed and blue. He whipped up a costume that mimicked the sleazy outfits worn by streetwalkers: a gaudy red satin dress, a moth-eaten fur scarf, and a black wig that looked like it had never been combed. With the accompaniment of a thudding drum, he sauntered onstage, spotted the audience, and opened with a cackling laugh.

"I bet you wonder what I'm doing here tonight, dressed so beautifully. I have a date tonight with an eighty year old man. He's rich, generous, but I won't marry him. He's in the belt manufacturing business and I'm afraid his knees will buckle. He gave me a diamond the other night and I said to him, but it's green. Whoever heard of a green diamond? He told me to give it some time, it will ripen.

"I can't stay long. I'm on the way to the doctor's. I asked him at my last visit if I should have my face lifted. He told me I'd look better if I had it knocked off. I bet you think I'm awful, but honestly when it comes to men I'm a one-way street. Well, I used to be. Now I'm open for all traffic.

"The other night a gentleman took me to a fancy restaurant to eat. Afterwards we went back to his place. I asked him what business he was in. He wouldn't say. I'm sure he is an architect. Just look at the blue prints he left on my neck!

"Don't you just love my fur wrap. The salesman told me it was seal, but I said it looks more like monkey. He said don't blame me if someone has been monkeying around with the seals.

"Oh my dears, I wish you could smell the perfume I bought today. The snotty salesgirl tried to sell me something called Night On The Town at $10 an ounce. Can you imagine? I told her I always wear an exclusive French scent, *Nuit en Grange*, which means Night In The Barn, at only 50¢ a gallon."

This would be the cue for his music and he'd sing a song, exiting with exaggerated gestures and anything he could think of to milk the applause.

He was informed after a performance at a particularly seedy Vaudeville house in Connecticut that his one-week run was going to be cut short if he didn't jazz up his material. He was more broke than usual and desperately cast about for a solution. Maybe some physical gags could pad out his routine.

The gimmick of removing the wig at the finale of a drag act to assure the public you were a real man was nearly as old as female impersonation itself, a trick that even the uptown Eltinge resorted to on occasion.

That evening as he finished his song to only a smattering of applause, he snatched off his blonde curls to reveal a man's hair. There was silence. He then removed what was actually a man's wig, from which cascaded a mass of platinum curls. This third hairpiece was jerked off, finally revealing Ray's own thick dark hair. This time there was a hardy round of applause. He was pleased, as was the doubting manager for the moment. Unfortunately, he would need more than a strong finish to stay on. At the end of the week, he was informed his services were no longer required.

He was beginning the long process of learning the ethos of performance. The stage was gradually becoming the place where life was lived. What happened outside the proscenium was only there so he could retell that experience in a hopefully humorous fashion for the few minutes he was onstage to all those wonderful people out there in the dark. The theater is a hard mistress, and like any chosen partner, does not always provide the climax one would wish.

Rather than surrender to failure, he growled under his breath as he stepped out into the theatre's dank alley, his costumes under his arm, "Fuck it. Give me all you've got. I can take it. The life of any performer is hard; the lot of the female impersonator very difficult indeed."

He continued to audition, pounding the New York pavement constantly. At times, he called at a casting agent's office so frequently that he found the door barred to him. Countless auditions, not only as a comedy drag act but also a straight chorus boy, yielded nothing. In desperation, he began to scan the newspapers for any job, theatrical or not. He had never worked outside the theatre world and didn't know where to begin.

America was in a turbulent period. The worst war in history had been raging in Europe since 1914. Like the rest of the country, Ray followed the accounts of the conflict in the daily newspapers.

The publishing baron, William Randolph Hearst, tried in a very disingenuous manner to convince America to stay out of the war.

He was notoriously anti-British and used any excuse to keep America from lending a hand to the valiant struggle that would eventually threaten the civilized world. Hearst railed on a daily basis about the wrong impression that America had of Germany.

Ray had a very special connection to England. This was the country that had fostered him during his formative years, and he carried many fond memories of his time in London. He was particularly offended by Heart's constant string of journalistic lies.

America finally threw down the gauntlet in April 1917. Initially, the population was inflamed by the prospect of defending a noble cause. Reality would soon set in within a few seasons, with the arrival on American shores of the bodies of thousands of young men, who had lost their lives in the terrible conflict. A somber mood settled like a dark shroud from coast to coast. Soon, everyone was seeking a little escape from the horrors of conflict.

By 1914, movies had become the leading form of mass entertainment. Within a few more seasons, according to *Motography*, The Strand and The Rialto in New York averaged 60,000-70,000 patrons per week, an unheard-of patronage for theatres of any kind. For a few coins anyone could escape to the fantasies being projected on movie screens that were also popping up in every neighborhood across the land.

Ray had decided that his future in show business was over. He had borrowed money from friends, was two weeks behind on his rent, and more often than not, he ate one meager meal a day.

He often came to a neighborhood park early in the morning to avoid his landlord's constant demands for rent. The park was enclosed by a low ivy-covered wall and had a small garden and several benches, usually occupied by elderly gentlemen.

Ray took a seat next to an unusually well-attired man and decided to strike up a conversation. He could see from the front page of the paper that his seat mate was reading that it carried the inevitable headlines about the Great War.

When Ray inquired if there was any promising news from abroad, the man offered him the paper, saying he must be off to work.

The want ads were always the first section Ray searched for. Folding the paper in two, he spotted an unusually large advertisement:

"Wanted, movie 'dress' extras. Both men and women.
Must supply own wardrobe and have a working knowledge of stage makeup.
Apply in person; East 15th Street and Locust Avenue, Brooklyn, New York
Vitagraph Film Co."

Tearing out the ad, he stuffed it in his top coat and raced home.

Ray was aware of films, but had never considered them as a serious part of the entertainment world. He had seen more than his fill in the nickelodeons that sprang up in abandoned store fronts and offices. The earliest films often contained crude images of train wrecks and galloping horses, all silent, and generally very short in length, but *The Birth of a Nation* (1915), among many other films, catapulted movie going to a national pastime. Many American productions were now made in California, but the financial heart of the industry was still centered in New York and Chicago. The Hollywood that we now know came a little later.

Early the next morning, Ray boarded a streetcar for Brooklyn. He found he was among the first to arrive at the Vitagraph offices. The odd assortment of humanity waiting along the hall didn't resemble the type of theatre people he was used to. The line moved very quickly, as each hopeful was summoned to a small office. Within minutes, they left and were replaced by the next job seeker.

He found himself standing in front of a rather gruff and unkempt man, cigar clamped in his mouth. He quickly added Ray's name and address to a coffee stained ledger, and, without another word, handed him instructions how to get to the Vitagraph Studios on Long Island.

No questions were asked, no resume required. *What sort of an outfit is this?* he wondered, as he stumbled out into the early morning sunlight. He'd forgotten to ask the salary and the amount of work required, but at this point anything was welcome.

The following Monday, after a brisk walk from the end of the streetcar line that served parts of Long Island, he caught his first sight of the Vitagraph Studios.

It was a curious jumble of large and small buildings scattered between several dilapidated open sheds. The grounds were unkempt with large patches of weeds and wild shrubs surrounding the site. It took several inquiries before he found where he was to go. A tiny office marked only with a hand-written sign indicated the business within.

A long line had already formed. Inside, the manager took the names of each extra, directing them to stand together at the door. They were told the type of clothing they must bring the next day. They would also have a rudimentary lesson in how to apply makeup.

With a small satchel under his arm, Ray arrived the next morning an hour before starting time. His well-worn leather bag contained an assortment of stage makeup collected over the years. Tubes of grease paint in a variety of colors nestled among containers of powder, various cosmetic pencils, and rouges for the lip and cheeks. Scattered among the items were several pair of false lashes.

Ray found himself herded into a windowless space that served as a communal dressing room. A director's assistant instructed everyone to listen carefully as he quickly barked orders at each of them. Ray was swiftly sized up and informed he would be a cowboy after being handed an ill-fitting hat and an oversized buckskin coat that smelled of cleaning fluid and stale perspiration.

The first day's filming, a primitive two-reel Western pot boiler, *Pioneer Trail Master*, was interminably slow. Each scene required the sets, consisting of painted backgrounds, to be moved and re-set for the next scene. The stage floor was remarkably small, some 30 ft. by 40 ft. A rough-looking crew moved furniture and props while the director constantly yelled orders. It all appeared to be chaos at first.

The lighting was a series of mercury vapor tubes mounted on tripods just out of camera range and also suspended above the set. This garishly harsh illumination made all the performers look as if they were in the last stages of heart disease. This was necessary to get the images to register on orthochromatic film stock that was sensitive only to blue and green light and required very bright light to insure the faces and backgrounds would be sharp and visible. Some of Vitagraph's movie cameras also required the operator to turn the film by hand, a demanding and tiring process.

Ray followed the director's simple cues, which consisted of nothing more than standing in the background of a bar. He tipped his hat to the bartender, nodded, and exited by a swinging door. At one point, after several attempts to open the louvered mock-up of a saloon door, he pushed too hard and almost brought down the entire flimsy backdrop. This brought a brief comical relief to the other extras and a shrill reprimand from the director's megaphone. He was required to do this several times as the principal actors would constantly have to repeat their actions to satisfy the demanding director. At the end of the day, they were all tired from waiting around in between the long breaks in the scenes.

The next day was more of the same. After a short lunch break, one of those things you read about in trite theatrical novels occurred. A minor player, an older actress, stumbled on the staircase and severely injured her ankle. The next set was assembled, the extras stood waiting for the filming to continue, but the director could not find a suitable substitute at such quick notice.

Ray hesitantly approached the director and told him he could play the part. When the director gave him an unbelieving stare, he explained his background in England as a dame and in Vaudeville as a drag comic. The injured actress was about his height and dress size, and with a wig from wardrobe and his expertise with makeup he could quickly transform himself. The director, pressured by the expense of a lost day's work, readily agreed to the switch.

As there was no dialogue to remember, he simply imitated what he had seen the actress do and followed the director's instructions as the scene progressed. The film was silent, so anyone could say anything during a filming. This often included the frustrated screams of the harried director and the colorful expletives of the overworked actors.

To match the look of the replaced actress, the previous days filming was re-shot with Ray in the part. He was thrilled with this chance at a small role and the bigger salary it brought.

Although many productions were now filmed in and around Los Angeles, California, the locale had not yet experienced the boom that would later make it the film capital of the world. Despite the better California climate and the far brighter outdoor light that enabled filmmakers to shoot outside, New York and the surrounding area continued to dominate the infant film industry, turning out countless one-reel and two-reel films, as well as an ever-growing avalanche of feature-length films. Comedies often featured a great deal of slapstick and physical pratfalls. This sort of bodily comedy required performers with stamina and agility. Some top stars had a stand-in for the more dangerous scenes. The studio could not afford to have a star injured.

Some female stars always had a stunt double. Soon, Ray found his talents constantly in demand. The camera would follow the rough and tumble of his action, dressed as one of the female stars, from a distance. Close-ups of the stars were shot to show the expressions appropriate to the scene, but when it came to falling off horses, down staircases, and general physical trauma, it would be Ray in the long shot taking the tumble. For this, he was well-compensated, but the aches, pains, and sprains that accompanied such mayhem began to take a toll on his mind and body.

Vitagraph frequently split filming between two locations. Exterior shots, depending on the light and weather, were done at the Flatbush location. Interior work was shot at a number of studios scattered around town.

Most films had graduated to using inside and outside locations. Often, the actors and crew boarded a commuter train, carrying costumes and props of all descriptions. If the film was a modern-day story, the contemporary garments proved easy to transport or simply wear. If it was a period piece, the other passengers on the train might be treated to the sight of knights in armor clambering aboard, or ladies in wimples or great feathered hats. The accoutrement they carried, such as swords and spears, occasionally produced an uninvited goose.

One of the most troublesome Vitagraph locations was an open air studio on the roof of a four-story building on Nassau Street in Brooklyn. The light was usually good, but the weather was the enemy. More than once, Ray watched a sudden gale knock down a flimsy faux wall or rip a wig off an actor's head, his own included.

After several months of steady but difficult work as an extra, he realized he was no closer to making it in Vaudeville than when he first arrived in America. He loved the security the studio afforded him, but longed to return to the more satisfying world of live performance.

Vitagraph had begun filming *My Official Wife*, a five-reel feature-length turgid drama centered on a story of the attempted assassination of the Czar of Russia. Ray was playing both male and female roles. Every morning at six, he arrived at the Flatbush studio, ready to take on any extra role required. He was also assigned to double for the film's star, Clara Kimball Young. Up to this point, Young had been a work horse in Vitagraph's one and two-reel dramas, ground out on a weekly basis. Although she portrayed a variety of heroines, she had often been typecast as a virtuous heroine. Although Ray's coloring and eyes resembled the actress, he was considerably taller than her, so the director eventually dropped him as the double. Looking at the resultant rushes, neither the director nor the producer thought Ray was a convincing lookalike for the petite star.

My Official Wife was a tale of Russia before the Revolution, filled with intrigue, forbidden romance, and an attempt upon the life of the Czar. The settings and costumes were luxurious. The turning point of the story is a spectacular ball at the Imperial Palace.

Ray, as a male extra, was turned out handsomely as a Russian guard, complete with shining saber, knee high leather boots, and fur trimmed cape. For the ballroom scene in the Grand Duke's palace, Ray was sumptuously gowned and be-wigged as a matronly noblewoman of the Czar's court, fluttering an enormous feather fan and tugging at long satin opera gloves.

Though he had no assigned movement, other than to descend the grand staircase on the arm of a handsome guard, he played outrageously with his fan and batted his long eyelashes in the direction of the camera. With no spoken dialogue, actors had to improvise body language to convey their feelings.

During this production, Ray formed a significant friendship. This new friend would eventually open unimagined doors of opportunity for him. This unusual bond would grow over the next decade. Ray's new friend made his film debut as an arrestingly handsome Imperial guard in this same ballroom scene. He was a dark, compact, quiet man. His arresting looks had prompted the director to hire him the day before to play a Cossack soldier. He had arrived at the studio as a guest of the set decorator, a notorious queen, who made no effort to disguise his sexual preference. The decorator had introduced his friend around, but made it a point to avoid Ray. Ray couldn't decide whether this interesting young fellow was straight or gay. He would later discover he was both, a switch hitter, who used his good looks to further his career.

This newcomer looked superb in his trimly-fitted trousers and Russian military jacket, his jet black hair tightly dressed with heavy pomade. His eyes, as deep as his hair color, were mysteriously hooded. Even under a heavy layer of grease paint, it was obvious he had a bad complexion. None of that seemed to matter when he moved. A panther was the closest thing Ray could compare him to. He felt he must be a dancer. As it turned out, his hunch was right.

At the end of the day's shooting, Ray managed to introduce himself to this mysterious newcomer. He gripped Ray's hand firmly and flashed a sincere smile, introducing himself as Rodolfo Guglielmi, a recent immigrant from Castelleneta, Italy. Ray told him of his attempts at working in Vaudeville. Rodolfo responded that he, too, was attempting to break into show business. He considered himself a dancer and hoped that work in movies might lead to a career in that direction.

What Ray would discover later was Rodolfo's particular style of dancing was for sale to bored ladies, usually well-married, with a full purse. He frequented the best hotel ballrooms in New York, mingling easily with the rich and jaded. He looked acceptable in his one and only second-hand tuxedo and patent leather hair style. Seldom were there more than a few dollars in his pocket, but he found that women were willing to alter that situation after he had squired them about the dance floor.

His specialty was the most shocking dance style of the day, the Argentine tango. This sensational dance involved incredibly close body contact with very sexually suggestive poses and turns. Rodolfo excelled at this, pressing himself against the breathless bodies of the mature women who were often treated to the growing hardness of his spectacular manhood.

Ray also discovered from the endless pipeline of theatrical tattling that Rodolfo had gotten his entry into society through a handsome older actor, Harrison Ford. With the influence of this established matinee idol, Rodolfo had made several connections with some important show business figures.

He roomed with Ford for some time, despite the fact that the well-heeled actor did not need any financial assistance from a roommate. Rodolfo soon moved on to greener pastures when he met the set decorator on the current film.

This fascinating new face soon acquired a different name, one that rolled more easily off the tongue than Guglielmi. The newly minted Rudolph Valentino was destined for legendary stardom.

By 1919, Ray was saddened to hear his new confidante had migrated to the West Coast as a dancer in a touring musical. The catalyst for his sudden departure was his involvement in a shooting scandal. An enraged husband, returning unexpectedly from a business trip, discovered his wife straddling Rudy's engorged manhood. A gun was introduced to the scenario and somehow ended up killing the cuckold. Barely escaping a murder conviction, the terrified Valentino fled New York. He joined the show, *The Masked Model*, bound for California.

Ray missed his new friend, who constantly advised him to give up his dreams of a stage career and seek his fortune in Hollywood. He couldn't imagine a real future in the film world, but he appreciated Rudolph's faith in his talent.

The two very different men had one thing in common, their love of animals. Both had an almost childlike fascination for dogs and horses. They shared stories of their experiences with animals as children, Rudolph in Sicily, and Ray on the ranch in Texas. Ray, due to meager finances and a nearly gypsy like existence, could not have a pet. Rudy, through good times and bad, always had some variety of canine at his side.

At their last meeting, Rudolph promised to stay in touch. Ray assumed it was just to be polite. He could not have imagined the heights to which the Italian actor would rise, nor could he have guessed the connection their futures would have.

Finally, Ray received an offer in the mail from a booking agency, one of dozens he was registered with. The envelope contained a simple one-page contract calling for sixteen weeks with a touring company.

He had never traveled with a unit show in Vaudeville and was about to learn a valuable lesson.

9
Touring the Sticks

Thousands of Vaudeville theatres dotted the American landscape, each with its own very different character. Ray had signed on with the Interstate Company, an agency that would send him to Oklahoma, Texas, Arkansas, Missouri, Illinois, Kentucky, and Wisconsin.

Trains were the travel choice of most Vaudeville tours, a rugged and often tiring experience. The class of train used to transport the road shows was third class, always ancient, and often behind schedule. Many of these obsolete steam trains consisted of both passenger and freight cars. Ray often found himself in an antiquated passenger conveyance, with carloads of wheat and potatoes in front, and carriers of squealing pigs bringing up the rear.

Performance schedules were hectic. Vaudeville shows never brought down the curtain until at least 10:00 p.m. Performers doing a one night stand had to catch a late train for the next town. Most small-town restaurants closed before the Vaudevillians had finished their show. When they got to the train station, the lunch counter would be shuttered. In addition to the lack of a decent meal, there was the matter of the passenger cars being uncoupled from the rest of the train so they could be sidetracked while the freight section continued on. The luckless passengers sometimes sat shivering in the dimly-lit coaches until they were reattached to another locomotive.

Because contract performers paid from their own meager purses for travel expenses, Ray found the cheapest method was to share a sleeping berth on a Pullman car. The close quarters of the tiny single beds stacked one above the other combined with the peculiar nighttime habits of a bed mate often created comical but exhausting nights.

The location of the next town frequently made it necessary to change trains in the middle of the night, requiring long waits on cold uncomfortable platforms. Meals were a haphazard affair, as many of the cheaper trains had no dining facilities.

A seasoned Vaudevillian learned to pack something edible that would tide them over until the next stop. A typical trip between engagements often involved an arrival at dawn. Rehearsals began immediately on arrival, despite the lack of sleep and food.

In the winter, there was little heat during rehearsals. This was something reserved for the paying customers in the evening. The dressing rooms assigned to the players had few creature comforts. They were usually dirty and poorly lighted. Some were windowless and lit by a single bulb dangling from the ceiling. Applying makeup was particularly difficult under these circumstances.

During more than one booking, Ray found himself sharing backstage facilities with one of the many animal acts that were an integral part of small-time Vaudeville. A burro and a monkey act were remembered vividly for incessant noises and an overpowering smell.

The strangest act Ray ever shared the stage with was a group of trained goats. The biggest problem their trainer had was the unpredictable nature of the horned performers. Ray remembered standing in the wings waiting to go on when suddenly one of the animals leapt in a single bound over the footlights, landing on his feet in the center aisle. The critter suddenly stopped and lunged at a terrified woman, grabbing her elaborate hat covered with artificial fruit. While the audience was convulsed with laughter, the goat proceeded to munch away on the chapeau, oblivious to the screams of protest from the owner.

Lodging while on tour was also a problem. Cheap was always the choice, and best was the rooming house that catered to theatre people.

Bathroom facilities were always a problem. Nearly all boardinghouses had only one bathroom on each floor at the end of a long, dimly lit hall. Getting up early was no guarantee of a hot bath. As soon as the door to the throne room opened, lodgers all along the corridor burst forth. Particularly unsettling at that hour were some unwelcome anatomical views that inevitably appeared with all the coming and going.

There were rarely telephones for guest use in boarding houses. If there was a phone it would be on the wall in the hallway. Competing with as many as twenty or more lodgers, Ray learned to make his calls very early or late.

The sleeping quarters of a rooming house varied widely. Often they were tiny with no window. Few had a closet or even adequate lighting. Players often improvised late night impromptu rehearsals. If they were unlucky enough to be in a bedroom below a dance group, the violent slapping of their tap shoes pounded a deafening tattoo that made slumber impossible. This was usually followed by the screams of the landlady, "Stop that damned racket!"

The longer they booked a room, the cheaper the tariff. If they were lucky enough to stay a full week, the rate could be as low as $4. This sometimes included a plain but filling evening meal. Most landlords forbade any food in the tenant's bedroom, but most hungry Vaudevillians smuggled in a variety of edibles. Ray found tinned meats and soups easy to conceal in luggage, though he often ate them cold.

One of the nasty tricks used by some theatre managers was to delay paying until just before the departure of the performers. The actors were given the pretext that the manager was forced to use the cash box receipts for their salaries. Each member waited in a slow line to be paid with coins. In a rush to catch the train, they shoved the silver in their pockets and raced to the station. Onboard, miles away from the last town, they discovered they had been shorted several dollars. Ray had a quick eye for counting cash and seldom got short changed.

As the show progressed from one berg to another, Ray finally earned a billing on the printed programs. He was still dancing in the male chorus, but he had worked up a new short drag routine that seemed to please the citizens of these less sophisticated towns.

Combining costumes and wigs he had appropriated during his work at Vitagraph, he created two alternate characters, a dame and an elderly socialite. For the dame, he spoke in a Cockney accent. Dialects seemed to be a sure laugh getter with American audiences. The other figure had the faded glamour of a matron of indeterminate age, who appeared to be a little tipsy, and more than a bit risqué. The jokes stopped just short of being dirty, and the songs always contained more than one meaning.

By the second month of the tour, he learned that where an act was featured on a bill was almost as important as the material a performer used. The dreaded "door mat" was the opening act. Vaudeville audiences were not like those that attended the legitimate theatre. Legit theatre goers knew that they would have to be seated before the performance was scheduled to begin. Vaudeville audiences just wandered in, often after the first act had begun.

They visited, made noise, and frequently ignored what was happening on stage. Most opening acts consisted of dancers, trained animals, jugglers, and acrobats. They didn't talk or sing, and it wasn't necessary for the audience to be quiet to enjoy them.

Ray found himself at first in this unwanted spot. He learned to deliver his songs and jokes in a very loud voice, often hushing the chatterboxes out front with a clever verbal barb aimed in their direction. He was never at a loss for words when challenged by a disgruntled audience member. His instantaneous use of a cutting retort usually reduced a heckler to a mute fool.

He soon moved into the number two spot, not the top, but usually a position for anyone doing a song. He cut out most of the jokes due to the five minute time constraints imposed by the crowded bill, instead concentrating on delivering a quick tempo song with a catchy tune sprinkled with off color lyrics.

Fourth and fifth spots required big stars and some spectacle. Six preceded the intermission, a position few artists wanted. Seven required a strong seasoned artist, because the act that followed them was the star spot, the performer everyone was waiting for.

The last act was referred to as "the chaser," because this was what people often saw as they got up to leave. To hold this spot required nerves of steel and a lot of attention-getting comedy. Ray finally achieved "the chaser" halfway through the tour. He gave it his all every night, and was generally well-received, even though the applause came from an audience already part of the way up the aisle. He was learning how to capture and hold an audience, the sign of a true Vaudevillian.

Experienced Vaudevillians warned him to be careful of offending local morals and standards. The worst type of audience was the charity groups, society snobs, or fraternal organizations. These people did not seem amused by Ray's "blue" humor, a term that indicated off-color stories and a casual acceptance of sex. He learned to make inquiries from each theatre manager as to the "sensibilities" of the locals. For the Bible beaters, he kept it clean and corny. For the more accepting, he included a generous helping of double meanings and knowing winks.

Next to the type of audience in importance, particularly in small-time Vaudeville, was the theatre orchestra. If he was lucky, there could be up to eight pieces. Three was more common. This usually included a piano, a horn, and some type of percussion.

If an accompanist was not an experienced musician, it was difficult to get the timing right, particularly with an artist like Ray. A good pianist anticipated the pauses and retards that were so important to a comedian when delivering a punch line to a gag, or an important break to allow for laughter or applause.

Often, Ray was hindered with an oaf at the ivories, who failed to hit his mark and ended up bungling the humorous effect Ray had worked to achieve. It could all be ruined in a few seconds.

He envied the performers who traveled with their own accompanist. They often had less talent than Ray, but the precision with which they delivered their material belied the fact.

Once during a stop at a particularly miserable little Vaudeville house, Ray inquired how many members were in the orchestra. The manager gave him a wink and said, "Two, a piano and a stool."

Ray had begun to mold his stage personality into a definite and easily recognizable character. He would continue to sharpen his craft, until he was able to literally play off the mood of the audience, responding to their signs of restlessness or enthusiasm. He also learned to improvise, no matter what situation might arise.

One night, an inebriated heckler constantly attempted to interrupt his impersonation act with crude remarks about Ray's gender identity. Stepping to the footlights, Ray singled him out with an accusing finger. *"You are only half the man I am, and I'm twice the woman you could ever handle."*

One of the main objectives Ray always strove for when performing to an entirely straight crowd, whether in a club or a Vaudeville theatre, was to gain a mastery of the audience.

He used all his stage experience in addition to his own unique talent to convince them to accept the image he presented, whether he was an old char woman, a dizzy dowager, or a "hatchet-faced busy-body." (The last was a term he frequently used to describe any woman he felt was a meddling gossip.)

Putting an audience at ease was important to Ray. He found he could get away with more outrageous behavior only after he had gained their acceptance. He did this by making it very clear that he did not take his drag seriously.

Men in particular had trouble with the idea of cross dressing. Their masculinity was threatened. Ray laughed at himself first, making it easier for the audience to join in his slightly self-deprecating attitude.

A ploy he learned from an old-time impersonator served him well, when he felt the audience was becoming tense or bored. When a joke fell flat, or there was no applause, he came to the edge of the stage and singled out someone in the front row. He leaned as far forward as possible, smiled broadly, crooked his index finger until he had them stand up, and in a stage whisper that projected to the balcony, he baited them.

"You, yes you with that woman who obviously is your wife. That's not the same young bleached blonde you had here last night. Since you seemed bored, I think I will do a little strip tease. Would you like that?"

By this time the fellow quickly resumed his seat, while the audience chortled.

"The more you clap, the more I'll take off."

Grasping his well-padded boobs in both hands, he shook them back and forth.

"You say you want more? How about a good look at my you know what?"

As if about to undo the hooks in the back of his dress he went on.

"I see you are not interested. Well audience, how about this gentlemen removing his clothes and we can all have a big laugh at his shortcomings!"

10
Up the Ladder, Wrong by Wrong

Fellow performer, Mae, was beginning to express her preference for the legitimate theatre as opposed to regional Vaudeville. From an interview at the time, "A Vaudeville audience is not as sophisticated as a Broadway audience. I often find small towns to have country cousin standards."

Unlike Ray, Mae now shunned the small-town tour and focused on New York. If fellow comics like Eddy Cantor and Bert Lahr could make comedy king, Mae now set her sights on being a comedic but sexy queen.

The artistic experience was not one that Mae worked toward. Her single track vision of how her audiences should perceive her would eventually force her into a corner, a corner that was very much her own. Her double entendre gags, coarse language, and revealing costumes were beginning to draw fire from a relatively new phenomenon, the theatre censor.

As Vaudeville became an increasingly family trade, it automatically invoked a form of self-censorship. Theatre owners realized that it was safer to monitor their artist before he or she committed a serious faux pas, than to have the righteous regulators breathing down their necks. Vaudeville impresarios began to post lengthy notices backstage as to what to not say or do while performing. No artist can use profanity, nothing sacrilegious, nothing off color, no suggestive movements. Every time Mae came across one of these posters, she laughed to herself. To her, they looked like an outline of her next stage appearance.

Mae West was a sly fox. She often inserted alternate lyrics at the last minute, lyrics that the managers had not heard during rehearsals.

"If you don't like my peaches, don't shake my tree."

Sung by another chanteuse, this line could be construed as mildly amusing. When Mae crooned the same verse, all the while shaking her shoulders and grinding her ample hips, it became quite obvious just what she was referring to.

Audiences responded eagerly to this new kind of woman. Managers were torn between firing the songstress and counting the receipts from packed houses that returned night after night.

Savvy theatre owners eventually developed a system that surreptitiously watched for known censors. Worst of all were the vice squads, who had the authority to instantly shut down a show. If a policeman was spotted entering the house, word was rushed backstage to put the lid on an offensive song or joke.

Mae learned how to sing a straight lyric that no one could object to, underlining her intended meaning with a suggestive thrust of the pelvis, or her heavily jeweled fingers caressing her full figure with a tiny smirk of self-satisfaction.

It was the queen bee in Mae's very frank and sexually-charged performances that was honey to most males. One worker drone in particular was drawn irresistibly to the Mae West hive.

Mae was working second billing in Detroit to an accordion player, the star of the show. His big hands enabled him to play an octave and a half reach on the accordion. He had classic masculine features, wavy black hair, and very sexy body language that spoke strongly to his female fans. One look and Mae knew he had the goods.

His name was Guideo Deiro , a twenty-seven-year-old immigrant from Northern Italy. He was both jealous of Mae's popularity and mesmerized by the very things that made her popular. Used to being the center of attention with most women, he could not understand Mae's apparent cold shoulder, despite his repeated attempts to woe her. After years on the road, constant flattery had made Mae just a little cynical. Her explanation, "I'm subjected to more temptation in one day than most gals get in a lifetime."

Guido hadn't learned that Mae made the rules when it came to men, and his dogged determination to seduce her was the wrong technique. Mae always wanted complete freedom of action, even if she was involved seriously with a lover. She repeatedly told the hot-blooded squeezebox player, "I'm single, because I was born that way. A dame that knows the ropes isn't likely to get tied up."

Despite Mae's protestations, Guido did prevail, aided in no small way by the gift of an enormous diamond ring that set him back several months' salary. Surprising the petite object of his affection with the sparkler following a performance, he dropped to his knees in front of the whole cast. "This ring is not a family jewel. It cost me real money. Please wear it."

Mae eyed the impressive stone as Guido slipped it on her rather plump ring finger. Unlike the cool detachment Mae always displayed for previous lovers, she fell bleached blonde head over platform heels. Guido lit her fire. She couldn't shake her infatuation for him.

"I can't help myself . . . the sex thing was terrific with this guy. I wanted him morning, noon, and night. That's all I wanted to do. It was very deep, hittin' on all the emotions. You can't get too hot over anybody unless there's somethin' that goes along with the sex act, can you?"

The two managed to share their billing over the next two seasons. It was Guido, originally the bigger star, who changed his bookings to be with Mae. He took on the role of her conductor. This was a far less prestigious position with considerably less money.

Mae went along with it, and soon the two were an act, she in front of the footlights, and he in the orchestra pit. Following the last curtain, they stole away. After several weeks of this cozy arrangement, Guido popped the question.

Always on top, Mae countered, "Are you kiddin? Marriage is a great institution. No family should be without it. Men are my hobby. If I ever got married, I'd have to give it up."

Guido continued to propose marriage, storming the battlements. At last, the fortress fell. That summer, they were wed, with the understanding that Guido would tell no one, not even his extended family.

Bursting with pride, he persuaded Mae to meet his relatives on a trip to Washington. After a sumptuous meal washed down with a generous homemade Chianti, the proud groom was unable to contain himself any longer. He confided they were a married couple, at which point his garrulous family embraced the startled Mae with a group embrace.

It must have also been evident to the profession that Mae and Guido were hitched.

Variety reviewed their act: "Mr. and Mrs. Deiro are playing at Shea's Theatre, Toronto, Canada."

No less an authority than Joe Laurie, Jr. wrote of the pair in his *Encyclopedia of Vaudeville*: "Guido Deiro is Mae West's hubby."

The tour continued for another year. Mae finally persuaded Guido at the end of her act to join her onstage. She stood front and center, pretending to play the accordion, while Guido did the actual fingering from the wings. When the audience applauded, Mae dragged Guido from the wings and had him repeat what the audience thought she had done. It was a great gimmick.

Despite the obvious physical joys the union produced, Guido's Mediterranean temper finally put an end to their bliss. He had become impossibly possessive. A swank Italian eatery was the setting for their nearly operatic farewell, but it was certainly not "senza rancor."

Suspecting every man that approached Mae that evening had mischief on his mind, Guido played his cards and lost the game. As Mae engaged a well-meaning fan in a harmless conversation at her table, Guido leapt up and brandished a short knife, threatening to cut his throat. The admirer threw a mean right clip, nearly breaking Guido's jaw, followed by two more volleys. As a final insult, the victor began to throw plates from the server's cart in Mae and Guido's direction. Mae ducked, just as a platter of pasta slammed Guido in the face. His white tuxedo shirt, soaked in sauce, clung to his muscular torso. Limp tendrils of spaghetti hung from his hair like red seaweed.

The wait staff attempted to subdue the enraged Deiro. Soon, an all-out fight reduced half the restaurant to rubble. There were broken chairs, overturned tables, and the comical sight of the combatants bathed in sauces, soups, and the spilled contents of a dessert cart.

Mae fled for New York alone. Years later, she reminisced, "I see it was a cruel thing I did to Guido, without a parting word. He carried on like a Latin maniac, calling my mother at all hours, begging to know where I was. He threatened to have the police search for me. He turned to heavy drink, and ended up near death in a hospital."

There remains the unanswered question: Why did Mae insist their marriage be kept a secret? The waters become even more muddied when looking at recently discovered documents for Guido Deiro and Catherine Mae Belle West. These are filed in The Supreme Court of the State of New York, dated November 9, 1920, granting a divorce to Guido Deiro and Catherine Mae Belle West.

Guido would not see Mae again until 1943. By then, she was one of the highest-paid stars in the business, and he was totally forgotten. He contacted her, showing his former wife an article he had written, "Mae West and Me." He was planning to sell it to *Look* magazine.

Mae objected, saying rather disingenuously, "I have never wanted to flaunt my romances in public."

He acquiesced, despite his impoverished state, as Mae threw the tell-tale story into the fireplace. This led to a brief renewal of their friendship. Perhaps her conscience bothered her more than she wanted to admit. Mae helped her down and out ex with some cash and a few theatrical leads until he got back on his feet. Then, he disappeared from her life.

After Guido and Mae split up their Vaudeville partnership, she went solo. From her growing song repertoire, one for which she often failed to pay royalties, came two very typical and successful numbers, "Any Kind of Man," and the highly suggestive "I want a Caveman."

One of the tricks used by singers in Vaudeville was to pad the audience with enthusiasts. Mae would have her manager contact as many songwriters as possible, preferably those that were not terribly successful. Each aspiring composer was baited with the possibility of Mae possibly adding one of their songs to her act.

Few could resist the temptation to be out front should Mae introduce their little masterpieces. When their muse was announced, they were sure her next ditty would be something they had penned. More often than not, they went home disappointed.

III
Only Pansies Know How

Ray had a vivid memory of the first time he saw Mae. He had ended his grueling tour of the hinterlands and was out for an evening on the town in New York. For him, this was a busman's holiday, an evening as part of the audience of a Vaudeville show. His companions, a gaggle of noisy queens, were all talking about this sequined and slinky new singing phenomenon. He paid little attention to the hyperbole of those around him until the orchestra struck up the introduction to Mae's act.

She came on in the star spot, elaborately gowned in black shimmering fabric, trailing a long white feather boa. The orchestra played a percussion heavy beat as Mae began to sway ever so slightly, a chorus of handsome men on each side slowly kicking in rhythm to the low down and dirty Burlesque house motif. Ray expected her to break out in a series of stripper bumps and grinds.

Mae flashed a brilliant smile and began to sing a song that would have been considered harmless from any other chanteuse. A well-directed bump from her hip in the direction of the dancer next to her caused him to collapse into the arms of the chorus. The audience responded with cheers.

Mae cast her scimitar eyes upward and continued to wriggle while the audience roared. Her exit was a strong as her entrance. Slowly unwrapping herself from the fifteen-foot ostrich boa like a snake in molt she wound her way sinuously between the line of masculine beauties until she reached the proscenium. She began to rub the feathery wrap in a very suggestive manner and threw it to the chorus as she disappeared into the wings. At the end of the number Ray's party and the rest of the packed theatre were on their feet cheering.

Afterward, Ray found himself backstage congratulating a vision in black spangles and a towering headdress. The still gyrating Mae was surrounded by a host of enamored males. The straight shooters were hoping to get a chance to fire their guns, the queens came to coo and perhaps copy some of Mae's outlandish costume. One particularly handsome admirer bowed and kissed Mae's extended hand.

"Ummm," she droned, "Opportunity knocks for every man; but, you have to give a woman a ring. Women with 'pasts' interest you men because you men hope that history will repeat itself."

May turned her attention momentarily to Ray and his friends. She inquired what they liked best about her act. Unanimously, they praised her gowns and hats. She sidled a little closer to the group and in a throaty whisper purred, "Only pansies know how to look like a sexy woman."

She confided she had gotten a lot of her inspiration from the many female impersonators she had worked with. At this point, Ray blurted out that he was an impersonator and would love to perform for her someday. He mentioned a Greenwich Village club he was about to open in, and was surprised when Mae said she might come.

The next day was Sunday. An antiquated New York law declared Sunday Vaudeville performances were illegal. Theatre managers circumvented the law by posting billboards that advertised the Vaudeville shows as "concerts." Concerts were legal, even though the same Vaudevillians that had tread the boards the night before in a Vaudeville show were now performing a Sunday "concert." To make matters more inane, the law required the curtains to be completely closed between each act.

Ray started out many of his work weeks performing in "concert" on Sunday, and hoofing it in Vaudeville the remainder of the week. One of the most dreaded theatres he ever worked in concert was The Colonial. It was infamous for the rudeness of the audience it attracted. Obnoxious would be an understatement.

The Colonial was also known for a system called the "claque." The claque was operated by a con man that would bring in people to laugh and applaud an artist, if the artist paid him a certain sum. If a performer refused to use this system, the con man would sic the audience on him with a type of applause called the "Colonial clap." This consisted of endless clapping in unison that continued throughout the performer's act, making it impossible to hear anything. Even more insulting was the tossing of pennies onstage. Once was enough for Ray, despite the fact that he was not the object of the audience's wrath. No sense risking it twice.

Important booking agents and producers frequently scouted the Sunday concerts looking for new talent. One of the longest, continuous bookings Ray ever signed was due to his discovery by a Brooklyn talent scout.

He was trying out a new act with a "straight" partner, the premise built around an Egyptian theme. The program listed it as "Cleopatra and Her Asp." Ray was a delightfully outlandish Cleopatra, and his partner, in the shortest of togas, was a hunky Marc Anthony.

The act was an immediate hit with audiences. The innuendos and double entendres of Ray's comic Egyptian Queen and the good looks of the strapping Marc Anthony guaranteed bookings all over Brooklyn. He played the Orpheum, Novelty, Crescent, Gotham, Prospect, and many theatres razed long ago.

Ray tried never to become static, often adding a new line or song. As his act became more risqué in response to the encouragement from out front, he received warnings from several managers. Emboldened by the strong reception audiences were giving him, he refused to clean up his material. He was given a list of words and situations he could not use on stage. Something new in his book of impersonations brought the situation to a head.

Ray decided to rework an act he had done in England that had always met with success. Dressed as a doddering dowager in a long gown, tiara, and opera gloves, he tottered on stage, taking his place in the curve of a grand piano. Signaling to his pianist with the long rhinestone studded handle of his lorgnette, he began in a fluttering falsetto:

"Now when I was a child
It seems I was wild
And I wanted to play a piano
So my big handsome teacher
The son of a preacher
His name was Professor Romance
I liked my young teacher, you bet

He was so handsome, and so tall
And it simply was grand
When he played with one hand, ha ha!
But I liked my first piece best of all
My first piece, ah, my very first piece
I was so young and so sentimental
It was hard, ha ha, very hard
But he was so patient and so gentle
Now I've had many pieces since I was a girl
How many I'll never recall
But the first piece he gave me was ten pages long, ha ha!
But I liked my first piece best of all!"

Basking in unusually strong applause Ray stood in the wings, ready to take another curtain call. His instincts had proved him right and he had correctly judged the mood of the audience. They loved the off-color ditty.

Backstage, the feeling was not shared. Suddenly, he felt the strong arm of the burly manager propel him to the stage door. The last thing he heard was a massive slam and click of the lock behind him. Standing in the cold, dimly lit alley, he made a decision. He would find and cultivate an audience that appreciated his work and he would perform in venues that catered to his type of audience. This decision set him on a long and rocky career road, but it was one that he seldom regretted.

12.
Grab a Dyke, It's a Raid: The Law, the Latin Lover, La-La Land

Mae had discovered a new partner, pianist Harry Richman. His many talents included those of an expert accompanist, as well as stylish dancer. It certainly didn't hurt that this package was handsomely wrapped. His other "talent" fascinated the keen-eyed Mae even more. He displayed it at the drop of a zipper to every pretty face in the show. Mae went after him like a predatory bird. She caught her prey, and soon they were intertwined in every location possible: bed, bath, and beyond. Mae's observation of this tireless straight shooter was succinct. "He was a machine!"

When asked how his relationship with her was progressing, Richman offered, "Geez, that West gal rehearses me eight hours a day. Maybe next week, we'll use the piano!"

Harry and Mae displayed an obvious onstage chemistry that soon had them playing the better Vaudeville houses. Their bookings continued to multiply until she discovered that he was secretly negotiating with the headliner, Nora Bayes, to create a new revue.

Bayes was notorious for her romances, walk-outs, and terrible tantrums. Mae pointed all this out to Harry, but he was obviously too taken with her charms to listen. After a heated exchange that ended with Harry's departure, Mae found herself in a theatrical limbo.

This was a particularly hard time for Mae as a Vaudeville act. She was a known commodity, but not a real star. Bookings were often weeks or months apart, and when they came, she often found herself on a bill in Jersey City or Hoboken, just over the river from New York. Unlike New York, these cities were notoriously tough on entertainers. If they didn't like her, they threw pennies on stage or hissed like cats. Mae was never the target of such ridicule, but she was always on edge as she saw the acts that preceded her become the objects of such blatant derision.

Another tough town was Boston, but Mae was never put off by the attitude of the audience there. Her favorite venue was the Old Howard, a legendary Burlesque house. When there was no Burlesque show booked, they featured Vaudeville. The audience was usually filled with sailors from the Charleston Navy Yard.

You can imagine the rapport that existed between the earthy songstress and a house full of randy sailors. Whenever a woman with a down and dirty approach such as Mae's was on the Howard's bill, the theatre had to hire a burly policeman to maintain order. The balcony proved to be the biggest problem. When this eager enforcer of law and order found anyone out of line, he was quick to apply the hard end of his club to the skull of the trouble maker.

One night at the Old Howard, just prior to Mae's entrance, a fight broke out in one of the end boxes overhanging stage right. Fists flew and tempers flared. Before the police officer could make his way from the balcony to the box, the act on stage immediately below the box became the target of a volley of beer bottles. In addition to the flying projectiles, a stream of black tobacco juice was spat with deadly aim onto the white tuxedo front of a dancer.

The manager, in a panic, motioned to the orchestra to take up Mae's entrance music. She quickly shimmied onstage to screams of approval from the rowdy sailors, the previous offending act fled, and the show went on.

Mae realized that being but one of many on a Vaudeville bill was not going to lead to her dream. Mae, and Mae alone, should be the reason that audiences filled the auditorium.

She decided a production, perhaps a play, custom designed for her particular talents, was what she needed. Achieving stardom was a tough climb, but she was unwavering in her ambitions. To her detractors she said, "I'm the kind of girl who climbs the ladder of success, wrong by wrong."

During a theatrical hiatus, Mae wrote a play that was to become her best box office effort to date. *Sex* (1926) was the name of West's titillating tome. This three-letter word was not bandied about casually at the time. Not surprisingly, she could not find a single producer to finance her little drama with the dirty name.

The role she had written for herself was that of a hard-boiled dame, who had seen everything and wasn't afraid to talk about it. Her language was peppered with street jargon and references to sex, drugs, and murder. Part of the action was in a brothel, and several scenes were lifted directly from things she had seen in Burlesque.

In the first act, she is discovered welcoming back an old flame. The former lover, suggestively straddling a recumbent Mae, keeps repeating, "I have something for you, something all the women are fighting for, but be careful not to bend it."

The "something" turns out to be a fancy ostrich feather he suggestively inserts in Mae's heaving cleavage. This sort of dialogue made the script a difficult sell.

Finding one producer's door after another rudely slammed in her face, Mae finally turned in desperation to her mother for the backing. Tillie was well-heeled and more than happy to put up the cash to see that Mae could have her chance at a starring role on Broadway. There was considerable financial risk involved for an untested author, so the West family wisely decided to try out the play in a less critical environ before signing a lease on an expensive New York venue.

The out of town engagement began in Connecticut to packed houses. The very title created a furor of interest. A New York producer came up to see what all the fuss was about. He went backstage after the curtain and promptly offered to bring it to his theatre in New York. The publicity that the play had created in Connecticut, all of it scandalous, guaranteed a sellout each night of the New York run. The critics called it "Vulgar . . . nasty . . . crude," and audiences couldn't get enough of it.

There was running concurrently an equally scandalous Broadway play that shocked audiences and critics alike. The more that was written about *The Captive*, (1926), the more impossible it became to get a ticket. Block-long lines formed outside the theatre each night. Ticket seekers jostled to gain entrance to this sizzling drama. The verboten theme was lesbianism.

As part of the standing-room-only audience for *The Captive*, Mae experienced a sudden inspiration. She looked around at the packed house and it became clear to her: she would write a play of an equally scandalous nature. She claimed the entire story came to her as she rode home from the theatre that night. Her subject would be a familiar one for her: homosexuality, specifically transvestites.

In an amazingly short time for a new author, Mae ground out the flamboyant tale of an underground world seldom glimpsed by audiences. Increasingly aware of the growing plague of theatre censorship, she hoped to pass off her writing as a form of public sexual education. It was only a thinly veiled excuse to showcase the drag queens she had seen performing in the Greenwich Village gay clubs. Like the uniquely titled *Sex*, this expose of the world of the impersonator became simply *The Drag*.

Word spread like wildfire through the gay community that a new play was being cast with auditions at a club in the Village. There were many parts for gay actors and female impersonators. Ray was among those that packed the little club in anticipation of meeting the author of this daring play. Mae arrived late after finishing her performance in *Sex*.

Her keen eye looked over the colorful crowd. There were male impersonators in top hat and tails, some with glued on mustaches and beards. The usual assortment of female impersonators ranged from exquisite to hilarious.

One tall figure caught her attention. She felt she had seen this person but couldn't place him. Ray explained he had come backstage after one of her performances and they had chatted for a moment. He gushed how good he thought she had been that night.

"Why should I be good, when I'm packing them in because I'm bad?" she snickered, hand on hip.

She felt Ray would be perfect for her new play. The colorless woman who was her assistant dutifully wrote down the details of those in the crowd that Mae chose. She kept the selection process moving quickly. It was over before Ray realized what had happened.

He stepped out into the damp New York night, the rehearsal address for the Broadway-bound show, *The Drag*, tucked tightly in his little beaded evening bag.

Rehearsals for the show were a free for all. There was a very thin plot line with no actual stars. It was meant to be a florid spectacle. Ray played both a drag and a straight role. The latter called for a tuxedo, an absolute necessity for any chorus boy's wardrobe.

This time, his drag would not be comic. Mae wanted glamour. He pieced together a silver gown with a dropped waist line, long white gloves, a beaded headband, and an oversized ostrich feather fan.

Mae carefully inspected the actors' costumes and gave Ray's ensemble a particularly long look from top to bottom. As she sidled away, all the while looking him up and down, her voice trailed off, "Its better to be looked over, than overlooked."

The dialogue of the play was lifted directly from the street and the clubs that were meeting places of gay culture. The bitchy exchanges between the many impersonators were the meat and potatoes of the play. A typical scene emphasized the catty banter that was the lingo of so many drags.

> Minnie: Oh queen, aren't you a thin one.
> Jade: Not at all. I can hang onto any man and not give him a hernia. You are the one that is perfectly plump!
> Minnie: Men prefer a gal with meat. When I go to the ship pier at least half the Navy flags don't go to half-mast.
> Jade: You are full of nonsense. Men are mad for my hot stuff. When I cruise the boulevards you can smell their meat cooking in Hell's Kitchen.
> Minnie: Your face certainly looks tight. Your eyes slant like a China doll.
> Jade: They'd better. I spent a fortune on my lift. In fact it is so tight it pulled everything up, and I mean everything, and now I have a goatee!

Ray's big moment came at the conclusion of the play, which consisted of an elaborate drag ball with a full jazz orchestra. This occupied almost a third of the play, the preceding scenes a mere lead up to the entertainers that populated the ball.

The ball featured a raunchy "cooch" dancer, dirty-mouthed comediennes straight from the world of Burlesque, a chorus line of drunk, over the hill impersonators, and a big musical number. Ray was given a small solo, singing, dancing, and embellishing with an occasional caustic ad lib. Mae approved of the cast adding their own touches. She wanted the audience to see these performers as they would appear in a gay club, a seamy slice of life most of them had never experienced.

Typically, the untried play opened out of town in Patterson, New Jersey. The press reaction was immediate and savage. Some even doubted that Mae was the author. She had decided to compose under the pseudonym, "Jane Mast," but this fooled hardly anyone.

Ignoring the negative opinions of the critics, Patterson, a town steeped in the raunchy traditions of Burlesque, planted their working class butts in every seat for each performance. The spicy entertainment evoked an equally randy response from the blue collar audiences.

There were now two Mae West literary creations filling theatres, and filling the papers with juicy bylines about this daring author. What mattered most to Mae was that people were talking, and talk sold tickets.

All this discussion of sex, abnormal or not, couldn't help but fill the nostrils of New York's morality bloodhounds. Mae's old nemesis, the censors and the cops, had joined together in a dangerous pack and were on the trail of this voluptuous bunny. They were out to get her, by hook or by crook. The time was right to corner their quarry. Mayor Walker, Mae's old friend and frequent protector, was out of town, leaving Mae and her crew particularly vulnerable.

During a highly suggestive scene in *Sex*, uniformed officers charged down the theatre aisles. Pandemonium and screams erupted from the audience. There was a large contingency of queens in the audience that night, and several were heard to exclaim, "Quick, grab a dyke, it's a raid!"

A startled but not intimidated Mae was engaged in a lip lock with a burly actor who was lying on top of the buxom star. Hauled unceremoniously from the stage, Mae, and any of the cast they could catch, was crammed into the waiting police wagons. The destination was the police station of the Eighteenth Precinct.

The press, who had been tipped off by the law, was waiting outside the station. Flashbulbs popped as the cars pulled up, disgorging their screaming cargo, still in costume and heavy stage makeup.

Throwing off the rough hold of a masculine police matron, Mae walked confidently to the top of the steps, turned, and addressed the crowd as if they were an opening night audience.

"Unlike that lesbian play *The Captive*, my cast in *Sex* is all normal."

What she didn't tell them was "that lesbian play" had inspired her other play, *The Drag*.

Almost simultaneously, there had been an equally sensational bust of the cast from *The Drag*. Mae's sister, Beverly, was among those hauled in.

The New York Times carried the headlines the next morning: "Bridgeport, Conn. Feb 1. Edwin Elsner of 373 West Forty Sixth Street, New York, stage director of 'The Drag' which opened here last night, and Miss Beverly West of 50 Jericho Turnpike, Floral Park, N.Y., sister of Mae West, author of the play, were arrested at 5:30 o'clock this morning in Miss West's room at the Arcade Hotel. They will be arraigned in the City Court on Wednesday on technical charges of disturbing the peace. The police allege both with charges of misconduct."

After ten days in the local slammer, and invaluable free publicity in the newspapers, Mae was released to go back to business as usual. Beverly's fate was a fine and no jail time.

Sex had already racked up an impressive record of 340 sold out performances. Despite the obvious popular success of the play, critics continued to badger the brazen actress/author.

The *Herald Tribune* fumed: "I refrain from objecting to Miss West's over-conspicuous charms . . . she is a plump blonde whose ample figure overflows her girdle in graceful cascades . . . she talks through her nostrils. You wonder why she appeals to men . . . She is a menace to art, morals, and deserves an investigation."

Mae responded to this particularly personal insult during a press interview. "I would horse whip this critic should I ever meet him."

Waiting in the wings was yet another of her plays, *The Wicked Age*. (1927). Again, there was legal dispute, but not from the censors. The lead actor was replaced after Mae found him "lacking" in a certain department. He claimed in court that Mae had propositioned him, and he had refused her charms. He also pointed out he had an iron clad contract. It was the contract that held up the production, so Mae abandoned the play.

One of the most ludicrous cases against a Mae West play was the indictment brought by the County of New York against *Pleasure Man* (1928). The New York police raided the play at the Biltmore Theatre on October 1, 1928. Within hours, Mae's lawyers had an injunction in hand, and the play began for a second performance the following night. Undaunted, the police again raided the theatre, this time carrying off the cast still in costume—many in drag—to the local station.

The Grand Jury indicted Mae and the entire cast. The charges included the following:

> "Unlawfully preparing, advertising, giving, directing, presenting and participating in an obscene, indecent, immoral and impure drama, play exhibition and entertainment. Furthermore the court feared for the morals of the youth who might view this obscenity. The debauchery and corruption of morals of the youth would create in their minds inordinate and lustful desires. In addition, the play created a common nuisance of all the people, and against the peace of the People of the State of New York and their dignity."

It took several months for this legal travesty to actually come to court. What made it all the more dubious was the lack of an actual script for the judge and jury to study.

It was dependent on the State to prove that this obscene piece of theatre was a threat to the public without having ever seen the actual script of the play.

Mae's lawyer was a brilliant defender, known for his exceptional cunning. To demonstrate to the court just how really dangerous the play's dialogue was, he called upon two of the arresting officers to testify. Both were very large, athletic men, built like football players. When called to the stand, both were reticent to enact what they had seen that night at the Biltmore Theatre.

Under oath, they were forced to act out the terrible scenes they had witnessed as performed by the troupe of degenerate drags in *Pleasure Man*. Holding one enormous pinky aloft, the first red-faced vice officer imitated the mince and swish of the lead drag character, the Bird of Paradise. In a startling falsetto, the macho man exclaimed, "Oh, Mary! Get you girl!"

The entire court room burst into uncontrollable laughter.

Undeterred, the prosecution continued to call witnesses. Again, an officer who had been part of the raid was called to give testimony. When asked for specifics of the "lewd" dance Mae performed in the play, the policeman described what he saw.

"Miss West moved her navel up and down, and from right to left"

The prosecutor followed up with, "So you actually saw her navel?"

Flushed and hesitant, the officer blurted out, "No, but I saw something in her middle that moved from East to West."

Mae was subsequently called to the stand to present her version of the play. She had deliberately dressed down in a simple dark outfit with very little makeup. She wore a tight-fitting cloche hat that covered most of her famous bleached coiffure. Her one concession to glamour was a black fur-trimmed coat.

Her usually bold and inviting eyes were cast downward as she simply stated the play was a total success from the start, with appreciative audiences every night. She said she had not received a single complaint, written or verbal, about the supposed dangers of her work. She pointed out that the State censor had recommended removing only one number from the entire play, and she had done so before it ever opened. In other words, the State had seen the previews and had found no problems.

She continued that on opening night she had been present in the lobby of the sold out theatre. The first act received warm applause. She stood in a reception line during the intermission, shaking the hands of many of New York's prominent politicians and businessmen. There offered only praise and congratulations.

Always cognizant of her audience, Mae realized that the court appeared to be on her side. She decided to throw down the gauntlet. Standing as straight and as tall as her five-foot frame would allow, she turned to the jury as if facing an opening night audience. Raising her voice, she argued that this trial was all a conspiracy to run her out of the legitimate theatre business, endanger her investments and future, and wreak havoc on the careers of those involved in *Pleasure Man*. In her most theatrical manner, she stood head held high, pointing a well-manicured hand in the direction of her accusers. "What they are saying is illegal, arbitrary, and tyrannical."

The judge's gavel came down in her favor with a bang, as the courtroom erupted in cheers.

The indictment was dismissed, but there was little sense of victory on Mae's part. The bail alone for the large cast had cost her over $60,000, and she never recouped her large investment in the physical costs of the play.

1931 was another tumultuous year for Mae. Her highly controversial play, *The Constant Sinner*, created a firestorm from the critics and public. It dealt with sex, as usual, but the sex was interracial, a theme that was hardly even discussed at the time, let alone portrayed on a Broadway stage.

Against the wishes of the Schubert brothers, the play's backers, Mae went forward with her plans to hire nearly twenty Black performers from Harlem. Mae pointed out that several of them had already broken the color barriers by appearing on Broadway.

Her next announcement created a stalemate. Mae chose Lorenzo Tucker, a successful and very sexy Black actor to play her lover. The Schubert brothers threatened to shut down the play instantly if Mae did not back down. She gave in.

The powerful Schubert Brothers insisted Mae use a White actor in blackface with a curly wig. He was forced to remove his wig during curtain calls to reassure the nervous audience that he was indeed White.

Mae instinctively knew the issue that bothered most critics—all male—was the idea that a Black man could be more attractive, more virile, than a White lover. Black women had gotten away for years, on stage and in clubs, portraying themselves as sexual objects. They danced and sang provocatively, leaving little to the imagination. White audiences had no problem with this image, but the idea that a Black man was also an object of sexual desire sent most insecure White men into an apoplectic fit. The Schubert brothers had gone so far as to hint they would seek police intervention if Mae persisted with her original casting

The resultant furor over the depiction of miscegenation in *The Constant Sinner* finally got to Mae. Her habit of making a curtain speech at the end of her plays took an odd turn. She told the audience that she had heard rumors that what was depicted on stage was a slice of her own personal life. She denied ever having frequented "dives, nightclubs, cabarets." She claimed to not have personally experienced what the audience had just seen in her play. She must have called upon all her skill as an actress to convince those who knew her secret lifestyle of men of all description and race.

Her next stage role would become one that lifted her career to another level. Removing all outside distractions from her life, she began to devote her considerable energy and imagination to *Diamond Lil* (1928).

Mae's unusual method of authorship consisted of thinking out loud, saving the thoughts she wanted on paper in an almost childish scrawl, and dictating them to her secretary. In the evening, she retired to her bedroom and scribbled corrections and ideas on the day's script. As she often said, "I do my best work in bed." In a matter of months, the work sprang forth full blown. *Diamond Lil* was to be a landmark in her career.

The action of *Diamond Lil* is set in a particularly seedy borough of New York, the Bowery. It is infested with crime and easy women. Mae's character stands at the top of this nefarious heap. Lil is a thinly disguised portrait of a prostitute. The time frame is the turn of the century.

Mae already had a concept of the look for *Diamond Lil*. Her eye for costuming was learned from working with her mother, a talented designer and dressmaker. Tillie taught her the importance of tailoring and fit. Mae's own figure was not the easiest to dress. Her legs were short and her famous top could overpower the whole outline.

She was introduced to a costume designer during the preparations for *Diamond Lil* that understood just what her famous figure needed.

Dolly Tree carried very impressive credentials when she was first hired by New York's top costume house. She had created the exotic feathered outfits for the legendary *Follies Bergère* in Paris in 1922. She stayed on, creating the entire wardrobe for five further *Follies Bergère* shows.

Mae contracted her to design the costumes for both *Diamond Lil* and *Pleasure Man*. For *Diamond Lil*, set in the 1890s, Tree gave Mae an hourglass figure, small in the waist, topped by a more than ample bust, and full hips and bottom below the belt. The cleavage was further enhanced with a corset that shoved what nature had provided to new heights. The waist was squeezed with a series of painful wire closures. The whole gown was iced, as if it were a cake, with feathers, flounces, and a dramatic train.

Dolly found the frocks for the female impersonators in *Pleasure Man* to be a different challenge. The typically broader shoulders, shorter legs, and longer torso of the average man required a lot of illusion. Arms needed more coverage, as did the throat and Adam's apple. Ray loved the costume Miss Tree created for him. He purchased it after the show closed, using it in his act for many years.

Once the physical details of *Diamond Lil* had been sorted out, the all-important angel became the next worry. Angel is an old Broadway term used for the money man, the guy with the deep pockets who backs a show. Mae found that angel in the unlikely person of a notorious devil, mobster Owney Madden.

Nicknamed "Killer" Madden, he had met Mae during a Vaudeville tour in the Windy City. He liked what he saw and told her so. There was an immediate attraction between the dangerous Madden and the equally daring Mae.

Owney was dark and graceful like a feline, and, like a tom cat, he was always turned on. The tryst that developed between Madden and Mae was hot and hurried. He was so taken with her that he promised to help her should she ever need him in the future. The future was here, and Mae put the touch on Madden. Always able to put his hands on some ill-gotten gains, he coughed up the cash for *Diamond Lil*.

One of Madden's employees was a young George Raft. Raft would eventually catch the eye of Hollywood's Paramount Studios. The heavily pomaded part-time pansy possessed the slick ballroom skills required of any lounge lizard, a dancing partner for ladies at tea dances, an afternoon soiree held in smart hotels and bistros in America's bigger cities.

These languid and limp-wristed young dance partners, nearly always handsome, thrilled their more mature partners with dance styles that seduced and titillated. Clutching their victims in a shockingly sexual posture, they would grind and rub the willing women, often producing low moans masked by the seductive music of the Tango.

The women who paid handsomely for this afternoon delight usually checked their corsets at the door, thus allowing complete and unbound enjoyment of the supple bodies of the young "lounge lizards" that partnered them.

This decidedly pejorative nickname came from habit the dancers had of lounging on the sofas of the hotels as they awaited their next female meal ticket. To retain the services of these gigolos, the ladies usually had to purchase gifts or surreptitiously stuff wads of cash into the tight trouser pockets of their dance partners. This sometimes resulted in an opportunity to gauge the size of the gigolo's money maker. It was rumored Raft had blackmailed more than one foolish society matron who paid dearly for the privilege of feeling Raft's mighty member.

At the beginning, Raft was simply an errand boy for "Killer" Madden, who collected Madden's share of the box office take during the run of *Diamond Lil*.

Raft and Mae quickly became simpatico but never sexual. This strange friendship would lead to Mae's invitation to Hollywood and eventual film stardom. In the meantime, *Diamond Lil* was bringing Mae the best reviews of her career.

The critics' stamp of approval for the saucy star gave her a new standing in the eyes of the better folk on Broadway. They crowded her dressing room after each performance—writers, actors, society matrons—all in awe of the "world's wickedest woman." This was a description Mae had created. She made sure the press bandied it about in all their releases.

There was more than a little truth in Mae's "wicked woman" title. Every day at 2:00 p.m., she locked herself in her dressing room. Visitors were strictly forbidden. She told everyone in ear shot she had to attend to her "duties." This almost always included the lover of the moment. Following this afternoon delight, the stud of the day departed and Mae prepared herself for her evening performance, a performance often inspired by her afternoon activities.

The Drag and *Pleasure Man* had aborted runs.

Ray was again at loose ends. He could possibly find another Vaudeville tour, but neither the pay nor the conditions seemed to justify the hard work.

He appeared vocally on several recordings. These began in the days of the 78 rpm sound recordings. (Later, he was captured on 45-rpm and finally 33 1/3 rpm vinyl discs.) His recording career would span more than thirty years.

Ray first set foot in a recording studio in March 1931. The label was Brunswick, a highly respected name. The record producers were trying to take advantage of the "Pansy Craze" that was then sweeping the country. Every label wanted to include at least one well-known female impersonator or gay performer in their catalogue. He was spotted by a talent scout from the record company during a performance in a cabaret revue and offered a one-off contract.

Ray recorded "I Want to be Good" (1931) for Brunswick, but, like Mae West, he took the lyrics of the old chestnut and bowdlerized them in a blue fashion to suit his raunchy style. What he committed to the B-side of the platter is unknown. Apparently, the executives at the company found his material "too hot," and so the recording stayed in their vaults.

He then moved on to a label called Western Record Company. His material was released incorporating his own name on the label, Bourbana. This studio was in-tune with the Ray Bourbon style, and released a long series of successful recordings over the years.

Under the Counter (UTC) was another label that signed him. (A partial list of the long-playing albums that he recorded for UTC is included in the appendices.)

These recordings were part of a niche style that was not sold openly in record stores. The subject matter was low down and blue, in the terminology of the business. Barely disguised tales of sex in every form, and some not so disguised, were the meat of this style. His material was not as crude as so many who recorded these "party records." This term was a code for "dirty."

Ray's style relied heavily on the double entendre, a la Mae West. He wrote many of the lyrics, and all of the patter that would accompany the introductions to the songs. There was an intimate feeling to most of the recordings, as if he were in your living room at a private party, telling the guests a naughty story. Most of these sounded as if they were personal recollections, and they often were.

Full orchestration backed him on several recordings, but most often he relied on a skilled personal pianist who also accompanied him in his live club shows. A favorite accompanist was the budding pianist and songwriter, Chet Forrest. Forrest and Ray collaborated on many songs and material. Forrest had a lover named Bob Wright, who would often accompany the act as they toured.

Forrest was a very talented composer. He felt that Ray's lightning fast improvisational delivery, unique among impersonators, enhanced his compositions. Their partnership ended after a few years in the 1930s. The composer went on to work at Paramount composing film scores.

Ray found several weeks work at The Flower Pot and other gay night spots in the Village. His experiences in the Mae West plays, though short-lived, were major theatre productions that gave him new confidence to play almost any character with assuredness and flash.

He added a new patter song at his opening at Frank's Place, one of Greenwich Village's more chic gay night spots. Dressed in an orange Mandarin dress and a black wig, he suddenly appeared from behind a curtain. In one hand was a large oriental fan; in the other a mallet used to strike a brass gong as his accompanist began a tinkling pseudo Oriental melody:

"Now in old China far away, lives a Mandarin they say,
Known as the honorable Mr. Tong.
He controls a bandit band,
Rules it with a sturdy hand,
And in China land they call a band a tong.
Now other Mandarins have tongs

But all the ladies say, Mr. Wong has the biggest tong in the
Orient today.
Mr. Wong has got the biggest tong in China,
And it's said there's really nothing finer.
Other tongs have mascots for which they are renowned
But Mr. Wong likes to have his draggin' 'round.
Mr. Wong has got the biggest tong in China.
Mr. Wong has got a short and rather ugly nose
But he has got a tong that grows, and grows, and grows!
Mr. Wong has got the biggest tong in China!
I'm leaving for Shanghai this very minute!"

Ray cackled in his peculiarly clangorous voice as he left the stage, buoyed up by waves of laughter.

At the time, Greenwich Village was home to the best-known enclave of gays and lesbians in the country. It was an inviting destination for gays, both as an address and a place to be entertained. Greenwich Village offered charming winding streets replete with a style reminiscent of old Europe. Rents were relatively cheap, and there was little that was truly bourgeois. Residents there could be as eccentric as they chose. Social experiments of all types could be seen on any street corner.

Gays seldom stood out among the artistic types that inhabited Greenwich Village. Unusual dress or costume drew few stares, except from the occasional suburbanite. A scattering of newspaper articles criticized women with mannish haircuts and men with long locks. Few residents of this new bohemia paid any attention. Sex was openly discussed and men could be seen kissing on the street. Women openly embraced and walked hand-in-hand. Unconventional sexuality was almost mainstream.

Homosexuality was as much a part of Greenwich Village as the then burgeoning free love movement. Being gay was considered chic, just as a certain mode of dress. Greenwich Village was now known as the home of lesbians and pansies. A colorful feature of this new found social freedom was the "drag ball."

At first, these parties were populated mostly by gay men and a scattering of lesbians. As the press began to seriously cover these events, the general public's curiosity grew, attending in increasing numbers. Straight New York entrepreneurs from other boroughs wanted in on the action. Those who promoted these balls profited tremendously, particularly those who advertised and charged ever-higher ticket prices.

Soon, the drag balls, originally created to offer a sophisticated evening entertainment to the citizens of the Village, became more of a public circus. Professional drags were encouraged to create spectacular tableaux for the entertainment of the masses. One enterprising impersonator, swathed in gold lamé from head to foot, was carried onstage by a dozen muscle men in matching codpieces, a la Cleopatra. Ray was frequently a guest and entertainer at many of these affairs.

The balls were originally intended to give some sense of identity to the diverse population that made up the New York gay community. Queens didn't invent the concept of a drag or costume ball, but these events held in most major communities of the eastern United States were a significant part of the pansy craze of the 1920s-1930s.

Masquerade balls had been a social fixture for centuries. A costume and mask allowed people to engage in all sorts of promiscuity and naughty behavior. Prior to the creation of the drag ball, many gays attended the straight masquerades. Since costume was the norm, they were indistinguishable from the other guests. Cross-dressing was acceptable and even favored by some straight groups.

Men's fraternal orders were notorious for encouraging cross-dressing among their members. Amusing, perhaps, but also very suspect. There are many unopened closets.

Webster Hall in Greenwich Village was the most important venue to host the balls and masquerades. Built in 1886, the entire façade was covered in rosy terra cotta stone with elaborate arched windows outlined in bas relief carvings. The vast interior was encircled by ornate balconies. It was from here that onlookers and curiosity seekers jammed the mezzanine to look down on the madcap antics of the outrageously costumed impersonators who filled the enormous dance floor.

Many fashion designers made it a point to attend these flamboyant events. They could be seen sketching some of the marvelous creations worn by the drags. It was a private joke among queens that many of their own creations would appear as exact copies in the shop windows of the so-called designers.

The queens spent months of painstaking hand labor cutting and sewing the materials for these fantasy frocks. The designers stole the artistry of these creations and contracted the work out, to be cheaply copied by the hordes of immigrant workers, who labored in sweat shop factories in New York's Garment District.

Other ball venues included such well-known emporiums as the New Star Casino in Little Italy, the venerable Astor Hotel, and even Madison Square Garden.

Mayor Jimmy Walker was one of the enablers of this unconventional entertainment. His police force usually looked the other way at such gatherings. Maintaining order and safety was their concern, not the gender of the bodies in the britches or ball gowns. Ray was familiar with the liberal character of Walker's administrations, as was Mae. On more than one occasion, she used her friend Walker's influence to get her cronies out of legal trouble, including Ray, who would experience a number of incarcerations during his long career.

Almost all of the balls were climaxed by a contest. As many as one hundred contestants paraded in the glare of the spotlight. The prize was a substantial amount of cash. Shimmering bugle-beaded gowns competed with yards of rare Bird of Paradise plumes, sewn by hand onto silk chemises. Great opera coats of gold lamé swirled in a fashion war competing with the ten-foot-long trains of brocaded ball gowns.

The best-known gay club in Greenwich Village was Paul and Joe's. The streetwise owners had learned to avoid problems with the law during the early 1920s. This was a period when certain particularly homophobic elements of the police department seemed to take great pleasure in raiding the many gay and lesbian bars that dotted Greenwich Village.

Paul and Joe's had a special room constructed above the regular club that had no obvious entrance from the street. Looking at the outside of the building gave no indication there was even a second floor. This was a particular haunt of not only the gay world, but the famous . . . from all walks of lives. Screen actors, opera stars, and curious members of the Mafia could be seen rubbing elbows with the local queens and lesbians as they sipped gin rickeys and other potent potables in this secret get-away.

The Flower Pot, snidely described by one reporter as "a receptacle for pansies," was a frequent venue for Ray's talent. Here, you could find the usual assortment of cross-dressers, chorus boys, men-on-the-make, and unemployed artists.

Greenwich Village was home to a large colony of artists. One of these was a painter Ray had met while working for Vitagraph Studios. John Kelly illustrated the title cards that contained the written dialogue used in silent movies. He was a slight figure of a man, but had impressed Ray with his sincere demeanor and intelligence. He was also very creative. At Ray's suggestion, he was hired to paint a large mural in the nightclub where the impersonator was working. It gave the two a chance to renew their friendship.

Meeting John for lunch one afternoon, Ray was startled to see a uniquely handsome young man already seated at the table. He possessed an innate elegance and a physical beauty that was striking. During the course of the lunch, Ray discovered that the two men were roommates.

They shared a one-room walk up in Greenwich Village. An immigrant from London, John's friend was in show business. This turned their conversation to tales of Ray's days in the British music halls. John's friend quickly warmed to the topic of London where he first worked with an acrobatic troupe that had come to America. At first, they had experienced success, but eventually the bookings became scarce. When he left the troupe, the actor told a familiar tale of struggle to make it in the hard world of the theatre.

Kelly and his buddy were far apart in age and looks. Kelly was twenty-five, and his partner barely seventeen. They shared a common work ethic. They supplemented their irregular incomes by selling neckties that were hand-painted by Kelly and modeled by his handsome roommate. They hocked the stylish cravats on the streets of New York, but even this failed to adequately supplement their sparse combined income. Things became so tight financially that they had been forced to add a third party to their already confined quarters.

As so often happens during a cocktail lunch, tongues were loosened and talk turned to who knew who and what. Ray instantly recognized the name of their third renter, Charlie Phelps. Ray knew him better by his stage name, Charlie Spangles. He had worked with him once at the Metropole Club in the Village.

Charlie's act was unique, playing a hermaphrodite, a black-bearded man on one side of his face and full drag on the other. His costume was one half man's tuxedo, the other half, a frilly evening dress. He placed one hand on his opposite shoulder when viewed from the back and appeared to be a couple dancing together, a clever and difficult illusion.

Ray was familiar with most female impersonators in show business. He catalogued the names of some of the famous he had known. Julian Eltinge, renowned for his wardrobe and solid success in legitimate theatre and silent films, had been an early inspiration for Ray.

Eltinge was not only a great entertainer but also a fashion icon with an enormous female fan base. His distinct style sense made him a role model for women of fashion during his era. What Ray found repulsive about Eltinge was his desperate attempts to prove to the public that he was "straight." This often led to staged fights, for the benefit of the newspaper reporters, with those who questioned his virility.

There was a brief lull in the conversation until Ray and Kelly both mentioned the impersonator, Barbette, at the same time. Kelly deferred to Ray, who had met Barbette on more than one occasion, to describe to Kelly's friend, also an acrobat, the uniqueness of this female impersonator cum acrobat.

Ray recounted the time he had seen his amazing show. He described how, against a backdrop of purple velvet panels, Barbette was lowered from the ceiling of the stage by an invisible wire. A tiny spotlight followed his downward spiral. He wore a platinum wig crowned by enormous plumes. This man-woman was wrapped in an extravagantly long cape of gold brocade. Reclining on a silver chaise lounge, he began to disrobe, until nothing was left except ruby pasties on his breasts and an elaborate gold filigree cod piece. He then ascended a ladder until he reached a tight wire extended across the stage. He walked precariously forward and backward, balancing with a thin pole. The spotlight cast reflections off his sequined eye makeup, like an exotic peacock. At the climax of the act, he leapt from the wire and landed on top of a veritable mountain of Oriental rugs. He bowed deeply to the wild applause, snatching off his wig to reveal a bony and masculine athlete's head. For a second, the audience gasped, and then resumed their thunderous applause.

Kelly's handsome partner began to lose some of his shyness with this last story. He surprised Ray with the story of his work in England with a pantomime group. His part in this amateur theatrical presentation had been to play the children's fairy tale favorite, *Old Mother Hubbard* (1893).

He took great delight in describing in detail his drag costume, a full-skirted muslin gown trimmed with lace collar and cuffs. On his head, he had worn a puffy satin bonnet. Continuing in the same vein, he told of coming to America with a revue. Their first engagement had been at the famous Hippodrome Theatre in New York. The production was called *Better Times* (1922). Again, he donned a drag costume, this time as a beautiful young girl in a spectacular number during the grand opera ball scene.

When the show folded, he was on his own. Luckily, he had made several close friendships with older men in New York. When he reiterated his hard luck story at a bar one night, he was offered free lodging and board by Lester Sweyd, the former female impersonator, "Fonzo, the Boy Wonder in Skirts." They lived together for several months until John Kelly came into the picture.

The next friend Ray mentioned was the famous impersonator, Francis Renault. This elicited a quick look of recognition from Kelly's boyfriend, and an uncomfortable look from Kelly. Ray mentioned that Renault was as handsome a man as he was beautiful as a woman, something that brought him a strong gay fan base. Kelly's friend quickly agreed. He described how Renault had offered to mentor him when they had shared a Vaudeville bill. Kelly attempted to change the subject, but was cut short. Renault had not only mentored, but had housed the handsome hopeful for a year prior to his present living arrangement. Ray quickly sized-up the situation.

As the pair took their leave, Kelly suddenly apologized for introducing Ray without doing the same for his roommate. Wrapping a protective arm around the broad shoulders of his significant other, he proudly announced that this was his Archie—Archibald Leach.

This was a name that would soon be familiar to Ray and the entire world, not as the Cockney-born-and-bred Archie Leach, but as Cary Grant. John Kelly would eventually become a world renowned costume designer in Hollywood, taking the name Orry-Kelly, and later winning three Academy Awards for Best Costume Design for *An American in Paris* (1951), *Cole Porter's Les Girls* (1957), and *Some Like It Hot* (1959), and he was nominated for a fourth for *Gypsy* (1962).

The afternoon had turned to twilight, as Ray sat alone at the empty café table. He was beginning to feel a little self-pity after dining with the handsome pair. Mulling over the memories of the years that had led up to this time, during which he had yet to find a true soul mate. Never one to dwell for long on any shortcomings, Ray began to recount some of the more exciting moments of his life. He suddenly recalled a life-changing event that had begun with a simple suggestion.

In 1920, at the urging of a professional photographer friend who worked at Vitagraph Studios, Ray's life had taken a startling turn. The photographer, who specialized in portraits, had taken several glamour drag shots of him just for fun. He was impressed with the reality of Ray's look. He showed him a recent copy of *Photoplay* magazine that contained an entry form for a beauty contest, a tool used at the time to sell magazines. He offered to photograph Ray at his most flattering and feminine angles, a project that resulted in some convincing portraiture.

The photographs were forwarded to *Photoplay*, along with a brief resume. The document was signed, "Rae Bourbon." This was the first time the gender-ambiguous spelling appears to have been adopted by him. The response four weeks later left both of them dumbstruck: Ray had won first prize.

The winner was to be transported to Hollywood at the magazine's expense and given a beginner's contract with the up-and-coming Paramount Studios. This ambitious studio not only created movies but set out to capture as many of the movie houses around the country as they could purchase. This way, their films would always be guaranteed a booking. Contests for Hollywood hopefuls were just one of their many promotional gimmicks. These contests, a steady feature for many years, held out hope to the masses that anybody might become a star.

Ray was met at the Los Angeles train station and taken to Paramount, where a publicity event had been arranged, complete with reporters and the studio's own public relations men.

The studio chauffer had been given Ray's winning photograph in order to identify the model at the bustling station. About to give up when he couldn't find a single female that matched the photo, only the driver's handmade sign with Ray's name finally connected the two. The chauffer was almost speechless when he realized this tall, slightly effeminate man was the lovely lady in the picture.

On the ride from the station, Ray was warned of the situation he would be facing. The photographers and studio executives might not be amused at the switched genders.

The concerned chauffer first took Ray to the makeup department, where he was quickly transformed by a sympathetic gay makeup artist into the image the studio had first received. While Ray was being revamped into "Rae," the driver hurriedly informed the studio big wigs of what had happened.

Paramount had no choice but to go ahead with the publicity event. Ray was warned not to speak, or get too close to the cameras or reporters. The studio press agents would do all the talking. Flash bulbs popped and questions flew in rapid succession. Ray posed and smiled, deferring the answers to the studio's savvy staff, who fielded all the inquiries. Surrounded by a phalanx of business suited executives, Ray was hurriedly escorted out a side door after a very brief session.

Now there was the problem of what to do with this surprise package. Ray suggested that he might be a stunt double for some of the studio's film actresses, a common practice when he had worked at Vitagraph in New York.

A director, makeup team, and cameraman were consulted. They all felt that Ray bore a striking resemblance to screen goddess Estelle Taylor. Miss Taylor had enjoyed a meteoric career, rising from a typist, married at fourteen to a wealthy tycoon, divorced at eighteen. This led to a modeling career and then a stint as a showgirl. She was spotted by a studio scout and quickly became a film star. The studio's makeup team agreed that Ray's eyes, eyebrows, and mouth were very much like Taylor's. With the right brunette wig and shot from mid-camera range, they felt he would be Taylor's perfect double and stunt person.

In the makeup studios of Paramount, he began to hone his talent at doing his own face. During the time he worked in the New York studios of Vitagraph, everyone did their own faces, and rather crudely for the most part. The only thing available then was greasepaint, a heavy product in a tube that had been created for use on the stage. It was thick and heavy and, once applied, dried into a mask. This hampered the actor's ability to use facial expressions. Too much movement and cracks would appear in the visage. This didn't matter as much when viewed from the distance of a stage, but the movie camera caught every little flaw.

Ray watched in wonder as the Paramount makeup artist transformed his look with an unfamiliar product he squeezed from an avocado-colored tube. It was dabbed on with a natural sea sponge on the entire face and then lightly dusted with a little powder. The effect was soft and natural. A deft use of a pencil around his eyes and on his brows came next. The finish was well-angled rouge application and skilled shaping of the mouth with lip color. He looked at the sepia photo of Estelle Taylor on the wall and was amazed at the resemblance to what he saw in the mirror.

The next day, Ray was on the set doing what he had done in New York, but this time, he had the guarantee of a year's contract. This meant a weekly salary whether he was working on a film or not, and a bonus with each day of actual work.

The first day of shooting brought back all the sensory images that were an integral part of filmmaking: the harsh lighting of the makeup rooms; the distinct smell of cosmetics; and, the naked faces of the extras awaiting the expertise of the artists who would paint their film faces.

From makeup, everyone progressed to hairdressing, a room filled with sweet-smelling lotions and the pungent glue used to attach wigs and hairpieces. Flat-haired hopefuls became luxuriously-coiffed queens and receding hairlines disappeared beneath youthful toupees.

What amazed him the most was watching a veritable face-lift accomplished in a matter of minutes, not with makeup or surgery, but with the actress's own hair. This little miracle was performed on an aging star that had been relegated to secondary parts, still desperate to hold on to her career. The lead hairdresser brushed the former star's hair straight back from her face and secured it with a band. He then picked out tiny strands of her thinning hair all along the hairline. These he braided into extremely tight strands, attaching hairpins to the end of each and twisting them so tightly she grimaced. A wig was then placed just behind the hairline and the painful hair ropes were pulled straight back into the coiffure. The result was a nearly youthful and temporarily tight face.

At first, Ray imagined that being the winner of a *Photoplay* contest must mean certain eventual success. He never failed to mention his prize when talking to anyone he thought might further his ambitions. His expectations were quickly dashed, when a studio hairdresser told him a rather cynical story.

Ray was being fitted with an elaborate court coiffure for a scene in another costume drama. As the beautician struggled to secure the weighty wig, Ray decided to see if this technician was as gossipy as most he had met. "What ever happened to Travesta Turbinata, that hatchet-faced little thing that won first prize in the *Hollywood Tattler's* beauty contest? I understand she was given a starring engagement in a picture and paid $500 a week for six weeks work." The hairdresser fidgeted for a moment, stuck his comb in Ray's half-ratted pompadour, and began his tale:

"Listen Miss Thing, the studio paid her the money all right. As for the rest, there was no more work for the poor kid. She had the brains of a gnat, and the rats that run this organization knew it. They made a few long shots of her for the movie, just like they do with most contest winning extras, and then they doubled her with a dame who could act. When her six weeks were up the director said she could hang around and learn the movie ropes, sans a pay envelope. It got her no place, and so she packed up what was left of the $3,000 and made the rounds of the other studios. She was not discouraged at first. She still believed all the stories she had heard of quick success. Down to her last dime, rumor is she did herself in, but not until she had hit the skids, selling the only thing she had left under a street lamp on Hollywood Boulevard. She fell for that old contest gag, oldest gimmick in the business. It is just an advertising stunt for the studios and the magazines that run the contest. All the studios do it. I've seen dozens of 'em come and go, sitting right in this chair, and very few make it."

Ray filed this pertinent bit of Hollywood wisdom under his enormous wig and vowed to take off the rose-colored glasses in the future.

Hollywood in the early days had more than a fair share of beautiful people. It was an irresistible lure for the hopeful and the dreamers. Any handsome profile or sexy figure seemed drawn by this shimmering magnet, which pulled them in and just as quickly dropped them. Natural selection did the rest. The endless demand for perfection insured a steady supply of physical beauty.

Almost as disconcerting as this tidal wave of beautiful flesh was Hollywood's architecture that Ray saw those first weeks. Everywhere he looked was a vast spread of jarring styles: Spanish haciendas; faux chateaus; Colonial mansions; and, a mélange of styles that could only be described as bastardized castles-in-the-air. It was very easy to succumb to this seductive world of fantasy and artificial beauty. He had come up the chain the hard way and decided not to let all this glamour without substance seduce him.

The 1920s are referred to "The Golden Age" in the motion picture film industry. The number of films ground-out on a weekly basis was staggering, and the financial returns could be enormous. The grist mill that turned out all this loot and lunacy demanded a cruel payment from some of the hopefuls who flocked to Hollywood. The tales of madness, drugs, and debauchery that made up this era are myriad. The career-wrecking scandals followed one after the other.

Ray was still young and tireless. Opportunity for pleasure presented itself at every new encounter in the make believe world of Hollywood. Drugs and alcohol fueled the endless parties and pleasure spots of the night.

Homosexuality was part and parcel of the film kingdom's lore. It was generally accepted, as long as it did not get into the press, particularly if you were a valuable money maker. He was not even a featured player, so he and all the other little cogs in the Hollywood dream factory went about enjoying their own particular perversions and peccadilloes.

Men, as well as the fresh-faced young women who sought their moment to shine in the film firmament, were subject to the demands of the "casting couch." This term loosely describes the exchange of an artist's sexual favors, which came in many forms, for the opportunity to gain fame on the silver screen. The director, or his assistant, was the usual taker and giver in this bizarre sexual market.

Tall, nicely built, and "straight' in demeanor when required, Ray was often the object of offers from his superiors. To his credit, he seldom acquiesced to these offers unless they were from a prospective partner that actually interested him. He found it very difficult to perform if he wasn't really attracted. This honest attitude was admirable, but it also meant the loss of several career-building invitations.

The first big Paramount production that he worked in was *Manslaughter* (1922), a typical Hollywood Victorian melodrama, directed by the powerful Cecil B. DeMille. It contained everything that audiences loved, sex, splendid sets, violence, and more sex. There were contemporary scenes of drunken youth living it up in the style of the Roaring 20s. Flashbacks included ancient Rome with glistening gladiators in the briefest of costumes, violent battles, and the glamorous decadence of the emperor's court. He was used as both a male and female extra.

In the same year, Ray worked on another film that starred his old friend from Vitagraph, Rudolph Valentino. Rudolph was now a major star. Ray was chosen from a large casting call for Valentino's new film, *Blood and Sand* (1922), produced by Famous Players-Lasky. Although he was under a standard extra's contract to Paramount, the studio looked the other way when minor actors sought outside work. It didn't hurt that Valentino singled him out at the final casting session.

At about nine minutes into *Blood and Sand* is a scene of a fatally wounded matador, played by Ray, who expires while being embraced by Rudolph. Ray jokingly remarked decades later that he was probably the only queen who ever died in the arms of Valentino. The touching sequence involved Rudolph playing the aspiring, young matador who cradles the dying matador, and then kisses him. Ray is seen later in the film as a bodyguard to Valentino, who has become the most famous master of the bull ring.

During the filming, Ray received an invitation to be a guest at a party at Wedgewood Place, the Valentino's mansion. That evening, greeted by the dramatic trappings of the house, black marble, black velvet, glowing orange drapes, and amber lighting, he entered the fantastical world of Rudolph's home.

The partygoers were as outlandish as the décor. Rudolph's wife was the beautiful, bisexual, Natacha Rambova. A multi-talented artist, she was currently involved with the exotic actress, Alla Nazimova. Rambova was designing the sets and costumes for Nazimova's latest film, *Salome* (1922). As the party progressed, the conversation turned to the troubled negotiations surrounding *Salome*. Every guest was fascinated with Nazimova's vivid descriptions of her visions for this Biblical tale that already had a scandalous theatrical history. She was worried about casting the extras for the crucial banquet scene, where the demented Princess Salome dances for her incestuous father, King Herod, and in return demands the severed head of John the Baptist.

Ray, sensing that this edgy actress wasn't looking for the normal extra, asked if all the parts had been cast. Rudolph interjected that Ray had played both genders to good effect. He had seen this first-hand during their days at Vitagraph in New York. Rudolph's wife agreed to test Ray, and several other obviously gay party guests, the next day. As it turned, out Nazimova hired only gay extras for *Salome*.

During the course of the evening, talk turned to technical matters of filming, costumes, hair, and makeup. Ray took the opportunity to compliment how good Rudolph looked in his latest film, remembering how poorly his skin had photographed when they had worked together at Vitagraph in New York. Rudolph, in a rare, candid moment, related how much trouble he had had when he first began acting in movies. His skin was a very dark olive, and the only products available then turned to a ghostly white under the harsh lighting. When he came to Hollywood, he was introduced to Max Factor, the man who would revolutionize the world of cosmetics. Rudolph complained bitterly about his bad cosmetic experiences at Vitagraph, and Factor promised him a solution. The two worked together for over a week at Factor's studio, trying and retrying formulas. When Rudolph began to grow bored with all this experimenting, Factor handed him a mortar and pestle and told him to get to work grinding the various pigments they were using. The next day, they hit on the perfect shade for the Latin lover's swarthy skin. Rudolph's smoldering good looks catapulted his successful film career.

Ray was very aware of the rumors swirling around Rudolph, not only in the film colony, but also among the gossip hags like Louella Parsons, a serpent-tongued part of the publishing empire of William Randolph Hurst. The *Chicago Tribune* had targeted the Italian heart throb with a scathing article:

> "Do women like the type of 'man' who pats pink powder on his face in a public washroom and arranges his coiffure in a public elevator…? Chicago has its powder puffs, London has its dancing men, and Paris its gigolos. Down with Decatur; up with Elinor Glyn. Hollywood is the national school of masculinity. Rudy, the beautiful gardener's boy, is the prototype of the American male?"

Ray chuckled silently over the reference to Chicago powder puffs and dancing men in London. He had certainly been both.

Rudolph was enormously popular and enjoyed the privileges that such fame brought, but fame came with a price tag that demanded absolute adherence to the image the public held in their narrow little minds. When Rudolph divorced both his wives, claims were put forth he had not consummated either marriage. America's greatest lover could not "get it up." The press, of course, ignored the fact that wives, Jean Acker, and Natacha Rambova, were both overt lesbians.

As the California sun disappeared on the horizon, Rudolph's party progressed to levels of both euphoria and numbness, triggered by alcohol and other ingested pleasures. The enormous ornate Empire clock chimed midnight from the foyer. Rudolph sat silently in his massive black chair, analyzing the body language and facial expressions of his guests. The copious crystal stems of fine Italian wine, coupled with the lateness of the hour, gradually loosened Rudolph's tongue.

Whenever he had an appreciative audience, he loved to spin a tale of his claim to a royal lineage. Guglielmi, his real surname, was a very common one in Sicily, where he was born. At some point in his youth, he had preceded Guglielmi with di Valentina, though no other member of his clan had such an important sounding name. He explained he had done extensive research and discovered that he was, indeed, the holder to this title, one that gave him direct lineage to the Papacy through the infamous and murderous Borgia family.

Looking around the room filled with a few famous faces, and the larger number of those that do their bidding, Ray was struck with the expressions of credulity he saw. Perhaps he should tell his tale of a possible title and royal claim to the Bourbon dynasty that had followed him to Texas where he had been born? He had grown up with the oft-repeated gossip that his biological mother had been impregnated by a minor member of the royal Bourbon family while she was boarding in a French convent. He seldom spoke of it, but it was the decisive factor in his choice of Bourbon as a stage name. He then thought better about trying to one-up his host. Rudolph could be instrumental in persuading Nazimova to hire him.

With all eyes still on Rudolph, the stories continued. He waxed sentimental about his Italian childhood. From a very early age, he had not accepted his lowly station in life. He always imagined himself as a knight or hero, dashing and elegantly dressed. This was his dream. He had an innate restlessness that finally led him to seek success on distant shores. He was struck with the similarity of Rudolph's childhood longings and his own desires to escape the ordinary future that his Texas birthplace held.

From his fanciful tales of titles and ambition, Rudolph suddenly spun-off into more mundane worries. He told the guests he was in the process of breaking ties he had formed with his studio. He felt he was underpaid and bitterly resented it. His contract called for one last film. He wanted out. The studio refused to meet his demand for a bigger salary.

"The Boss," Rudolph's sobriquet for his butch wife, repeatedly demanded Paramount give him his due. Her constant interference on the set, demanding more money for her husband and bigger parts, led to her banishment from the studio. Rudolph was furious that his soul mate and advisor was now barred from the set. He felt he had no choice but to sever all ties with Paramount.

The attention of his guests had begun to wander, as Rudolph's tale of woe continued. Realizing that he had said enough, he bid everyone goodnight. Rudolph pulled Ray aside as both were leaving, promising to see that he was hired for the upcoming Swanson film. Turning to leave, he was aware that Rudolph's two handsome Great Danes were trying to follow him out the door. They had developed an instant attraction to Ray, and sat like imposing guards on each side of his chair during the evening, each vying for his attention. Rudolph observed that this was unusual behavior for the two usually aloof dogs. Ray replied that he missed having canine companions, but his erratic lifestyle didn't permit it.

If Ray had found the Valentino mansion to be unusual, it couldn't begin to compare to his reaction to the goings-on on the set of *Salome*. It was like nothing he had ever experienced. The entire production was literally copied from the famous illustrations of Aubrey Beardsley. These daring Art Nouveau designs were used as stage décor in Oscar Wilde's sensational play, *Salome* (1893).

The hair, makeup, sets, everything, were stark black and white. The cast, on the other hand, was neutral . . . gender neutral. Both Nazimova and her art director, Natacha Rambova, insisted on an entirely gay cast and crew.

Nazimova, as Salome, was coiffed in a fashion that resembled an explosion of black cotton candy. This frothy concoction was topped by a head piece that consisted of gleaming wires supporting a bouquet of glittering white balls. The sparkling orbs were in constant motion, catching the splintered beams of the klieg lights with each turn of the actress's odd movements.

Ray was one of three courtiers costumed in the most outlandish drag he had ever seen. Each was bewigged with a tall fantasy coiffure of goat's hair capped with a pair of horns, not unlike the headgear of the Valkyrie in a Wagner opera. He felt all he needed to complete the image was a brass brassiere and a long spear.

Nazimova, the star and co-director with Charles Bryant in this ego-driven production, gave the barest of directions to Ray and his two flamboyant co-workers. They were given no action cues by the director, just told to remain seated next to the thrones of King Herod and his debauched queen. They were basically left to their own devices.

Despite this paucity of information, Ray did his best to look animated and eccentric. He would have stood out in a more conventional production. In *Salome*, everyone and everything in every frame of the film was a study in the eccentric. He felt like a participant in a freak show.

When it came time for the crucial dance sequence that is the crux of this gruesome tale, Nazimova insisted the maintenance engineers drop the temperature of the studio. The scantily clad members of the cast, many only in the skimpiest of tights, complained about the cold sound stage. He overheard Nazimova tell her dresser the frigid air would keep her nipples erect and visible under her flimsy chemise as she executed her dance of seduction.

The infamous dance of the Seven Veils, as performed by Nazimova, made him laugh. He knew many Burlesque strippers who generated twice the heat of icy Nazimova. He remembered seeing Eva Tanguay and Mae West in their versions of this veiled dance, both hot, licentious, and more than worthy of a visit from the vice squad.

The pseudo screen siren mistook spasms for orgasms, as she grimaced and rolled her eyes in a ludicrous attempt to look lascivious. Nazimova, stung by the harshly critical reviews that would follow, haughtily informed the press that her interpretation was, "a highly stylized performance." Ray found the whole film to be "a load of hokum."

The reported budget for *Salome* ran well over $300,000, an enormous sum for a movie at that time. The backers found it hard to justify such extravagance, considering the entire picture was shot on a single set. The initial budget had been half that, but escalated on a daily basis, as Nazimova insisted that all costumes be made by hand with the finest of detailing. Fabrics were imported from the notoriously expensive Maison Lewis of Paris.

When the shooting finally ground to a halt, the finished product sat on the shelf for months. The distributors who previewed *Salome* all turned thumbs down. For over a year, no distributor would touch the film.

Hollywood was being rocked with one scandal after another. There were unexplained murders, rapes, and dope dealings among the screen idols of 1923. Righteous America was shocked and demanded a clean-up of Hollywood Babylon. Distributors who had seen *Salome* wanted no part of the overtly gay overtones that pervaded Nazimova's film.

Finally, an obscure distributor picked up the film's option on a limited basis. As predicted by the film colony, this celluloid oddity failed miserably at the box office. It played to lukewarm critical reviews and was withdrawn.

Ray was again in front of the cameras soon after *Salome*. This time, the subject was the bestselling book, *Beyond the Rocks* (1906), by the English writer, Elinor Glyn. She had shocked the world with her first literary effort, *Three Weeks* (1907), a tawdry tale of a sexually aggressive queen in a fictional kingdom. Women were seldom portrayed with such candor. Glyn's offer to sell the novel to Hollywood studios resulted in one version directed in 1914 by Perry N. Vekroff and starring Madlaine Traverse and George C.

Pearce and a second version directed in 1924 by Alan Crosland and starring Aileen Pringle and Conrad Nagel.

One of her later efforts, *Beyond the Rocks*, was considerably tamer in tone. The rights to film her book were purchased at a record sum. Shooting began in December 1921.

Rudolph's co-star in *Beyond the Rocks* (1922) was Gloria Swanson. The petite and powerful star was cut an enormous paycheck—$20,000 per week—for each film. The studio was not willing to risk an equal sum for the emotional Italian star. Rudolph paraphrased a conversation that he and Swanson had had that very afternoon. Swanson advised him to stand his ground and demand a salary commensurate with his box office appeal.

The entire cast and crew were shuttled to the island of Catalina, a location that offered a variety of backgrounds for outdoor shots. The minor actors were housed in low-rent hotels and small bungalows. As frequently happened, the extras tended to break off in groups of similar interest. Ray managed to bunk with a noisy group of gay actors that displayed a penchant for partying long into the night. Despite the early morning calls to film, everyone soon found the many nightspots that dotted the central part of the island. Gambling was a very popular tourist attraction, and with it came the dance halls and bars that were open twenty-four hours a day. The set the next morning saw some very hung-over actors. Only the serious efforts of the talented makeup department helped to conceal the effects of the previous night.

Beyond the Rocks (1922) is an improbable tale of a beautiful young woman named Theodora Fitzgerald, set in the 1920s. Theodora marries an elderly millionaire to please her demanding father, a retired sea captain. On her Swiss honeymoon, the bride falls over a mountain cliff while taking a photo. She is rescued by a handsome young man, Lord Bracondale, who had coincidentally rescued her in an earlier scene from a boat accident near her father's sea-side cottage. The geriatric groom and his accident-prone spouse now set off for Paris, with Bracondale in hot pursuit. Again, the bride and Bracondale meet while touring Versailles. This yes/no scenario continues for the rest of the film, the bride and her young stud playing cat-and-mouse in a variety of colorful settings.

After viewing the initial rushes, the Paramount executives felt that the public would want to see Swanson and Valentino in more elaborate costumes and settings, so they added even more icing to this overdone cake. The Versailles scene lacked impact, so the director suggested a flashback in the garden to a much earlier time, thus allowing the two super stars to gussy-up in finery befitting a royal pair. Both Swanson and Rudolph were notorious clothes horses. Rudolph was poured into skin-tight breeches that clearly displayed his calling card. Swanson, never one to shy away from extravagant over-dress, was swathed in layers of silk and satin, to which were added half the accessories from the wardrobe department.

Ray, no stranger to excess, wore the costume of a mincing dandy, complete with high-heeled court slippers, satin breeches, and a powdered, white wig. "Rae" later appears in drag in a contemporary evening gown as one of many in a crowd of party goers at a high-society ball. The shot opens as the guests enter an impressive mansion and proceed to a grand staircase that is surmounted by enormous, crystal chandeliers.

Slowly, "Rae" ascends the stairs, one narrow foothold at a time, arm in arm with an elderly escort. In one gloved hand, he deftly maneuvers an outsized ostrich fan. With the other, he steadies himself. Never really comfortable in high heels, he had substituted lady's house slippers that constantly slithered on the worn marble. Ahead of him was the tiny figure of Gloria Swanson, standing imperiously at the top of the staircase, waiting to shake hands with the party's hostess.

The director wasn't satisfied with the scene, or Swanson's facial expression . . . more like an imperial pout than that of an innocent ingénue. Raising the enormous megaphone to his mouth, he bellowed, "Remember Gloria, the book says, and I quote, 'it all seemed like Fairy-Land to Theodora . . . as she mounted the steps with the rest of the throng.'" "Rae" had to hide his smirk behind his feather fan, nearly losing his balance on the precarious stairs.

That evening, Swanson invited the entire cast to her impressive twenty-four-room Beverly Hills mansion for a cocktail party. Her home was as overdone as her costumes. Everything was gilded and glittering. Black marble and gold gilt abounded. Even her bathtub was covered in the precious metal.

The stars worked very hard all week, putting in as many as fourteen hours a day. At night, out came the finery. Even though everyone had dressed up all week long under the blazing klieg lights, tonight was to be another costume party. Swanson's favorite entertainment was a costume ball.

Most of the extras arrived late after the long trip from Catalina, still wearing the period costumes they had donned that day for filming. Purchasing an outfit for this one-time affair was beyond their meager means. Ray decided to wear the men's court finery, rather than the cumbersome ball gown he wore in the crowd scene.

Among the many famous figures arriving through the impressive arches of Swanson's portico was the author of *Beyond the Rocks*. She had not been invited, but that mattered little to the abrasive Madame Elinor Glyn. She had conned actor John Barrymore into believing she was on the guest list, vaguely hinting she would use her influence to secure a role for him in the filming of her next novel. He escorted the already inebriated authoress up the steps to the mansion, stepping unceremoniously on the train of her gown, part of her costume as Catherine the Great of Russia. When the odd couple arrived at the grand entrance to Swanson's home, Barrymore was at first denied access. His costume as a street tramp was so realistic that the haughty butler barred his way.

Hearing the fracas in the hallway, Swanson arrived to investigate. She was spectacular in a green and gold gown encrusted with shimmering bugle beads. Thin panels covered with the costly crystals hung by the thousands from the multiple trains of her dress. They trailed several feet behind her, making an odd scratching noise on the gleaming marble floor.

"John!" hissed the barely five-foot actress, as she pushed her butler aside to rescue handsome John Barrymore. The two stars strolled away, arm in arm, leaving drunken Glyn behind.

When Ray spotted the acid-tongued authoress heading in his direction, he made a bee line for the bathroom.

When the coast was clear, he rejoined the happy mob at the elaborate bar and buffet the generous star had provided. Extras were always hungry and thirsty, as evidenced by their voracious assault on the rich edible and potable offerings. Despite the laws of Prohibition, a river of intoxicants flowed freely, well into the early hours.

Swanson loved a party as well as anyone in the film capital. Standing on the staircase of her great entry hall, the petite star raised her arms and called for attention. "Oh, what a party we are having! The public expects us to live like kings and queens. So, why not? We all love life, and we are making more money than we could ever have imagined. There is no reason to believe it will ever stop!"

Ray suddenly felt the enormous gap that existed between those at the pinnacle and all the rest who struggled on the assembly lines that were the studios. This brief glimpse into the rarified world of the privileged only emphasized that gap.

One of the few comic breaks everyone enjoyed during the long weeks of filming were the visits to the set by Madame Glyn. Most were stunned when they first laid eyes on this vision: a pasty made up face that resembled a road map; tiny squinty eyes rimmed in snake green; eyelashes like black whisk brooms; and, cranberry-colored hair wadded into a shape that resembled a fur turban. Blood red lips outlined a mouth crammed with oversized snow-white dentures, clacking and clattering at the most inopportune times.

In addition to books, Glyn frequently wrote for movie magazines, the type of rag that seldom told the truth about the Hollywood crowd. One of her favorite themes was to ask a series of thinly veiled questions alluding to the true masculinity of certain actors. This usually had to do with whether they had responded in-kind to her romantic advances. Ray and the rest of the gay camp found her to be intolerable.

Things began to get out of hand, as Glyn attempted to usurp the director's role. She interrupted filming and argued with the actors. The problem came to a head when she insisted on authenticity in the wardrobe, particularly Swanson's and Valentino's.

One afternoon, she stopped the cameras to inspect a gown that Gloria was wearing, berating the wardrobe mistress and her assistant. She wanted real silk, antique lace, sable rather than mink, and priceless chinchilla furs. The studios had long used faux fabrics and furs that photographed like the real thing.

The studio stepped in when they discovered that Glyn had approached a jeweler about lending over $1 million in jewels to encircle Swanson's tiny neck. They were not about to insure such a mother lode that would require a security guard to constantly trail the petite Paramount star. When Madame Glyn threatened to bring the production to a halt unless her wishes were obeyed, the harried director objected. Throwing his enormous megaphone in the direction of the addle-pated old Brit's grotesque figure, he called for security. The bestselling bitch was promptly escorted off the set by two burly guards, never to return.

The next morning, Ray was called as a last-minute extra for a scene onboard a yacht with Swanson and Rudolph. As the day wore on, there were constant delays in what should have been a quick take. Rudolph was not satisfied with a love scene with his co-star. It didn't seem authentic to him, so he demanded that Gloria kiss him again and again.

Seeking any excuse to take a break, Swanson told the director she had to use the head on the yacht, and returned a few minutes later.

Filming resumed, and Rudolph again clutched Gloria tightly, giving her that fiery look for which he was famous. Just as their mouths came together, he retracted, spitting and wiping his lips, giving everyone a quick lesson in Italian expletives.

Gloria had chewed a handful of garlic, which was still in her mouth when hot-blooded Rudolph attempted to insert his tongue between her tiny rose bud lips. Despite his familiarity with the odoriferous component of all Italian dishes, the wet wad of half chewed garlic produced his shockingly unromantic response. After his initial shock, they both had a good laugh.

When he finished *Beyond the Rocks*, Ray's contract with the studio concluded. He continued to work steadily as an extra, both at Paramount and other studios. The difference now was that there was no weekly salary guarantee; only a per-hour wage.

Paramount was experiencing a series of enormous scandals that were a press agent's nightmare. In September 1921, "Fatty" Arbuckle, one of their biggest stars—in the literal sense—was accused of the rape and manslaughter of Virginia Rappe, a promising starlet, during an all-night orgy. Arbuckle, a mountain of a man, loved booze, broads, and bedroom kink. Supposedly, the hapless victim's bladder had been ruptured during the violent sexual attack by the whale-like "Fatty." She died four days later. After Arbuckle's first two trials resulted in hung juries, he was acquitted in a third trial and received a formal written statement of apology from the jury.

On the heels of this scandal, another erupted. This one involved director William Desmond Taylor. Ray heard the story first-hand from Taylor's Black manservant, Henry Peavey. They had become friends when Ray first arrived at Paramount. Peavey had introduced him to the many temptations of Hollywood's notorious underground gay life.

On February 1, 1922, Peavey discovered his employer's dead body inside his bungalow at the Alvarado Court Apartments at 404-B South Alvarado Street, Los Angeles. Peavey went berserk, running through the streets of the quiet upscale neighborhood. The neighbors were awakened to his high pitched screams, "Dey've kilt de Massa! Dey've kilt de Massa!" Peavey sounded for all the world like Prissy in, *Gone With the Wind* (1939). The hysterical manservant continued to wail and moan until he was collected and calmed by the police.

The papers had a field day with the sordid details of the director's murder, including a cache of pornographic pictures that the indiscreet Taylor had taken with several of Hollywood's most prominent actresses. The press described in detail how, "the soprano-voiced manservant, Peavey" had wailed liked a woman on the night of the murder. There was even an item that detailed Peavey's love of crocheting doilies and scarves.

One peculiar bit of information from a witness was a report of seeing someone who looked like they were in "drag" running from the scene of the murder. Peavey later revealed to Ray that Taylor had asked him about several notorious, "queer meeting places," ones that might cater to cross-dressers. Taylor insisted it was only to buy illegal drugs, but Peavey doubted his explanation. Drugs were available anywhere in Hollywood for those with the cash.

Ray later learned from Peavey that William Desmond Taylor was, indeed, bisexual. That came as no surprise to street-wise Ray. What did shock him were the lengths to which a film studio was willing to go in order to tamper with evidence at a crime scene. Peavey swore that someone from Paramount had gone so far as to create a cover-up for Taylor's gender orientation by leaving starlet Mary Miles Minter's, black lace panties on the floor of the bedroom.

Peavey confessed he frequently provided young male hustlers for his boss with the understanding that it all must be kept strictly confidential.

1923 proved to be an extremely scandal-ridden year for Paramount, and the film industry in general, when the industry's third most popular star, Wallace Reid, died from complications resulting from a morphine addiction while he was attempting recovery.

Ray's experiences in the make-believe world of Hollywood had taught him much. He learned that the supposedly open search for extras was not as open as he had supposed at first. Those in charge repeatedly chose performers they knew, or had been recommended to them. Every studio he had worked for gave first pick to relatives of studio employees, provided they met the physical requirements. This made it very hard to get his foot in the door.

When his Paramount contract concluded, he found himself in a salary situation that was tenuous, at best. If an extra did not have an especially interesting look or talent, they could go for weeks without a paycheck. Playing in a mob scene was particularly frustrating. It was very hard to catch a director's eye. Ray had the edge at times because he could play either sex, but his drag persona was usually confined to stunt doubling for an actress, or filling in a crowd scene.

Ray never made the breakthrough that impersonators such as Bothwell Brown had experienced. This cross-dressing actor had made a series of successful pictures playing a woman, a highly unusual career achievement at that time.

Most think the history of Hollywood is comprised of big stars, big studios, and the big power that drives them both. Time colors the memory in ways that blur and soften, much like the camera filters used on an aging actress to erase the years.

Ray, from his beginnings in silent movies, frequently worked in many of the small studios. These little brothers of the Hollywood giants ground out "quickies," vastly scaled-down film formats that attempted to mimic the prestigious efforts of the big boys. Small studios in the 1930s had a nearly impossible task competing with the bloated budgets of the top studios, MGM, Paramount, 20th Century Fox, Warner Bros., and others. The big difference between the "Poverty Row" studios and the "Kings of the Hill" was disrepute and perceived prestige.

One of the staples of the "cheapie" film factory was the Western. Ray often worked in this rough and tumble genre, primarily because of his ability to appear believably as a stunt double for female stars, such as Estelle Taylor, an actress who later became one of his close friends. Few of the rugged men who doubled for actresses were convincing. Ray had the advantage of years of female impersonation. This gave his image on screen a credibility his straight counterparts lacked.

Despite the frequency of his work in movies, there was lacking that satisfaction of a live audience and the reward that applause and laughter could bring.

Before making the final decision to return to a stage career, Ray accepted an invitation from a friend who had started a new business. The public was fascinated with Hollywood, the movie studios in particular. His enterprising friend sensed a new market: taking visitors on a tour of the Hollywood studios. Perhaps Ray, with his familiarity of the movie system, would like to be a tour guide. To experience what the work would entail, he was given a demonstration of a typical tour. Along with several prospective employees, the tour owner made a half-day circuit of the proposed routes. Several of the sites they visited were studios where Ray had never worked.

The first stop on the tour was an enormous, glassed-in stage that held an actual dirigible, or airship, a huge gas-filled balloon. Rounding the outside of the building, the group came upon an entirely different scenario . . . a mock-up of a Town Hall, complete with transplanted sod and fading artificial flowers in buried pots. Giant trees had been hauled from miles away to add a touch of realism. On the other side of the brick street stood a high arched wall with a tall turret and a balcony. If visitors squinted, it looked like a scene from a medieval world. Within yards of this Arthurian structure was a tableau that was thousands of miles distant in time and style, a street from old Peking. As Ray continued to walk the vast lots, he was greeted with scenes of New York's East Side and a complete Mississippi River town. Of course, he knew from experience that all the buildings were just fronts and behind their doors was an empty patch of dirt.

A cavernous stage held a giant water tank, used to float large models of sailing ships and ocean liners, which, when cleverly photographed, looked to be the real thing.

The next stop were the workshops, where movie scenery was manufactured, a property warehouse, where hundreds of props ranging from chandeliers, staircases, and the thrones of kings were stored and tagged.

The wardrobe warehouses held upwards of 5,000 costumes. Neatly hung on endless racks were the outfits for bull fighters, Chinese warriors, sailors, harem girls, cowboys, and evening clothes from every era.

The tour came to an end at one of the studio's casting offices. Ray was allowed to look into the rows of filing cabinets, where thousands of men, women, and children were indexed by card. Many of these cards had a photograph of the subjects in what they must have imagined was their most alluring pose. Looking at all of those impossibly hopeful faces, most long forgotten, he made up his mind what he must do.

13
East is East, West is West

After Ray wrapped his role in, *Beyond the Rocks* (1922), he returned to New York. Meanwhile, fellow New Yorker Mae West wrote a play, *The Hussy* (1922). The project was stillborn for lack of financial backing.

The Wicked Age (1927) was her next hoped-for success, but it wasn't. It was found to be "Gross, disgusting, tiresome, vulgar, without a single excusing feature or reason for being." It was certainly a disheartening review for almost anyone, except unstoppable Mae.

Sex and *The Drag* legal troubles dragged on for several years, including court appearances, but it was all part of the game in Mae's mind. Any publicity, good or bad, was welcome in the eye of this self-promoting performer.

Undaunted by the little hiccups in her master plan, Mae turned her attention to more successful matters. She was packing them in for *Diamond Lil* and now it was time to take the show on the road before the New York buzz died down. *Diamond Lil* had given her the best reviews she had received to date:

> "Miss Mae West has become an institution, the theatre is crowded at each performance, the star and author is now more admired by her fans than Lynn Fontanne, Helen Hayes, or Eva La Galliene." -*The Tribune*
>
> "Mae is to the New York stage what a match is to a scuttle of gunpowder . . . Mae West in a sizzling drama that sets Times Square to roaring." -*Evening Telegram*
>
> "Glamour Mae West undoubtedly has . . . she astonishes, shocks, engages, and puzzles." -*New Republic*

Backstage, Mae answered reporters' questions on closing night before the tour of *Diamond Lil* began. They wanted to know what her secret was, what she did differently than other authors and actresses.

"It isn't what I do, but how I do it. It isn't what I say, but how I say it."

Mae's famous style of delivery left no question in the mind of the press as to her meaning.

The first weeks of the tour were hectic. Mae was a total trooper, but even her famous stamina began to fade. She developed a mysterious stomach disorder. Several doctor visits revealed no cause for the persistent pain. In desperation, Mae decided to follow up on an article she had been given by a cast member about a faith healer who was holding a public meeting the next evening.

Disguised in a dark wig and toned-down street clothing, Mae was among the audience for the Indian Yoga's lecture. Impressed by what she saw that evening, she invited the guru to come to her hotel. He gave her a series of dietary instructions and other non-conventional methods that soon had the star fit and in form.

Mae ploughed ahead. She was in Chicago for fourteen weeks, then Detroit, and finally San Francisco. In the meantime, she received word that her mother was ill but was expected to recover. It was in the City by the Bay that Mae eventually learned her mother was dangerously ill. The diagnosis was liver cancer.

Mae, remembering the Yoga healer, sought in vain to locate him. On January 26, 1930, she arrived in Brooklyn just in time to say "Farewell" to her beloved Tillie. It took the normally unflappable star a year to regain her usual outlook on life. Even in the twilight of her eighty-something-year career, Mae continued to feel an honest and ongoing sorrow for the loss of her mother.

A tired and much slimmer Mae was back in court two months later to settle the legal situation over *Pleasure Man*. After fourteen days of testimony, she was given an acquittal, along with Ray and the other cast members.

The following year was filled with aborted shows that played to half-empty theatres. She was more fascinated with the anatomies of her paramours than their brains, and this often applied to the men she chose to act opposite her on the stage. Often a male co-star was simply a good-looking prop for Mae to ogle and tease.

Whenever she saw a man who tickled her fancy, he was almost always a slice of beefcake.

Mae had a penchant for men who were boxers. Her father had been a pugilist, who had awakened in his young daughter a love of boxing . . . and boxers. The young Black heavyweight, Joe Louis, was one of her conquests, as were Max Baer, and the world-class featherweight, Albert "Chalky" Wright. Wright would eventually become Mae's chauffer when his ring days came to a close.

Mae was having a hot and heavy affair with muscle-bound boxer Gentleman Jim Corbett during the run *Sex*. He loved being seen with the voluptuous star in all the hot night spots. Mae didn't mind either, as it gave both of them excellent newspaper coverage.

One night, they dropped in on Texas Guinan's Club. There were wall-to-wall celebrities, including matinee idol Rudolph Valentino, George Raft, surrounded by members of the Mafia, and Humphrey Bogart. Both Bogart and Raft were just beginning what would be long careers in Hollywood.

The owner of this sizzling speakeasy was a blonde and brassy girl from Texas, Mary Louise Cecilia Guinan, known to her public as "Texas" Guinan. She had come up through the ranks, dancing in a chorus line, and eventually starring in silent film Westerns. She was a friend to mobsters, stars, and politicians alike. The atmosphere of the club was sophisticated and sleazy.

"Well, hello suckers!" shouted the big mouthed Texas Guinan when she spotted Mae on Corbett's ample arm. She escorted them to a prominent table near the dance floor.

As Mae was being seated, she recognized several members of the party next to her. Among the celebrities was Broadway actor and soon to be film star Humphrey Bogart. Mae acknowledged his broad smile with a nod, and inquired about his wife, the actress Helen Menken, who was then starring in the scandalous play, *The Captive* (1926), a tale of lesbian love. What really irked Mae was that Menken's play was stealing some of the thunder from *Sex*. There was no love lost between the two actresses, and Mae made it clear to Bogart just what she thought of his wife and her play. "If you see Helen, tell her that most of the people want to see a looker like me enjoying sex, in a play called *Sex*. Who wants to see a bunch of dykes discussing pussy all evening!" Bogart told Mae she could tell his wife just how she felt in a minute when she returned from the powder room.

A welcome interruption to what could have become a headline-grabbing, hair pulling contest came in the handsome form of Rudolph Valentino. Valentino presented himself to Mae's table, exchanging greetings all around. Bowing, he kissed Mae's jeweled hand and gallantly requested a dance.

The crowd parted as the odd couple entered the dance floor: the ample, little blonde in towering heels, and the dark lover of every maiden's erotic fantasy. Completely in his element, Rudolph held his leonine head proudly as he pivoted and prowled the floor, molding Mae's famous torso into a dozen different lustful positions. Mae was responsive but breathless as the dance ended and Rudy loosened his lubricous grip on her hourglass figure. It was obvious she was very taken with this swarthy master of the dance.

Mae thought about Rudolph often after that. His death, almost to the month after their brief encounter, shocked and saddened her. She sought some closure by hosting a séance in Manhattan, attended by Texas Guinan, her brother Tommy, and a few close friends of Rudolph. Among them was the mobster, Owney Madden, known both to Mae and Rudolph. Mae insisted that the medium officiating at the séance be Italian. She felt that he would be simpatico to Rudolph's Mediterranean nature, and could translate, should the spirit of the dead star revert to his native tongue.

Two years later, while touring in a play, Mae continued to hold séances. Witnesses swore they heard Rudolph's voice warn Mae, "Your enemies are many. You must trust no one!" For several years, she relied on Rudolph to be her spiritual guide.

The Great Depression had settled in for a long run, but Mae's literary efforts were no longer experiencing a long run. Store windows were boarded up. People stood in line for blocks in the cold to get a cup of soup. Too many Americans were jobless.

The jobless don't spend money on entertainment. The glittering lights of Broadway were dark, Vaudeville houses began to show movies to anyone who had a dime. Vaudeville was breathing its last gasp. Mae, for all her spunk, couldn't fight this downturn that was enveloping the entire nation.

In retrospect, it seems odd that the impresarios and showmen who gave birth to Vaudeville now seemed unaware that movies were the wave of the entertainment future. Vaudeville really hit its zenith in 1913 when the magnificent New York Palace Theatre became the peak of any performer's career.

At the same time Vaudeville peaked, movies became an important part of the entertainment world. Audiences, for a fraction of what they paid for live shows, could see the world's greatest stars for much less than the price of a Vaudeville ticket.

The writing was on the theatre walls, but some of the moguls who controlled Vaudeville seemed blind to the warning. They were too busy fighting among themselves for a piece of a pie that would soon grow stale and unwanted.

The end of this once enormously popular entertainment form has been blamed on many factors. One of the strongest culprits in its demise was the theatre mogul, Edward F. Albee. His Keith-Albee-Orpheum Corporation had a monopoly on the world of Vaudeville. In its halcyon days, Vaudeville was controlled by enormous circuits. The Keith-Albee-Orpheum Corporation was a python, with a strangle hold on the necks of the performers who worked their circuit.

Albee said to anyone who would listen, "I am Vaudeville," and he was for many years. He was also a total bully. He blacklisted any performer who disagreed with him, no matter how successful they were with the public. If the artist wanted to advertise in a publication that he didn't approve, such as the highly influential *Variety*, he made it clear that they were not welcome on the many stages he owned around the country.

Albee, for all his initial success, seemed to seriously misjudged Vaudeville's future. He never admitted it was the people's escape, a way to forget the cares of the day. Audiences wanted topical humor, a way to laugh at the social, political, and economic trends of the time.

Albee also took Vaudeville from a twice a day performance to five times a day. This was an almost impossible schedule for any performer. Eccentric singers, dialects, and nutty comedians prevailed for many years. Albee wanted to give Vaudeville a fancy new set of clothes. He dressed up Vaudeville fit-to-kill, and so it died a slow but well-dressed death.

This gave rise to a number of smaller independent organizations that lured away the more important names in Vaudeville. The market now had competition, and an all-out war ensued to snag the former big fish from the stranglehold of the monopolistic likes of Keith-Albee-Orpheum Corporation.

Mae had frequently appeared on the Keith-Albee circuit. As she watched bookings drop all around her, she knew it was time to find another employer for her special talents.

This fierce competition among Vaudeville circuits produced a new breed of impresario. Marcus Loew was among those considered to be fair and sensitive to the needs of the artists who worked for him. He realized a happy performer was an inspired performer, and this translated into an ideal relationship for the audience, artist, and box office.

The Orpheum Theatres were run by Martin Beck, again a simpatico employer. He insisted in lodging his top stars in only the finest hotels, and seeing that they were catered to. Mae reveled in this velvet glove approach, seldom refusing an offer to sign with Beck.

The Jazz Singer (1927), a Warner Bros feature-length motion picture with synchronized sound-on-disc, premiered on October 6, 1927, at Warner Bros.' flagship theater in New York. The film's success heralded the commercial ascendance of sound films and the decline of the silent film era. This opened doors to seasoned professionals from the legitimate stage, artists who could sing and dance, and who had a readily identifiable voice. Mae West more than fit the bill for this new innovation.

Just as the once ample opportunities in Vaudeville also began to shrink alarmingly, Mae was contacted by George Raft. He now supplemented his income by dancing in the chorus of Broadway musicals. One night, he was spotted by a Hollywood agent. The film studios were scouring the Broadway shows in search of new talent. Raft's first movie role was in a small part with Texas Guinan in *Queen of the Night Clubs* (1929). He often was type cast as a dancer or a gangster . . . not much of a stretch for man who had associated for years with mobsters.

After working at Warner Bros., RKO Radio Pictures, and 20th Century Fox, Raft finally appeared in a hit, *Scarface* (1932) starring Paul Muni. A few months later, he was now working at Paramount pictures. Studio heads were even considering the always natty Raft as a replacement for the deceased Rudolph Valentino. Rudolph's premature death had left Paramount without a replacement to fill his elegant shoes. Raft was one of the many Valentino copies that the studios rushed into long-forgotten films.

Raft was just beginning work on his next film, *Night After Night* (1932). It had a small part for a hard-boiled woman of the world of an indeterminate age. Paramount was considering several Hollywood actresses for the part, but Raft insisted the studio test his friend, Mae. With no offers on the theatrical horizon in New York, she wisely decided to accept his timely invitation.

All up and down Broadway the theatre marquees were darkened. The former street of theatrical promise was now the boulevard of broken dreams. Actors everywhere joined the ranks of the unemployed in long breadlines, where a few months before hundreds had stood in line to buy theatre tickets.

Mae, rising star and authoress, was not immune to this great calamity. At the moment when things looked bleakest, Raft's intervention brought her an offer of a $32,000 contract on a one-picture deal. She couldn't afford not to take the gamble.

Mae tied up loose ends, borrowed some funds from her manager, Timony, and bid farewell to New York. Always aware of her image, she instinctively knew she would have to arrive in style. Mae and her ever-present maid boarded the luxurious *20th Century Limited*, changing to the *Santa Fe* in Chicago. They were headed for the land of sunshine.

After a three-day trek across the great American landscape, the locomotive chugged to a crawl as it entered the imposing Los Angeles station, a strangely beautiful series of domes, archways, and tall palm trees. This enormous Moorish-styled structure was the gateway to Southern California.

Through the large window of her private compartment Mae spotted a throng of reporters watching the train's arrival. Double checking her body-hugging frock and theatrical makeup in the mirror, she tilted her hat and prepared for her entrance.

She stepped into the doorway, striking a well-rehearsed pose. Flash bulbs popped and questions flew. Holding up a gloved hand, she flashed a dazzling smile.

"I'm not a little girl from a little town making good in a big town. I'm a big girl from a big town making good in a little town."

The studio heads did not completely agree. Not only was she asked to do a screen test, but she heard whispers that questioned the wisdom of using a woman of forty, who had never set foot on a film set.

To add insult to injury, she hated the part she had been assigned. It was a minor role with dialogue as uninteresting as a bowl of oatmeal, and with about as much color. She wasted no time in informing the studio she was returning to New York.

One of the Paramount bosses had seen what Mae could do on the New York stage. He convinced his partners to allow her to rewrite her own dialogue, just as she had done in her many plays.

Mae immediately penned an inspired vision of her first screen character, the hard-boiled Maudie Triplett, even supervising her flashy costumes and jewels.

In her first scene, Maudie enters a night club and sidles over to the hat check girl, handing her the spectacular white fox furs that are seductively draped across her ivory shoulders. As Mae stuck out a diamond encrusted hand and arm, the girl behind the stand gasped in amazement. "Goodness, what lovely diamonds!"

The irrepressible Mae replied, "Goodness had nothing to do with it, dearie."

Turning her back to the camera, she slowly ascends the staircase leading to the club. The veteran cameraman knew a good thing when he saw it. Against the director's orders, the camera followed Mae's undulating hips and bottom, encased in a shimmering silver gown that left little to the imagination, all the way up the flight of stairs. When the Paramount executives viewed the scene's rushes the next day, they were thrilled.

The picture's star, George Raft, told the press on the night of the film's premiere, "In this picture, Mae West stole everything but the cameras."

The press was even more excited. *Photoplay* said of her performance, "Blonde, buxom, rowdy Mae West was like a blast of fresh air in the smoky atmosphere of Raft's swell speakeasy."

Mae had taken her years of stage and Vaudeville experience and distilled them into a form that fit the screen of a movie theatre. Audiences were instantly taken with her undulating walk, her blunt approach to love, and her insinuating voice that colored even the simplest dialogue. Theatre owners were swamped with demands for more Mae West.

The studio offered her a range of pictures, all modern, in an attempt to cash-in on her sensational popularity. Mae simply could not see herself as a modern heroine, and in an amazing display of self-assurance, refused all offers. She was adamant that she film one of her plays.

Rather than lose their hot new property, Paramount capitulated to her demands and filming on *Diamond Lil* (1933) began immediately. By the time the cameras began to roll, Mae's very successful play, which had been banned from the screen by the Hays Code, had been heavily censored and renamed *She Done Him Wrong* (1933), a decision Mae always regretted.

Still on the Vaudeville grind, Ray, along with most of the country, saw Mae's first film. Vaudeville now ran first-run films along with a two-a-day performance schedule of live shows. He read in the trade papers the enormous deluge of fan mail that Paramount was receiving for their new star.

The Depression had deepened and Hollywood was feeling the pinch, particularly Paramount Studios, which had suffered a series of disappointing movies, Adolph Zukor's over-expansion, and his use of overvalued Paramount stock for purchases that forced the company into receivership in 1933.

Night After Night was an overnight sensation, quickly but temporarily refilling the coffers of the studio, which officially went bankrupt in 1935. Originally intended as a George Raft film, Mae had stolen the thunder from the star. Ray was but one of millions taken with this disturbing new sex symbol.

By the early 1930s, Ray had purchased an ancient Ford sedan. He now took bookings that allowed him to drive, rather than use the train. To cover expenses and pad out his act, he had teamed-up with fellow impersonators, Billy Richards and his boyfriend. The amount of costumes, luggage, and paraphernalia the trio required necessitated the addition of a small trailer to the back of the wheezing vehicle.

On their way to Denver for a lengthy engagement, things suddenly took a wrong turn. Their exhausted vehicle began to cough and sputter as it lurched forward, straining from the altitude and the added weight of the trailer. Alighting from the driver's seat, Ray, who could "butch it up" with the best, popped the sedan's bonnet. "Carburetor trouble," he mumbled to his amused and doubting companions.

Rather than risk driving on, he decided to backtrack to the little town they had just passed. The trio unhooked the weighty trailer. Ray climbed back on board, sharply wheeling the sputtering Ford in a bone-jarring u-turn.

The two left behind decided to make use of this enforced delay. Rummaging among the mounds of frocks and furs in the trailer, they extracted their antique, pedal-powered sewing machine. They drug the heavy contraption to a clearing alongside the shoulder of the bumpy two-lane road.

Startled motorists blinked at the sight of the two willowy impersonators pedaling furiously as they stitched a frock, bellowing an operetta duet in a piercing falsetto as they rehearsed their act.

It was during the trio's engagement in Colorado that Ray formed a lasting friendship with another drag artist, Tommy Martelle. Billed as the "Boy in The Pretty Gowns," Martelle had begun his career in 1911, when Ray was still cutting his theatrical teeth in London. Now, they were both appearing as impersonators, but Martelle was enjoying frequent success touring in his own musical shows as the star. Ray was still forced to accept engagements in less than stellar establishments, with frequent lapses in his booking calendar.

Ray had come to see Martelle's show on the recommendation of a friend. What he saw impressed him very much. He made his way backstage to congratulate Martelle on a job well done. Ray praised the costumes he had seen that night and wondered if they were professionally made. He mentioned that his two fellow performers made nearly all their costumes with the help of an ancient sewing machine they drug with them to each engagement. Martelle suggested they get together on a day off and evaluate Ray's costume situation. Over the next weeks, Ray learned invaluable information about altering existing gowns with simple sewing tricks that added greatly to the wardrobe. Martelle even gifted Ray with a number of chic accessories that he no longer used.

Despite this new look to his stage persona, bookings still remained elusive. When the trio he formed could no longer get a booking, he struck-out as solo. After banging around the country in a series of one night stands, he made a difficult decision. A week-long booking in Boston would be his last.

By this time, Vaudeville was only part of what theatres now offered. Half of the day was filled with showing motion pictures. Ray was to be on the second half of the bill at the Boston Theatre, but due to a ferocious winter storm, the train carrying the other acts never arrived. The management cancelled that afternoon's performance.

Rather than waste the remainder of the day hanging around the theatre, he decided to take in a nearby show that featured a friend of his, the impersonator, Jean Barrie. Typical of the varied acts that comprised Vaudeville, there was also an animal act that featured a team of enormous elephants. He loved animals and was excited to see the pachyderms. They were to follow Barrie's big number.

As the glamorous Barrie, who had a trained operatic voice, began to back dramatically toward the wings in preparation for the sensational high note that always ended his act, the audience began to noisily stir. The singer naturally assumed it was in anticipation of his climactic high C.

What actually set-off the audience was the sight of the enormous rear of an agitated elephant backing on to the stage. The poor pachyderm was about to collide with Barrie who was now belting out that signature note.

In unison, but in a different key, came the bellow of a constipated elephant that had not been properly exercised due to the inclement weather. The animal's desperate trainer had lost control of the creature as it sought relief.

Suddenly, a brown waterfall engulfed the startled Barrie. It drowned everything in its path, including those in the orchestra pit, but not before hitting the electric footlights and shorting out the entire lighting system of the theatre.

There sat Ray, choking on his laughter in the darkened theatre. Surely this was a sign from above that both Vaudeville and he were full of "you know what" and needed a definite change.

Following the trail that Mae had blazed, Ray returned to Hollywood. He wasn't a contest winner this time with a contract in hand. Returning to the cinema would mean a lot of casting calls and even more competition than before.

Rather than leave his theatrical wardrobe with friends as he had done on his first Hollywood venture, he packed everything he could manage. He could always don drag and make a buck in a gay club if steady work as a film extra didn't materialize.

Gay men and transvestites had been a fixture of the night life of Los Angeles for many years. Prohibition suddenly gave them a spotlight in the entertainment world.

The phrase "Pansy Craze" was born. Newspapers, films, books, and plays featured this new fascination with an age-old lifestyle. The craze grew as a parallel to the jazz era and the development of the newly "out" gay culture. Hollywood had an entire enclave of gays who thrived in the entertainment factories of the film studios. Makeup artists, hair dressers, chorus boys, actors, costume designers, and the whole industry that surrounded them were part and parcel of this short-lived pansy paradise.

Ray's persistent nature finally paid off. After pounding the pavements for more than a week, he dropped by The Horizontal Room, a well-known pansy club. He needed a drink and a job. He made straight for the bar to inquire if the management were hiring entertainers. He was introduced to the owner, who told him to come back that evening to see the current show and afterward they would talk.

Officially, clubs were not supposed to serve alcohol. There was a bar in every club that served "refreshments," cups of tea and glasses of soft drinks. The contents were usually 100-proof. Ray noticed that evening that many people were pouring their own liquor discreetly from a flask into a glass of mix that carried a pretty stiff tariff. The entertainment he saw at the Horizontal Room was a good deal weaker than the gin that he was graciously offered by a gentlemen seated next to him at the bar. After the show, Ray was asked to return the next afternoon to audition. He was positive he could top anything he had seen that night.

The club was empty when he arrived, except for the pianist and drummer, the serving staff, and the owner. Coming onstage from the changing room, he handed his sheet music to the accompanist. The club was shuttered and rather dark, making the lone spotlight the owner aimed at him all the more dramatic. He had chosen a form-fitting beaded white gown and a long stole covered in yards of black and white feathers. His wig was platinum, smartly waved in the style of the day.

The pianist pounded out the first chorus of a Dixieland evergreen. Ray did an enthusiastic bump and grind. He repeated the bump, aiming it directly at the drummer in perfect synch. In a good imitation of a Burlesque stripper, he swirled his feather boa, cupping the feathery wrap in a suggestive manner across his derriere:

"I don't want to be a madam, I just want to be one of the girls.
I know I'm not pretty, I know I'm not cute.
I want to kick my heels up in a house of ill repute...."

The piano tempo slowed to a tinkling background as he segued into one of his patter songs, a theatrical device he had learned long ago in the music hall:

"Now historians tell of a wishing well,
And you may repeat as the truth.
Its' water sublime in a southern clime,
For restoring old things to its youth.
Now Ponce de Leon was a very curious don,
For his youth was just flitting away.

He'd sailed the world over and in times of yore,
Was known as THE best of his day.
With his gun in his hand, always up at the crack of dawn,
But there came a sunrise when much to his surprise,
The spring in his gun was gone.
Though he tried in vain he always missed his aim,
For the damned thing was just a flash in the pan.
At first he cried, and then he sighed,
For the gun is the life of a man.
It seems that some screw has been lost from you,
He said to his sad little gun.
You're so old and so tired,
And your balls have been fired,
So I guess it's the end of our fun.
But never the less, as you might have guessed,
Poncey never lost his desire.
For he'd heard it told when his gun was too old,
A certain spring of youth would make it re-fire.
But a curious thing is Poncey never found this spring,
And his search ended one beautiful day,
For while leading his band without fear,
He forgot to cover his rear.
And Mary, he learned to love it better that way!"

Ray's main concern was not his material, or his delivery. It was just harder to audition in the cold atmosphere of an empty cabaret. He need not have worried. The staff had gathered around the stage, obviously enjoying his animated gab, and they rewarded him with a hardy hand. The owner signed him on the spot.

Word soon spread of the new talent featured nightly at The Horizontal. Within a short time, Ray was billed as the headliner. As his fame grew, he began to attract some of the well-known show business faces to the club. On any given night, out front he might find Joan Crawford, Bob Hope, or a lean and hungry-looking young Howard Hughes, the eccentric movie producer. Hughes always surrounded himself with several beautiful women. Often included among his party was the ruggedly handsome cowboy star,

Randolph Scott. Ray heard all the gossip through the gay pipeline. Scott was whispered to be Hughes' latest love interest.

Later, Scott would be Cary Grant's roommate, at a time when neither star needed the financial benefit of shared living quarters. It was common knowledge that movie studios went to great expense to hide the sexual proclivities of their top stars, including Grant and Scott. Reporters and papers were paid-off to look the other way.

Pansy clubs were tolerated by the police, as long as there was no obvious sale of alcohol, no same-sex dancing, and no evidence of fondling or embracing. Nudity was never an option, male or female. It was in this touchy atmosphere that Ray and several other well-known impersonators plied their risky trade. When outside a gay club, entertainers had to walk the straight and narrow, and that meant no makeup, wigs, or gowns.

It wasn't like old New York, where drag was a well-known and accepted tradition in the theatre. The accepted eccentricities attributed to theatre people in New York did not provide as good a cover for a fairy in California. In New York, widely recognized gay styles in dress and demeanor went virtually unnoticed.

California seemed to be the center of hypocrisy, grinding out uncensored smut and violence on film, yet raiding the establishments that featured legitimate entertainers in one of the oldest practices in theatre, cross-dressing. The club owners and theatre managers in Hollywood were aware that this gay, new angle was attracting a crowd. By boldly challenging the conventions of the time, and catering to an audience's appetite for new sensations, the pansy craze was born. The resultant craze, like any new idea, had a dark side.

The sudden success of these queer clubs only increased vice and police harassment. Despite the ever-present threat of raids and arrest for almost a decade, the public was fascinated with this other world. Not only did it fill the clubs and juke joints, but made its way onto the silver screen and serious novels. The public avidly followed thinly veiled depictions of gay life.

A sudden anti-gay sentiment reared its ugly head in the mid-1930s. The public began to feel uneasy about the blurring of the gender lines. Suddenly, what was funny—a comic drag or a butch lesbian impersonating a man—now seemed threatening.

Across the country, the gossip magazines carried headlines like "Fag Balls Exposed," in an article about a drag ball in New York. Magazines such as *Variety* delighted in telling their readers about a food fight that broke out in a restaurant when a waiter showed up in a "red evening gown with long white gloves, finger waved wig, and high heeled shoes." The resultant melee ended in complete chaos with several patrons taken to the hospital.

Part of this new attitude was engendered by the terrible suffering brought on by the Great Depression. This economic disaster wiped away all the conventions held dear by the public for decades. They wished to return to a more stable and clearly defined society. Suddenly, the public wanted to slam the doors of the closets from which so many queens and lesbians had escaped. Several acts of violence, including unexplained shootings at gay clubs, fanned the fires of fear.

In truth, some of this was due to the Mafia's warring gangs involved in territorial rivalries involving liquor distribution and club ownerships. This was all the authorities needed. It was the perfect excuse to clamp down and eventually close those clubs that featured female impersonators.

This was a frequent topic among impersonators when they visited each other's shows. Ray went on his nights off to see such established queens like Francis Renault, the star from New York, who had housed a penniless Archie Leach before he was transformed into Cary Grant. Renault could be seen nightly at a club named Clark's.

Karyl Norman, billed as "The Creole Fashion Plate," held forth at the swank La Boheme. Norman had been a well-known fixture in the New York gay scene. Ray had worked with him when they were both beginning. Ray received a lavender engraved invitation to his opening night in Hollywood. Norman relied heavily on his $100,000 wardrobe and a chorus line of ten hunky and handsome young men. There was never an empty seat when this dark-skinned drag performed.

Through Norman, Ray was introduced to the owner of a more upscale club, Jimmy's Back Yard. Norman brought him backstage after the show to meet the proprietor. The following week, Ray received an invitation to headline at Jimmy's at a considerably higher salary than he was currently receiving. He felt it only fair to give his current employer a chance to match the offer. When this didn't happen, Ray walked.

He arrived at Jimmy's just as serious legal issues in Hollywood began to surface. For the past two seasons, there seemed to be little enforcement by the authorities, other than an occasional harassment outside the clubs. This usually involved amateur impersonators that would leave the bars while still in costume. Drag was tolerated as long as it remained safely on stage. To flaunt it on the street posed a threat to the "sanctity of the family and marriage," as one particularly righteous publication declared.

Overnight, the legal climate changed. Both La Boheme and Jimmy's were raided. Straight customers and queers were hauled-off to police stations. They were met with the press, who had obviously been tipped off. The resultant photographs of the bedraggled queens and their admirers made sensational copy for the morning papers. Even more damaging was new legislation forbidding "one gender from wearing the clothing of the other." This was a temporary death knell for the art of female impersonation.

Ironically, screen luminaries, such as Marlene Dietrich and Katherine Hepburn, were donning men's tuxedos and pants. Suddenly, Norman and Ray were prohibited from appearing on stage in their beautiful costumes, an integral part of their acts. Norman tried to continue, singing and dancing in a tuxedo, still heavily made up, but the audience was not interested. Another desperate impersonator wheeled his rack of impressive gowns on stage, holding them up to his body as he sang. Again it was futile.

Ray was not about to give in. He packed his frocks and fled to San Francisco. The famous Tait's Club offered Ray a starring spot. Soon, the long arm of the law extended to even that liberal bastion by the Bay. Ray's short-lived engagement came to a dramatic end. That night, a local radio station had set up at Tait's to broadcast the show. A deep voice announced the star of the show, "Mr.

Ray Bourbon." This was followed by a long harp arpeggio. "Ray" burst through the curtains, dressed in a tightly-belted silver and white lamé gown, to enthusiastic applause:

> "Now when Penelope Swope,
> Married Bennington Slope,
> He was as thin and as trim as a willow.
> They could cling face to face in a lover's embrace,
> Just as close as a sheet to a pillow.
> She'd be his dear wife for the rest of her life,
> In his arms she would sigh and he'd hold her.
> Now they both realized on account of his size,
> It was increasingly hard to enfold her.
> It's so sad to relate he had taken on weight,
> Since they stood up in front of the preacher.
> He would no longer woo her, can't even get to her,
> He has too much damned stomach to reach her.
> Poor Mrs. Bennington Slope simply cannot cope,
> With the slope of her husband's abdomen.
> And all of his ardor just makes everything harder,
> When Swope thinks of their love in the gloamin.'
> He's willing to try, he'll never say die,
> There's plenty of life, but no hope.
> He's so padded with suet, he just can't get to it,
> Poor Mrs. Penelope Bennington Slope!"

As Ray began to take his bows, a great ruckus came from the back of the stage. Several partially dressed drags ran screaming from behind the curtains. Hot on their six-inch high heels were six of San Francisco's finest. Ray was hit full-force by this wall of wailing would-be women, sending him backwards into to the arms of a particularly burly gendarme. The local radio station continued to broadcast during the entire melee. Their listeners were convinced that the raid was just part of the show. The next day the papers told the real story:

"Rae Bourbon was arrested when his San Francisco performance was raided by police . . . Tait's Café was the scene . . . Monday night was a colorful affair, that incidentally was broadcast by KWFI . . . after Rae Bourbon had sung and danced in feminine attire Captain Lane blew his whistle and half a dozen coppers nabbed the boys. They gave them time to take off their dresses, hustled them into the wagon, which clanged to the station house with the gang of mascaraed, rouged, lipsticked impersonators who floored the tough Irish desk sergeant upon their entrance."

Variety ran a column in a tongue-in-cheek campy style that would have made any drag queen proud:

"San Francisco is a manly town that likes show suggestive and liquor straight. When it comes to pansy floor shows, that's a different matter. Tait's Cafe was the scene of a raid when great big gorgeous policemen descended on the club and carried off seven members of the "Boys Will Be Girls" troupe, and shoved them in a nasty old jail cell. That blindfolded woman, Justice, pulled her eyeshade awry, looked out at the gowns and makeup of the girls and with tongue in cheek, scheduled a hearing for the Women's Court. The Judge dismissed Rae Bourbon, Jean Russell, Neil Dorney, Sam Silvers, Eddie Lee, Francis Blair, and Fred Notl. The manager, Daniel Carson, was held. The City rescinded the Café's permit, and is doing everything possible to make it tough for the club."

Ray was a seasoned trouper, and the night in jail was only a nuisance. Unable to sleep, he asked the guard if there were any newspapers. He reached through the bars for the well-worn remnants of a week-old tabloid. Turning to the entertainment section, a name from his past caught his eye: "Tommy Martelle. Foremost delineator of feminine types. A laugh guaranteed to last the entire week . . . acclaimed by critics in many cities as America's foremost female impersonator."

Ray paused there, not entirely in agreement with the reporter's assessment of Martelle's talent. He was undeniably gorgeous, but "foremost?" Hardly. Martelle did seem to be in the news in many cities Ray booked. Ray had to grudgingly admit his raunchy approach to material often slammed theatrical doors to more mainstream productions that were Martelle's bread and butter. Like Mae, Ray had chosen a rougher road. "Tommy can give the girls pointers on how to wear clothes, many or few. He knows the shrug that best displays white shoulders and the gestures that show off soft whiteness and flexibility of lady like hands."

Ray put down the paper, looking at his rough un-manicured hands. They would never be mistaken for those of a lady, nor would he. Hell no, he was a hard-boiled dame, a broad, a whore with a heart of gold. Long evening gloves covered a myriad of problems and his signature laugh often covered his deep-seated insecurities. He tossed the paper aside, as the guard came to release him. He pulled himself erect, head up, and blinked as he walked out into the bright California sun. After a nights' incarceration, with the splotchy remnants of his makeup still visible, Ray was met by reporters as he left the jail. When asked why he continued to risk arrest by performing in drag, he borrowed a quote from Mae West. "An ounce of performance is worth a pound of promises. The best way to behave is to misbehave."

Ray packed his bags and returned to Hollywood. Films were at least legitimate work, even in drag. Apparently, the law thought impersonators were harmless as long as they were safely up there on the silver screen.

Gay life in Hollywood was as prolific as ever, if only a bit more under the radar than it had been. There was a certain level of tolerance that permitted matinee idols and film divas to romp in the forbidden garden of gay life, particularly in the suddenly fashionable drag clubs. Here, it was acceptable to rub elbows with all manner of dubious genders, and for a short time it looked like a trend that would endure.

As it has happened throughout history, gay men and women still managed to meet and love, but homosexuality was becoming more of a consequential matter, due in part to changing social attitudes. Many of these changes were brought on by the gender conflict that had deepened due to the Depression. Men, the primary bread-winners at that time, were now neutered and made to seem less manly by their inability to support their families. The new found craze for pansy entertainers in clubs and movies somehow seemed to fly in the face of the fundamental building blocks of the great American society.

In this unclear atmosphere of growing intolerance to unacceptable public social mores, Ray found he had to walk a tightrope of sexual behavior. Being obvious on the street could land you in jail for the night, if for no other reason than it offended the homophobic nature of a cop. No longer was it wise to frequent the steam baths scattered on the fringes of Hollywood, where it was possible to entertain as many tricks as could be lured into the tiny cubicles of these notorious gay hangouts.

Ray, like so many people in the entertainment world, was a bit of a gypsy. Constant travelling and an uncertain income are not conducive to long-term relationships. As an aging queen, he also found it harder each year to find a suitable partner, the best alternative to the dangerous world of anonymous sex. It seemed a good time to strengthen existing friendships, scoring the occasional sex partner when it was safe, and concentrate on career.

Ray's return to Hollywood found him in front of the cameras again, this time with his former club pianist, Bart Howard, in a Marion Davie's picture called *Ever Since Eve* (1937).

He also landed a weekly gig as a regular on a local radio program called *Back Stage at Earl Carroll's*. In between, he appeared frequently at the Holland Inn. So successful was his spot as the Inn's house comic that he was made manager. This lasted briefly, due mainly to his overly generous bar credits for all his friends.

Despite Ray's frequent change of clubs, *Variety* continued to follow his career, a sign of his growing importance in the impersonator world. A legitimate theatre engagement elicited the following: "It is Rae Bourbon all the way. Those who have reveled in this nightclub performer's antics will want to see him in a whole evening of his best routines. The show contains a few other acts, but they are merely breathers for Bourbon."

Another performance brought a more specific report from *Variety*: "It is a romp for Bourbon, donning skirts and violent pastels most of the way and having a really gay time. He calls for a drink after each strenuous session at swishery and pantomime, and real stuff it is too, or so it looked. Don't take along anyone who is squeamish, for they will be shocked to no end."

Ray's answer to the paparazzi's questions was like most things from his mouth, a many-sided reply. He told a reporter during an interview:

> "It is difficult for me to say what I am. I am more about comedy. Am I a drag queen? I do specific characters, and there is always a little of me in that character. Drag is about what you wear, and I do wear some fabulous gowns, but I got my start in the tradition of the English dame. It is not about being queer, though that is what most people assume about impersonation. The history of the dame is that you are portraying a character, not the fact that you might be in a woman's dress. I grew up on a ranch in Texas. My father taught me to do all the things you would expect, ride horses, shoot rifles and hunt. I didn't really appreciate the things I was made to do when I was ten years old but I understand now what he was trying to do, prepare me for the real world. I know how to shoot a gun and ride a horse. I do it in movies as an extra."

*Little Ray Waddell (Ray Bourbon) had found a home...
a desolate and hard place.*

*Ray was now almost thirteen, in London at a
boarding school for problem boys.*

With the sound of cheering still ringing in her ears, Mae informed her mother that she would be a stage star someday.

He perfected his singing and dancing in the chorus in company with a bunch of dames (the British term for "female impersonator"). Ray had something extra, a bit more flair.

Malcolm Scott helped Ray, gave him expert advice drawn from his long career as an impersonator.

Audiences were never quite sure just what Mae was up to. Was she spoofing sex?

One of Mae West's earliest influences was the impersonator Bert Savoy, who dressed in elegant gowns but behaved in an outrageous manner.

Variety wrote, "Unless Miss West can tone down her stage presence... she might as well hop right out of Vaudeville and into Burlesque."

Mae seemed to be on the road to laying the ground rules of early feminism in 1919.

Gladys Bentley. A few more libations and a firm masculine handshake with this bull dagger sealed the deal.

Lestra LaMonte. The Crepe Paper Fashion Plate.

"Wanted: Movie dress extras. Apply in person, Vitagraph Films."
Ray was thrilled with his chance at a small role on the Vitagraph set.

One extra caught Ray's wandering eye. He could not have guessed the connection their futures would have. Rudolph Valentino would quickly become a worldwide sensation.

Bobby O'Neill, Harry Laughlin, and Mae were doing a particularly energetic dance. A provocative series of bumps and grinds created a serious wardrobe malfunction.

Countless auditions, not only as a comedy drag act, but also as a straight chorus boy, yielded nothing.

A dapper Ray Bourbon from his chorus boy days.

One of the most troublesome locations was an open-air studio on the roof a building. Ray watched a sudden gale rip-off his wig.

The Herald Tribune fumed, "She is a menace to art, morals, and deserves an investigation." A photo from Mae's highly successful play, Sex, landed her in jail.

After ten days in the local slammer, Mae West was released. The publicity was priceless.

Rudolph Valentino with his favorite pet. Valentino and Ray both had an almost childlike fascination for dogs and horses.

A director, a makeup team, and a camera man were consulted. They felt that Ray bore a striking resemblance to Estelle Taylor. He would be her perfect stunt double.

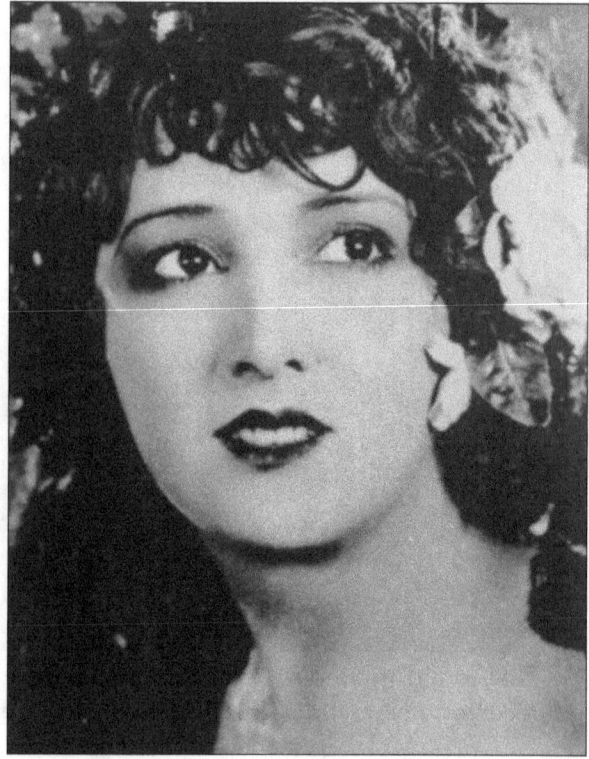

The costumes in Salome (1922) were like nothing Ray had ever experienced. He is pictured here bewigged with what appeared to be horns wrapped in goat hair.

Nazimova as Salome (1922), coiffed in a fashion like an explosion of black cotton candy.

In, Beyond the Rocks (1922), Gloria Swanson and Rudolph Valentino were tricked-out in period finery. Ray played a mincing dandy in the background.

Mae in the play, Diamond Lil (1928), which was infested with crime and easy women. She would parlay this role into a million-dollar ticket for many years.

Ray escorted his friend, the fading silent film star Estelle Taylor. He and Estelle appeared in several films together.

In, Night After Night *(1932), Mae West stole everything but the cameras. Her co-star was George Raft.*

"Hello, suckers!" was Texas Guinans' famous quip. Pictured here with Mae West, Guinan was a notorious nightclub owner. She introduced Mae to Rudolph Valentino just one month before his untimely death.

Mae West while making Belle of the Ninetes (1934). Her character's low morals were initially against the rules of the 1930 Hays Code that the studio had agreed to follow. Will B. Hays sometimes installed watchdogs to verify that retakes adhered to the Code.

Rudy Valentino starring in Blood and Sand (1922).

William Haines, Hollywood heartthrob. By the time he and Ray worked together, Haines had been seriously demoted in salary and star billing.

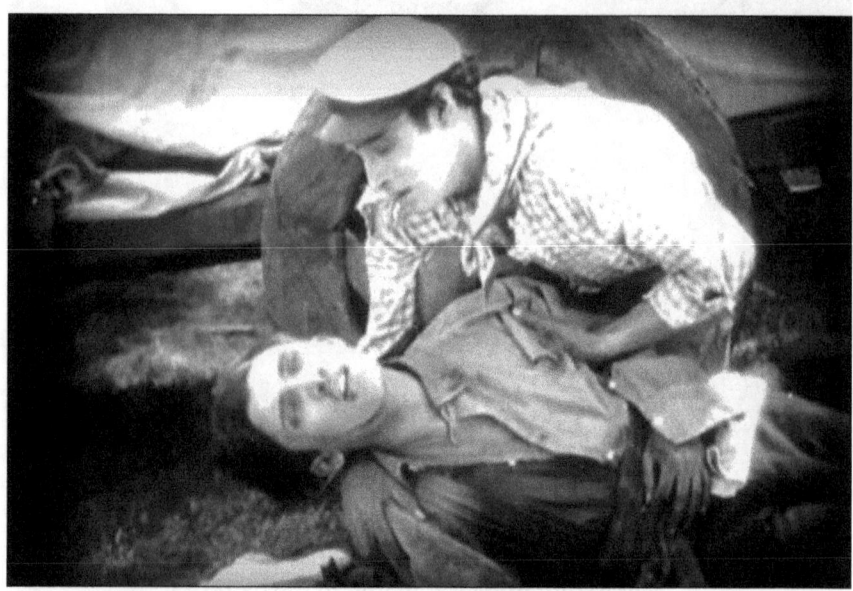

Ray, in a scene from the first reel of Blood and Sand (1922), dies in the arms of the dashing Rudolph Valentino.

A radio skit on the very popular Chase and Sanborn Hour. Mae is pictured with Edgar Bergen and his marionette, Charlie McCarthy. The result was more publicity than she could ever have imagined, and it led to Mae's banishment from radio for a decade.

Mae's biggest flop, The Heat is On (1943). The New York Times felt, "The heat is definitely off." More than twenty-five years passed before Mae appeared in another movie.

Mae's Many Faces. Artist, A. Tillman.

Lupe Velez, the Mexican film sensation. She confided to Ray, "I would rather kill myself." She did.

Boxer Rocky Marciano. Mae liked 'em rough. She once said, "It takes two to get one in trouble."

One of Mae's many court appearances with her ever-faithful and long-time manager and friend, James Timony, by her side.

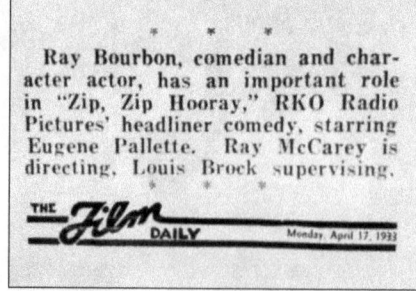

Ray Bourbon was arrested at Tait's Café, when half a dozen coppers nabbed the boys. San Francisco Chronicle.

Ray's most important film, RKO's Zip Zip Hooray (1933). The U.S. Catalog of Copyright Entries lists this 2-reel film being copyrighted by RKO on March 31, 1933. The Film Daily publication announced the film on April 17.

Ray's favorite scene in Golddiggers of 1937, produced in 1936. Dapper in the latest fashion, fedora hat, and bow tie, his signature mustache gave him a slightly cynical touch.

Ray was having the time of his life with Mae in the play, Catherine Was Great (1944). His take on Florian was quick, comic, and oh-so-queer.

Florian in Catherine Was Great (1944). He delighted in his elaborate costume. "He ... drew delicious laughs ...."

Catherine Was Great (1944). Mae strutted and stalked the stage, tossing off her lines, followed by the billows of a 75-pound, jewel-encrusted cape.

Mae in Las Vegas, 1954. If randy men can ogle firm young flesh, why can't ladies be treated to succulent slabs of beefcake?

"I don't want to be considered just a man dressed as a woman. Yes, they are outlandishly dressed, frequently bitches, campy, and always worth imitating." Ray, in a strapless gown, standing in the midst of his once large inheritance, now just faded costumes.

Command performance for King Edward VIII and Mrs. Simpson. Their hands were making the motions of polite applause, but their faces were set in stone.

Command Performance. Ray had been bamboozled by The Crazy Gang into participating in a politically incorrect song in front of the eyes of misguided King Edward VIII and his mistress, Mrs. Simpson.

Ray Bourbon said, "Josephine Baker was the most sensational thing I'd seen in years... all she had on was a tiny jeweled crotch cover... the ovation was thunderous."

Ray was called back to tour with Diamond Lil, a cross-country odyssey between 1948 and 1950.

Wearing black and white, false eyelashes, heavy perfume, and a five-o'clock shadow, Ray Bourbon, actor/actress, enters Beverly Hills Municipal Court, to deny that he (or, she) was guilty of impersonating a woman. Los Angeles Examiner.

Mae West and Tallulah Bankhead. Talullah said, "But daaaahling, I know that old broad. We both worked Vegas. Mae was bumping and grinding... I, too, was surrounded by queer chorus boys."

Rae's glamour shot, in pearls.

Ray as Bowery Rose in the touring company of the play, Diamond Lil, with Mae West, 1948-1950.

Mae West and Rock Hudson stopped the show cold at the 1957 Academy Awards Oscar show. The Examiner.

Ray Bourbon, still a name on the impersonator circuit, had been invited to join the tour of the world-famous Jewel Box Revue, New York City.

Kansas City's Jewel Box Lounge, Troost Avenue. Like a faded and jaded old hooker, Jewel Box Lounge promised an exciting and affordable night on the town.

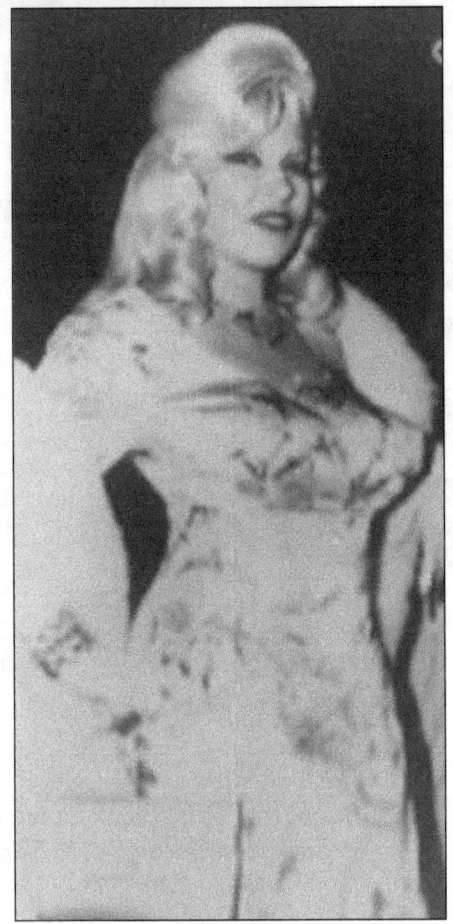

In the 1950s, Ray got in on the ground floor of America's fascination with comedy records, typically risqué vinyl platters.

Mae West at seventy-one, appearing on the TV sit-com, Mr. Ed. (1964).

*Ray's co-stars at the Jewel Box Lounge in the 1960s.
Front row: Joey Block; Butch Ellis; Jaimie Greeney.
Back row: Carrie Davis; Skip Arnold; G. G. Allen.*

Mae reveled in the attention, as she was delivered daily in a Rolls Royce to the studio set of Myra Breckenridge (1970).

Ray said, "I've been around a long, long time. When the man said 'Let there be light,' I'm the bitch that flipped the switch."

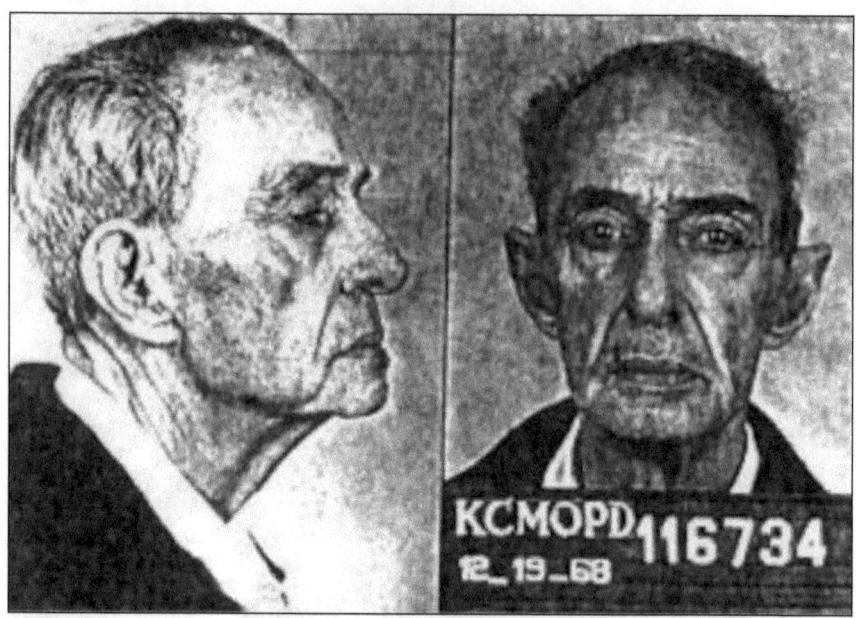

Ray's mug shots from his 1964 arrest reveal much about his downward spiral, and the condition he was in near the end of his life. "Whatever I've wanted to say, I've said it. You can laugh and leer at the life I've led, but Mary I'm glad I've led it!"—Ray Bourbon

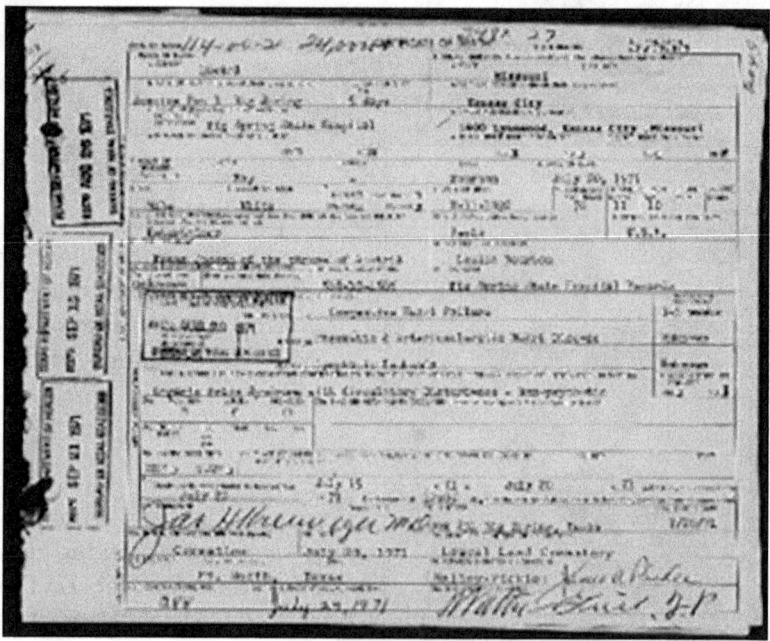

Ray Bourbon's death certificate, 1971.

Mae, the octogenarian, still truckin' and trickin.'

Rex Reed, reviewing Mae's final film, Sextette: "She looks like something they found in the basement of a pyramid."

Mae West's death certificate, 1980.

A pair of overly chic impersonators of days gone by. The author, Patrick C. Byrne, in yards of black fox, with Phillip Beard, in white mink, borrowed from their Mission Hills clients. This one-night-only amateur night contest at Kansas City's Jewel Box Lounge (at Ray Bourbon's suggestion) was their only foray into the wonderful world of performance.

Author, Patrick C. Byrne, and one of his Mae West creations, waiting to go on at the historic Uptown Theatre in Kansas City, Missouri.

14
Cut, Don't Print That!

While Ray was feeling the weight of the law, Mae was beginning to feel the sting of the Motion Picture Producers and Distributors of America (MPPDA). Their mouthpiece and President, Will Hays, was a thoroughly narrow-minded Presbyterian elder from the Hoosier state. Hays had been involved in the dirtiest of politics in his earlier career, taking enormous bribes from corporations to help elect President Harding, who ran an administration that was one of the most corrupt in U.S. history.

Hays feigned shock at the moral tone in Hollywood. His $150,000 salary from the MPPDA was an impetus to spur him on to clean up what he perceived as "filth" on movie screens everywhere.

His first act as "the little white father of the cinema" was to distribute a set of rules to every movie studio. To be avoided at all cost were "improper sex scenes, white slavery, attractive vice, nakedness, prolonged love scenes, the underworld, gambling and drunkenness, ridicule of public officials, offending religious beliefs, violence, vulgar body language, and salacious advertising of movies." Mae took one look at the list and laughed out loud.

During the first years of talking pictures, the studio formula aimed at drawing in the Depression weary was to give them a plate full of sex and violence. The MPPDA's list of forbidden items ran into a wall of resistance from all sides.

Because pictures now "spoke," there was a rush among studios to hire artists who had had stage experience. They often came from Vaudeville, Broadway, and worst of all, Burlesque. These performers could speak and sing, and what they said, and how they said it, often raised red flags among the morality watchdogs.

Nothing points this out more strongly than one of Mae's favorite witticisms, "It's not what I say, but how I say it." Mae was a master of the double entendre. Anyone who had theatre experience knew that you covered any glitch with a quick comeback, and sometimes the written script wasn't nearly as funny as what popped into a performer's head, naughty though it might be.

One of the major flaws in this hypocritical system was the placement of too much emphasis on monitoring the sexual content of a film. Violence was far more prevalent in movies at this time, particularly the glorification of brutality in gangster films. Violence was not considered distasteful at this time, but sex, the most natural and one of the strongest urges, was taboo.

It is not hard to understand this when the names of those who tried to enforce this very unbalanced code were Joseph Breen and Martin Quigley. They were both the main ingredients in a mutton-flavored Catholic stew. The Irish, at this time, did not condemn violence, thinking it was part of "manliness." Sex, on the other hand, was certainly part of the Devil's plan. Never mind that those who held to this notion often reproduced like rabbits.

Some people thought of the MPPDA as prigs put in charge of monitoring the morals of the film industry, but the studios had all agreed to the policies in order to circumvent government censorship. Hays and his staff found Mae West to be a singularly threatening departure from the Code. Her image was that of a woman who controlled the situation. She was in charge of everything, including the men who flocked to her. She was a threat to the dominance of men and the sacred order of the household. Women were meant to be under the thumb of their lover or hubby.

It didn't help that Hollywood's scandal magazines, such as *True Confessions*, found Mae West to be such a delicious item. In a two-part interview published in December 1933 and 1934, the publication ran a feature titled, "Mae West—Queen of Sex."

> "No stay-at-home-wife-life would do for the versatile performer from Brooklyn, New York. The more than forty year old actress learned to do black face imitations at an age when other children were doing long division.
>
> "There is practically no line of stage work that one can mention that Mae West has not tackled. By twelve years of age she was a fully developed woman. Her curves were as solid and firm and alluring as they are today. Imitations

and child parts, to which she had graduated, were discarded and Mae became a Burlesque Queen at $500 a week when she was thirteen!

"Vaudeville, musical comedies, even engagements at Coney Island where she became a strong woman in an acrobatic act. Dancing lessons with Ned Wayburn led to musical comedies. Big money in Burlesque, pin money in small roles in comedies. Any job that came along, Mae West could do it."

This sort of publicity was a double-edged sword, fascinating the public and giving ammunition to the censors who sought to put an end to the Mae West phenomenon.

The 1930s were a period of severe social unease. Men no longer possessed the authority they once held as the bread winner, the patriarch, the brute that drug the inferior female by the hair from their cave.

The character that Mae portrayed in film, and the character that inhabited the real body of Mae West, was having none of this.

At first, the studios refused to cave to censor's ludicrous standards. Their product was not somebody else's idea of morality; they were hawking entertainment. Hollywood was one of the few bright spots in a collapsed economy, and the studios wanted to keep it that way. They would continue to give the audience what it wanted as long as they could.

Production on *She Done Him Wrong* continued. Mae tested most of the studio's leading men as a possible co-star. Many were good-looking and talented, but they didn't have that spark that lit Mae's fire.

One day while exiting the Paramount lot in her enormous chauffeur-driven limousine, Mae's eagle eye spotted a good-looking man leaving a sound stage. He was obviously an actor, but one she had never seen. Directing the driver to stop, she rolled down the window and asked the startled young man, who immediately recognized her, if he was under contract to her studio.

He turned out to be Cary Grant, then a relative unknown, despite having appeared in eight films, including prominent roles in

Devil and the Deep (1932) with Tallulah Bankhead and Gary Cooper, and *Blonde Venus* (1932) starring Marlena Dietrich. Impressed with his natty good looks, Mae continued the conversation, filling him in on the possibility of doing a screen test with her.

"If you can talk, you'll do," insinuated the mega star. When Mae heard his unique British sound, she was sold.

Grant immediately charmed the knickers off Mae with his captivating voice and bedroom eyes. A legendary film pairing was born in the streets of Paramount Studios.

The studio was astounded when she finished the picture in only eighteen days. She was astounded at how unprepared some of the crew had been on her first picture, and vowed there would be none of that on her first starring picture.

She insisted that everyone, from her co-stars, down to the smallest walk-on, know exactly what was expected of them in advance. She had worked out every detail of her character before the cameras ever began rolling each morning. What appeared to be part of nature, the walk, the swagger, the rolling shoulders, were all carefully orchestrated.

A contributing factor to that famous Mae West oceanic roll was something her audiences almost never saw, the towering platform shoes painfully strapped to her little feet. These cruel shoes added at least six inches to her petite figure. Just maneuvering in those unnatural elevators created the undulation that audiences took to be a naturally sexy walk. This also explains why Mae preferred the long dresses of the 1890s that seldom allowed the slightest peek at her imprisoned feet.

She Done Him Wrong allowed Mae a chance to give film audiences what her Vaudeville audiences had enjoyed for decades, her unique way with a song. "A Guy What Takes His Time" is a case in point. As she says, she likes to see a guy arriving in low and there certainly isn't any fun in getting something done when you have to rush to make the grade. If anyone can spot an amateur and appreciate a connoisseur at his trade, it was Mae.

When queried by reporters as to the plot of her latest cinematic effort, they got a typical bit of Westian wisdom. "It's all about a girl who lost her reputation but never missed it."

What many did not realize was that she was already forty years old when she brought *Diamond Lil* to the screen as *She Done Him Wrong*. Most female film stars would be looking at a demotion to character parts at this juncture. Mae was just beginning her film odyssey and she was top-billed and in charge of the whole package. She was still sexy and shocking, and, worst of all, she dared to mock sexual mores.

Had a less confident actress attempted the same thing, she probably would not have appealed to as large and diverse an audience as those that flocked to see this new sensation. Mae was perceived as the genuine article.

At last, the bawdy blonde, who had worked her act on stages across the continent, was able to reach audience numbers no Vaudevillian had ever dreamed of. The film had sold out bookings across the land, from the backwoods to Broadway. It also elevated co-star Cary Grant to starring roles with his next appearance in *The Woman Accused* (1933).

To Paramount's surprise, Mae suggested she do a series of cross country personal appearances to promote her new film. She loved live audiences and reveled in the applause. The waves of love that poured across the footlights in the form of applause and laughter worked on her like an aphrodisiac. This was a constant throughout her career, perhaps more meaningful to her than the string of temporary liaisons that dotted her memoirs. Audiences supplied the true love that didn't seem to be part of her personal life.

At each stop, she appeared onstage before the film ran, acting out brief skits and singing at least one of the songs that were associated with her. Mae was devoted to the ardent fans that turned out in droves to applaud and laugh. They served to constantly remind her of her hard-earned successes.

While the receipts from her films were money in the bank, the people who were out there in the darkened theatre to award her with their live approval confirmed her worth. They were her measure of success and perhaps her real one true love.

Although Mae always managed to look years younger than her actual age during her live tours, it was becoming increasingly difficult and time consuming to keep up the illusion. Her hectic travelling schedule did not allow the necessary time for experts to work on maintaining her platinum locks.

After a series of chemical disasters in various salons, her always fragile hair succumbed. Her notorious frugality also played a part in her hair-do's demise. On more than one occasion, she sent her dresser to the local drug store to purchase a bottle of peroxide bleach, a particularly dangerous decision in the hands of a non-professional. The end result led to her dependence on wigs for the rest of her life.

Paramount's future was now secure, thanks in no small part to the girl from Bushwick. Mae would eventually write eight films. Most would be "box office boffo" in the lingo of *Variety*, that Bible of show business.

She summed it up when asked about just what made her so special. "Diamonds is my career. Personality is the glitter that sends your little gleam across the footlights into that big black space where the audience is."

That big black space was filled with faces that flocked in record numbers to see that glittering personality on the screen.

A unique feature of all Mae West films was their lack of true romance. Mae, completely self-occupied, never seemed to connect with any of her co-stars, except in her obvious physical desire for them. She would get them in a clutch, turn on the heat, and when the potential paramour got too familiar, she'd push him at arm's length and sidle away. Art often reflects life.

Mae's newfound fortune paid for her first home in Hollywood. It was a classic apartment building. The Ravenswood on Rossmore Blvd. was built in the grand manner, full of fine woodworking and old world craftsmanship. The spacious, elegant lobby was beautifully furnished with Oriental rugs and crystal chandeliers. Mae's income had increased so dramatically after her first film that she decided to buy the entire apartment building.

Her penthouse suite was done in glitzy faux Louis XIV. Her idea of accessories ran mostly to photographs, paintings, and statues of herself. Along with the Ravenswood, she invested in several expensive properties. So strong was her dislike for the buildings across from her apartment that she bought them and had the façades changed to complement her taste.

Crime was rampant in the early 1930s, not only in the Mafia-centric cities of New York and Chicago but all across the land. Hollywood was no exception. America was in the throes of the worst economic period in history. Poverty and the subsequent desperation it produced created the test tube that grew the national infection, crime. Movie stars became primary targets for kidnapping and extortion.

One night in October 1932, Mae was to make a rare appearance at one of Hollywood's elegant nightclubs. She was seated in the back of her enormous black Cadillac limousine parked in front of her residence. While arranging her bleached locks one more time and studying her makeup in a jewel-encrusted Cartier compact, she was startled when her door was suddenly flung open.

Before she could cry out, a masked figure demanded her jewelry. As usual, she was dripping in diamonds valued at over $15,000. In seconds, the thug had stripped her bare of her hard-earned rocks. He nearly tore her ear lobe as he roughly pulled at her enormous chandelier earrings.

Her chauffer leapt to her defense, his pistol at the ready. When he saw Mae's assailant had a gun aimed at her head, he decided to drop his weapon. By the time Mae had regained her composure, the robber had fled on foot.

After an intensive investigation, the guilty party turned out to be the chauffer. He had set up the entire incident with the help of some of his underworld friends. Mae was forced to testify at the trial, something she did not want to comply with, given her own association with some rather shady characters from her past.

Her hunch was right, for she received numerous death threats and warnings of disfigurement to her famous face, threats she did not take lightly. She was familiar with these characters and she knew they often followed through with violence. Her face was her fortune and any disfigurement meant the loss of her career.

Only after promises of round the clock protection at her apartment from the Los Angeles Police was Mae willing to issue a public statement, saying that she refused to be intimidated and would launch a campaign to see that those guilty would be brought to justice.

The newspapers ate it up. The result was a priceless publicity coup for the petite sex pot that had previously been regarded by some as a crude and classless upstart with a questionable background. Suddenly, she was a torch carrier for law and order.

As Mae's star burned ever-brighter, Ray was taking anything that came his way. He signed on at the Chesterfield Motion Picture Corporation on his return from the scandalous raid in San Francisco.

One of several poverty row film studios, Chesterfield didn't actually have its own physical facilities. Universal Pictures rented them one of their unused old lots for filming. Here, they ground out cowboy, mystery, melodrama, and other "quickies" that were shorter than the usual motion picture.

Ray worked nearly every day, including Sundays. He did his usual cover of stunt roles for the actresses, and in between, any work offered as an extra.

One of the responsibilities of any extra wearing a wig or hairpiece was to make sure it wasn't damaged or lost. When Ray first worked in movies on the East coast, the quality of the wigs given to the extras, and even some of the stars, was almost laughable because the costume department frequently substituted goat hair, wool, or even Spanish moss for human hair. For long shots it didn't matter, but close-ups picked up every particular in a scene.

When Ray was doubling for a film's star, he had to be coiffed with an exact and expensive copy of her wig. Most film studios had begun to rent wigs rather than own them. These were made by hand, sewn with real hair, and carefully styled by expert hairdressers. They were prohibitively expensive, particularly for some of the smaller studios for whom he worked. Max Factor, later of cosmetic fame, manufactured almost all the wigs used in movies.

The Factor Company kept close track of their rented products and charged a hefty fine if any were lost or damaged. One of the big problems was the use of location shots for action movies. The film crew often used the rugged hills and deserts outside of Los Angeles for authenticity in combat and cowboy films.

Ray was not only an outstanding female double but an expert in the saddle. He rode breakneck across the flinty terrain, skirts flying and his wig firmly pinned to his skull. Even the painfully tight steel bobby pins did not always manage to hold his coiffure fast when he would take a tumble on a horse. The crew frequently retrieved these dislodged curly creations from spiny cactus or entangled in spiky tumbleweeds. If the hairpiece could not be rehabilitated by the experts at Max Factor, the studio was either fined or forced to purchase a new one. The money men who kept a close eye on movie budgets tried to pass on these added expenses by dunning the paycheck of the unfortunate actor who had worn the wig. The average price of a woman's wig could run into five times a typical extra's monthly salary. Because Ray had had such long experience wearing a hairpiece, he usually managed to salvage it and thus avoided any fines.

A lucky contact he had made while appearing at Jimmy's Backyard, in between film work was cinema heartthrob William Haines. Haines was not an infrequent visitor to the pansy clubs where Ray and Karyl Norman performed.

Though Haines always had a female companion on his arm, it was apparent to Ray that this was one of those covers the movie studios provided to conceal the true sexual nature of their biggest stars. The most famous of Haines' many dates was the enormously ambitious Joan Crawford. Crawford was a true "fag hag," always simpatico to Hollywood's gay crowd, and not averse to being a "switch hitter."

Haines usually invited Ray to join his table post show. The conversations were witty and peppered with the latest titillating rumors and chatter. Ray had developed the habit of downing a "stiffner" or two during performance, and so he arrived already well-oiled when he joined Haines' party. Surrounded by glamorous table mates, Ray held forth with off-color jokes and innuendos of the latest Hollywood gambols.

After a particularly hilarious evening filled with promises of future invitations, Haines reached in the pocket of his Davidoff tuxedo and handed Ray his card. This was accompanied by an offer to get him an audition at Metro Goldwyn Mayer (MGM). MGM was the gold standard among studios.

Haines and his lover, Jimmy, were the most obvious and "out" of the many gay couples that populated the world of movies. Unfortunately, MGM was the most homophobic of the studios. This created an immediate and lasting crisis for Haines' career.

Ray heard rumors of this tense situation when he began to work on Haines' latest film, *Are You Listening?* (1932).

William Haines had been MGM's biggest moneymaker for several years. He was also their biggest headache. He refused to hide his gay life style. This drove the studio's boss, Louis Mayer, to distraction. Mayer was a narrow-minded bigot. He lacked class and imagination, constantly surrounded by fawning lackeys and very few friends.

Despite the enormous profits generated by a Haines' film, Mayer began to secretly sabotage the career of the recalcitrant star. By the time Ray worked with him, he had been seriously demoted in salary and star billing, finding his name below the title of a picture rather than above.

The current Haines' film was a cheaply made melodrama with a tired script. Ray had only two days of work on the poorly planned project.

Haines had one more picture to make to end his contract, and Ray was invited to come aboard again. This time it was, *Fast Life* (1932), an action-filled tale with chases and boat races, but little else. Both critics and audiences were not impressed. It was a flop and ended Haines' career at MGM. It also ended Ray's entrée at that studio.

One of the saddest footnotes in Hollywood's long history of homophobia was William Haines' story. After being discovered by an MGM talent scout, he appeared in a handful of minor roles from 1922-1924 before MGM loaned him out to Columbia Pictures, where he received favorable reviews for his role in *The Midnight Express* (1924). Haines returned to MGM and became an instant movie star in 1926 with *Brown of Harvard* (1926). He quickly followed with more successful films, filling the financial accounts of the greedy studio head, Louis B. Mayer.

Haines was "married" to Jimmie Shields, a fact known to most Hollywood professionals but kept from the general public. This was just how the game was played in those days. Mayer loathed Haines and any other contract star at MGM who gave the slightest public indication of being gay. It might affect Mayer's bottom line, the only thing that mattered to the repugnant film huckster.

Elinor Glyn, who Ray despised from his contacts with her during the filming of Beyond the Rocks (1922), loved to "out" male film stars she suspected of being gay in the trashy tabloids she wrote for. It was widely-known she felt that way about any man who showed no interest in her.

She never blamed it on her advanced years or hideous appearance. Her pompous pronouncements about which star had "IT"—sex appeal—made her the laughingstock of Hollywood.

Her even more ludicrous endorsements of the Duke and the Duchess of Windsor with their treasonous connections to Hitler and Mussolini only served to emphasize her delusional nature.

Hearing of ghoulish Glyn's thinly veiled gay branding of Haines, Mayer insisted that he either marry a woman, or squire some brainless MGM starlet on the town to affirm his manliness. Stamping his well-shod foot in Mayer's enormous office, Haines refused to cooperate.

During this particularly heated confrontation, the pig-like Mayer squealed that Glyn had declared Haines to "have no sex appeal."

Haines, never at a loss for words, shot back that he had "been kept by both the best women, and men, in New York. Both sexes had the hots for me."

Enraged, Mayer repeated that Haines obviously didn't have "IT," the official Glyn stamp of approval.

Haines exploded, "*You* certainly do have 'IT,' but L.B., you left the 'sh' off of it."

Mayer never forgave him. In a cruel act of retribution, he flushed Haines' career down the drain, despite the fact that it cost the greedy producer a fortune in lost revenues. Anyone who placed that sort of blind hatred in front of simple common sense surely had something awful hiding in his own closet.

Ray, again, made the rounds of the studios, always carrying his now sizeable portfolio. It contained personal notes and recommendations from Mae West, Rudolph Valentino, William Boyd, and a long list of luminaries, alive and deceased. There were glamour shots from studio photographers and clippings and reviews from a lengthy career.

Stopping for a coffee break in one of the many little diners scattered along Santa Monica Boulevard, he struck up a conversation at the lunch counter with Edward Hearn, an actor he recognized from his days in New York.

Hearn had appeared in *The Drag*. Both he and Ray joked about the changes time had stamped on their looks since they had worked together and the things they had done to survive in the rough and tumble world that was Hollywood.

As their conversation lagged, Ray got up and said he had to, "hit the pavement and continue making the rounds."

The bulky folio slipped from Ray's grasp, as he got off the stool and spilled across the well-worn tiles. Hearn bent over to help retrieve the contents. As he stacked the photographs, he commented that they all were stamped with film studio logos. He suggested he might be able to help. He was on his way for a costume fitting at Mascot Pictures and invited Ray to tag along.

The two jumped into Hearn's shiny new green Studebaker convertible for the short drive to the studio. As they wheeled up to the front gate, a guard motioned them in. The car stopped in front of the administration building, a large stucco two-story structure with a manicured lawn.

Ray was introduced to several employees, as Hearn took him on a quick tour of the grounds. He was amazed at the size of the complex: two enormous hanger-shaped sound stages surrounded by smaller buildings that housed dressing rooms, wardrobe, a processing lab, and even a plaster shop, where craftsmen duplicated historical fixtures from ancient civilizations. Behind the sound stages was a vast grove of trees used for jungle backgrounds. Beyond the forest were replications of entire little towns used for exterior sets.

They ended up in the small windowless wardrobe building, where Hearn was measured and fitted with costumes for his new cowboy picture. His said his roles were usually secondary, but he worked steadily on a six-month contract that had been renewed several times.

As the actor tried on several outfits, with the help of an overly attentive male dresser, he introduced Raye to the assistant director. Hearne mentioned that his friend had a long career in film and that he had brought an extensive resume.

As the actor stripped off one costume to try another, he stood naked, oblivious to those around him. *He may have a few miles on him,* Ray thought, sucking in his gut, but Hearne's still firm figure had endured much better than Bourbon's paunchy form. Ray retreated to a corner couch, self-consciously pulling his slightly tattered trench coat around him.

The director thumbed through Ray's folio, commenting on the variety of photographs. He turned and said something under his breath to Hearn as he left.

Ray was surprised when he was told the director wanted him to report to work in the morning as an extra. Ray inquired which gender he would be playing. His friend laughingly told him, "Either or, from the looks of your photographs."

Mascot Pictures had been formed just a few years earlier by film producer Nat Levine, a self-made man with no education. He had learned the ropes from the bottom, quickly becoming the studio head. His skill as a gambler had played a large part in his success. His ill-gotten gains had enabled him to purchase the old Mac Sennett Studios, which he renamed Mascot. It was strictly poverty row compared to the industry giants, Levine found his niche. He even borrowed the symbol of MGM—a jungle cat—for his logo. This was a thinly veiled knock-off, a roaring tiger resting on top of a model of planet Earth.

The ambitious Mascot churned out B-picture serials, a genre that was shown in weekly segments at neighborhood movie houses across the country. The audience was young and the stories were action filled and cheaply made. They used former stars, thankful for any kind of work they could get, and a rare few on the way up.

Ray was shocked the next day, when he ran into his old friend, William Haines. The former MGM luminary had been reduced to secondary leads at this third-string studio. He had just finished, *Young and Beautiful* (1934) with Edward Hearn. Haines said it was certainly ironic to still be playing, "the brash and arrogant juvenile in a style I popularized over a decade ago." Ray had to silently agree. Haines was anything but juvenile, looking pudgy and definitely balding.

Sensing Ray's discomfort at finding him in these reduced circumstances he joked in an attempt to put his friend at ease. Haines mockingly referred to the camera as, "a one-eyed monster," and quipped that the monster would be, "no friend to him at this point."

His former youthful good looks had disappeared. His full head of shiny hair was retreating on a daily basis. Extra pounds also packed the formerly hunky Haines frame.

Unlike like so many eternally vain actors, Haines had no compunction about facing his present physical state.

Like the other Hollywood grist mills, Mascot squeezed every ounce of energy out of their stable of actors and extras. Ray worked ten-hour days for weeks, stunt doubling for such long forgotten silent screen ladies as Esther Ralston, and riding horses as an extra in dusty cowboy epics. He spent several days working with Hearn in a bargain basement serial, *The Vanishing Legion* (1931).

Haines visited the set often, exchanging dirty stories with Hearn and reliving their booze-soaked wild days before the clock had caught up with both.

Ray got a casting call for *The Marines Are Coming* (1934), the second of two films for which Haines was contracted. On the set, Haines introduced him to the swishy actor, Franklin Pangborn, who took an immediate liking to Ray and included him in several socially select soirees.

Haines moved in a much more select gay circle than Ray was accustomed. A room full of snobby queens always left him feeling a little uncomfortable, sensing he was the object of ridicule during these "piss elegant" functions.

He much preferred a night of hard drinking and dishing the dirt with a lot of street-wise queers.

He was sad to see that Haines, once a top matinee idol, could no longer summon the star quality that had made him a household name. *Young and Beautiful* received faint praise, but *The Marines Are Coming* was a disaster. He received the worst reviews of his career, and soon left the film world.

Haines later became one of Hollywood's most prominent decorators. Ironically, he created lavish homes for some of the studio heads who had once shunned him. He smiled internally as he presented his staggering invoices to these moguls for his services.

Ray continued to work steadily as an extra. This allowed him to save enough to put a down payment on a little Spanish-style stucco house on the outskirts of Los Angeles.

Within a few months of moving in, an unexpected windfall gave him the cash to pay off the mortgage completely. This would be his first and only real home.

His adoptive mother had passed away in Texas, leaving him an inheritance that allowed him to not worry about the immediate future. The amount of the bequest was never verified, but was rumored to be close to $300,000. Truth is, it turned out to be five times that amount, an enormous sum for that time.

The *El Paso Herald Post*, July 27, 1931, reported, "Juarez Actor Gets Fortune. Hal Waddell's Father Leaves $1,500,000 Estate."

> "The first thing Hal Waddell, female impersonator at Hugo's Lobby No. 2, contemplates after he gets some of the $1,500,000 estate left him by his father, is to quit working until midnight and getting up before noon. Waddell, whose stage name is Rae Bourbon, Monday was making plans for a future that he says contains $900,000 cash and $600,000 in Texas oil lands. He has been advised that his father's estate finally has been settled. 'I want to spend six months touring the world,' Waddell said, 'and then go for the legitimate stage.'"

When he arrived in Texas to lay claim to the legacy, he was questioned by the local reporters on his plans to use this inheritance.

"I will spend at least six months on a world tour, and upon my return work on the legitimate stage," bragged suddenly financially secure Ray. Both of these predictions would come true.

Like so many who had come into easy money, newfound fortunes took wings with equal ease.

Ray invested a great deal in designer furs, each costing thousands of dollars. He also purchased enough expensive imported cloth to open a fabric store. From this, he planned to have dozens of costly stage gowns created for his persona, "Rae." To accessorize his newfound glitz, there were Italian pumps, real jewels, and unending accoutrement.

He remembered the frequent success Mae West enjoyed as a writer, and so he hoped to emulate a little of her good fortune. In 1932, with his newfound leisure, he dedicated his time to writing *Hookers*, a novel. It was published by "House of Bourbon" in Philadelphia under the pseudonym Richard F. Mann, and dedicated "to Evelyn." The subject matter and the title were something about which Ray had first-hand knowledge. To promote it, he invested a large sum with an expensive advertising agency. After a brief initial success, the book ended up in the bargain bin without even recouping Ray's investment.

For the next several months, he simply did nothing, other than making the rounds of the gay clubs, indulging his habit of binge drinking, a habit that would spiral out of control in the years to come.

He also found time to strike up brief relationships among the many habitués of the shadowy world of gay night life. Unfortunately, he seldom chose a suitable partner, one with nothing to contribute. "What an impressive basket!" Ray sometimes exclaimed, as the dick du jour dropped his drawers.

As he aged, his taste ran to attractive younger men with a slightly dangerous and rough demeanor. These were the hustlers and call boys that preyed on older queens, selling their services for cash or expensive gifts.

There was a particularly ugly confrontation with a big-muscled trick at Ray's house one evening. They had connected previously in those shadowy places where quick and anonymous sex prevailed. This time, he foolishly let down his guard and allowed this handsome opportunist to spend the night.

In the wee small hours of the morning, Ray was awakened from a drunken slumber to find the young thug pillaging through his closet. In addition to the usual drag items stored on racks, there were several expensive fur wraps that been had purchased with the remainder of his inheritance. These were to be important wardrobe additions for future shows.

The would-be thief had the pelts wrapped around his arms and was starting to head down the hall to the front door. Still in the alltogether, Ray pulled a revolver from his nightstand and quietly tip toed naked behind the pilfering pick-up. The thieving trick heard a click and found himself staring down the cold steel barrel of Ray's revolver. The macho-looking gigolo shrieked, dropped the loot, and bolted out the door.

Ray was seldom without a gun, remembering the violent end his first lover, George, had met in Texas. The illicit world of the gay man was sometimes more dangerous than the Wild West.

Bored with his indolent days, Ray returned to work. He renewed contacts with several agents and quickly settled back into his old routine. He went where the work was available, crisscrossing the continent for the next several years, appearing in virtually every drag club of any importance. A partial list included the following establishments, big, small, chic, and shabby:

Drift Inn, San Francisco
Coon Chicken Inn, Salt Lake City
Sugar Bowl, New Orleans
Park Avenue, New York
Gaiety Theatre, St Louis
The Cave, Vancouver, B.C.
Cheerio Club, Idaho Falls
Carnival Lounge, Pittsburgh
Rondezvous, Los Angeles

At the Clover Club in Portland, Ray tried out a new routine. This was typical of the material that would comprise his act for the next twenty years:

"I'm tired of suppressing the desire I have of dressing
The way I have always thought that I should
I have no business in Sak's suits, or even lumber jack suits
Drag is always where I should have stood
Me and the models, in Harper's or Vogue,
are truly sisters under the skin
Oh, I'm back and delighted, so very excited,
I'm back, and in drag again
You can see it from my head down to my toes
But I got out of line somewhere in between
There's a thorn in every damned rose!
Now, I've improved on the works of Mother Nature
I know some things that old gal forgot
I always do a good job being what I am
But I do a better job being what I am not
I was never meant to be a tailor's dummy
You can see damned well what I was meant to be
So I'll be a lady if it kills me
And I'll go to Hell in mink, I guarantee
Oh, I'm back in drag again
I hope it is perfect
Perfume, jewels, and curls
But I've frightened away some of my oldest friends
They just can't seem to go for us girls!
Now I never felt my best in pants or tee shirts
I don't like to wear suspenders or belts
I don't like getting into BVD's or shorts
Unless they're on somebody else!
I'm back in drag, and lovin' it!"

For the next few years, Ray received almost universally laudatory reviews everywhere he played. For his appearance at Chez Boheme, the reviewer said: "Bourbon opened April 4 and patrons crowded in to welcome him. His appearances guarantee numerous reservations. Bourbon's monologue, against a background of piano music, wowed the crowd at all four shows last night. His material is cleverly done and presented. Bourbon leaves nothing to the imagination."

At Club Hollywood, reviewers felt the same about him: "Using double entendre material, Bourbon socks it across. There is no end to the clever material Bourbon has at his fingertips."

In New York at the chic La Vie Parisienne, the plaudits continued: "The laugh load is carried by Rae Bourbon, a West Coast comic who knows how to punch and pantomime. His first bit, a gal on the make in a cocktail lounge, panicked the mob. Top laugh material!"

Meanwhile, the Mae West phenomenon was the talk of the country. It didn't surprise Ray that he played clubs with more than one impersonator who attempted Mae West take-offs with varying degrees of success. Some mastered the walk, some the eyes that rolled back as they drawled that singular adenoidal sound that only Mae could expel.

When asked by a reporter why so many gays were such ardent fans, Mae replied, "They're crazy about me because I am so flamboyant. They love to imitate the things I say and the way I act, and they like the way I move my body."

Ray incorporated bits of the Mae West attitude, at times, in his show, but he never thought of being an imitator of the real thing. He had worked hard to establish the image of Rae, "the Bourbon bitch," and that was what he built upon.

In Hollywood, Mae was now the queen of Paramount. Her residence reflected her newfound cache with white rugs, white furniture, white piano, and giant mirrors above a white bed. These overhead reflections were there, as she told a reporter, "So I can see how I'm doin."

She was also her own best promoter and press agent. A perfect example of her publicity savvy can be found in a letter she personally sent to a theatre manager, extolling the merits of one of her first films.

Manager: Affiliated Theatres
"Dear Sir:

I'm no angel... but I've spread my wings a few times!

I know what every young girl should know... and a couple of things they ought to forget!!

'I'm No Angel'—and you can take that title as a warning from me—is my new picture. I believe I've got a story that's a honey! Something the neighbors will talk about over their back fences. My first starring picture, "She Done Him Wrong," got them all in a huddle. My new one will knock 'em for a goal!

There never was any kind of dame, anywhere, that worried more about her figure than a showman does about his! I mean the one he reads and either weeps or sings about at the end of the week.

I've produced shows of my own, so I know first-hand what co-operation between the show and theatre management means at the box-office. Let's co-operate.

Ask the locals to "come up and see me" in "I'm No Angel" ... and we'll both be proud of our figures!!"
Sincerely,
Mae West

Mae was now the second highest-paid person in the United States. By the time *I'm No Angel* (1933) had finished its initial release, the sultry star was raking in $500,000 a year. That was an almost unheard of salary at that time. The enormous success of the film also helped Cary Grant finally solidify his star status. In later years, he would always point out that "West found me, and made me, so to speak."

One of Mae's best friends at Paramount was the sultry German star, Marlene Dietrich. Mae was truly a diva when it came to other women. Other than her sister and mother, Mae had no time for her own sex. What the connection to Dietrich was is a mystery. Paramount had tried to create publicity based on the supposed rivalry between the widely divergent stars, but it was a fabrication.

Mae was earthy, unsophisticated, and far from intellectual. Dietrich was bright, brittle, bitchy, and extremely self-centered. This last trait was probably one of the things they had in common, that and an insatiable lust for the opposite sex. Dietrich went her one better by also bedding an occasional woman, something that Mae could not imagine.

Dietrich had become an enormous cabaret star in Germany in the 1920s. Like Mae, she learned a great deal about performing from the female impersonators who also worked these cafes. Unlike Mae, who copied the manners and dress of famous Vaudeville drags, Dietrich first went for the male impersonation, donning top hat and tails, and singing love songs to the women in the audience. When she did perform as a chanteuse, it was usually in a costume that might give pause to the most flamboyant of drags.

The glamorous actress and the earthy star chummed around on the sound stages of Paramount, having lunch together in their dressing rooms, and sharing secrets about their fellow actors over a coffee between takes.

Mae was a little jealous of the floral tributes that filled Dietrich's dressing room on a daily basis. Often, the highly scented offerings choked the small space, and many were left on the steps leading to the door. When Dietrich was filming on the set, Mae sneaked over and picked out the arrangements she liked, particularly the enormous rose creations. Dietrich hated roses, and pretended not to notice when Mae helped herself to the floral loot. If there were other flowers missing that were Dietrich's favorites, then the fun began. Both ladies liked to play practical jokes on each other. Dietrich finally got the better of Mae one afternoon.

Mae was expecting an extravagant new gown from her favorite designer, Travis Banton. It was an opulent silver lace creation swathed in yards of white fox fur. Dietrich had heard Mae brag about the outlandish creation.

She kept her eye out for the delivery from the wardrobe department to Mae's dressing room. Spotting the wardrobe girl with the sparkling creation on her arm, Dietrich intercepted the delivery and promised to give it to Mae personally.

Dietrich rushed inside to don the dress. Mae returned to her dressing room, only to see Dietrich standing seductively in the doorway, wrapped in the shimmering yards of lace.

"What are you doing in my dress?" demanded Mae.

"Mr. Banton created this especially for me. What do you think?" Dietrich asked, turning around to display the fit, her hands attempting to gather up the more than ample material that made up the bosom of the gown.

Mae saw that the flat front of the German star could not possibly fill the copious cups of the flashy frock.

They both burst into laughter, hugging each other as a startled crew watched the unlikely duo retreat arm in arm to Mae's room.

Mae's forth picture, originally titled *It Ain't No Sin*, ran into censorship trouble as soon as the ink was dry on the first draft of the script.

The plot spins a tale of a notorious character named Ruby Carter. The story opens with the police reviewing Miss Carter's records. She is suspected of murder, larceny, bank fraud, and a host of other crimes. Somehow she has managed to wriggle out of the clutches of the law.

The story set off a firestorm of protest from Joseph Breen at the Hays Office. He rejected "in toto" the first script. Breen wrote Paramount producer A. M. Botsford that he was incensed at the story's vulgarity and obscenity, glorification of crime and criminals, glorification of a prostitute, and the general theme of the story that he believed was "definitely on the side of evil and crime and [was] against goodness, decency and law."

Mae was livid, but powerless. She ranted to anyone involved in the decision, including the MPPDA. This made them ever more determined to clamp down on story elements that were deemed against the Hays Office Code, but wily Mae purposely wrote into the script material that she knew Breen would cut in his haste to emasculate the particularly dirty dialogue, hoping that the other material would remain.

In the midst of all the uproar that now dogged almost anything Mae did or said on screen or off, came this interview with *Picturegoer* magazine. Mae was still incensed with the censors but was wise enough to temper her words: "Love is a woman's stock-in-trade, and she should always be overstocked. The film public likes the characterizations I play, a real woman who is honest and fearless."

At first, Paramount's New York studio head, Emmanuel Cohen, was kept in the dark about Breen's lengthy objections. Once he was finally informed, Cohen agreed that "thematically" the picture was in violation of the Code, and agreed to make five major changes.

A severely altered script finally went into production. No longer satisfied to watch the rushes of the day's takes, the watchdogs installed a censor on the sound stage right next to the director to watch for any telltale signs of improper innuendo or suggestive movement from the earthy star. The bloodless prig watched each wiggle of those famous hips, and wiggled his ears at Mae's raw quips. What he didn't realize, when watching the particularly crude scenes Mae inserted, was that it was all a ploy.

Black performers had a very rough go in Hollywood at this time, relegated to minor roles as maids, servants, and boot blacks. Mae was a pioneer in pressing for recognition of those she saw as oppressed. This was underlined in current her fight with Paramount. Several big musical numbers had been scheduled for the movie, featuring Mae's vocal renditions of "Troubled Waters," "My Old Flame," and "Memphis Blues."

Mae wanted the best musicians to back her up, and for her that could only be the sensational jazz band of Duke Ellington. This involved big bucks, and the studio felt that they had invested more than enough in lavish sets, costumes, and a large crowd of extras.

"No," was the answer to Mae's entreaties to include the Ellington band. This was not a word Mae was used to hearing. She finally prevailed. The end result was a performance that is truly the best of Mae's musical career.

On June 1, 1934, the film was screened for Breen and the Hays Office.

On June 2, 1934, Breen sent Cohen a letter stating that the film was still "definitely in violation" of the Code.

On June 4, 1934, the scenes in violation were also outlined in a memo from Breen to Paramount President Adolph Zukor, specifying the "general low moral tone, immoral criminal theme of story, and lack of sufficient compensating moral values," including "the life of a notorious woman . . . her activities in a crooked gambling establishment . . . her doping of the prizefighter . . . her acts as an accessory to crimes of homicide and arson . . . her illicit love affair with an acknowledged ex-convict, thief, and killer."

To pacify Breen, all changes were made, and an additional wedding sequence was shot in re-takes and inserted.

Will B. Hays himself viewed the partially-remade film, and, in an interoffice memo of July 13, 1934, stated that he had advised Paramount to further show that Mae was a "burlesque queen and not a prostitute and that she really was good at heart." He also specified that the filmmakers should "show affirmatively that she was boisterous, robust, tough, indeed, but not a prostitute . . . ."

According to *Daily Variety*, after more revisions were made, the film was given the Purity Seal on August 6, 1934.

On September 4, 1934, the Catholic Legion of Decency condemned the film, while it was still known as *It Ain't No Sin*. They later rescinded their decision and officially approved the film . . . but for adult audiences only.

A ridiculous footnote to all this Papal pomposity is an incident that occurred in New York. A group of Catholic priests, hardly role models when it came to sexual aberration, were picketing in front of a theatre marquee advertising *It Ain't No Sin*. The parading Papist carried signs that read, "It is!"

Because of intense pressure from censors, whose standards varied somewhat from state to state, Paramount caved in and changed the title to the more innocent-sounding *Belle of the Nineties* (1934) and the film went into full release. Despite all their efforts, censors in some Eastern states continued to reject the picture throughout its first run and made cuts without studio approval, but enough raunchy material still remained—if only through innuendo and double entendre—to provide a victory for Mae.

Opera hardly seems like an art form associated with Mae West, but her next film, *Goin' to Town* (1935), allowed the husky-voiced contralto to belt out one of the better known arias from the opera, *Samson and Delilah*.

"Mae will slay you when she sings grand opera!" the publicity mill at Paramount crowed to the press. The story of her character, a nouveau riche society climber named Cleo, is an improbable tale typical of many comedies of the era. The heroine stages an operatic evening in an attempt to impress the snobbish high society she longs to conquer.

Maybe the Metropolitan Opera might not sign her up, but Mae displayed some remarkable musical skills in tackling this most demanding art form. She studied with a classical voice coach for weeks in preparation for the big scene and hired a well-known opera tenor to partner her.

Delilah's music is in the range of the contralto voice, a truly deep sound, but also rises at moments to top A and B. Mae more than mastered the depth of the range, but as her voice ascended the vocal scale, it took on a harsh, tight sound. She had cleverly chosen a big operatic tenor voice to partner her in the duet. He easily covered any unpleasant sounds she made, and those that did come through she wisely played for laughs. Unfortunately not everyone considered the film up to Mae's previous standards, but the *Herald Tribune* found Mae's Cleo to be "Rowdier, raucous, satirical, and more amusing than her last starring role."

Between club engagements, Ray returned to his little house in Los Angeles. It was a relief to settle in to the relative normality and quiet of "the Bourbon hacienda," as he affectionately dubbed the small stucco bungalow. It also provided a reliable mailing address.

One morning, while still bleary-eyed and nursing a whopper of a hangover, he sorted through the usual pile of junk mail. A large parchment envelope addressed in flowery calligraphy with the engraved return address of Edmund Goulding caught his attention.

Ray had known Goulding since the early 1920s. He was a scriptwriter for MGM and a party giver extraordinaire. Most of the soirees Goulding organized were mere excuses for sex orgies, gay, straight, and something in between. Edmund Goulding was openly bi-sexual and made little effort to hide his proclivities.

Ray had heard the many tales of trouble that Goulding had with the vice squad. After one particularly wild party, several women came forward with tales of extreme sexual brutality, claiming they had fled fearing for their lives. MGM had to pay off the District Attorney. The studio was forced to send Goulding to Europe until the threat of a massive scandal faded.

Despite his questionable reputation, Ray knew Goulding was on the guest list of most of the power brokers in Hollywood. For this reason, Ray had maintained a cordial but slightly distant friendship.

The impressive envelope contained an elaborate invitation to a costume ball, hosted for Goulding by none other than the Countess Dorothy di Frasso. Even among the fruits and nuts that populated Hollywood, this eccentric hostess stood out.

She was born Dorothy Tailor, the daughter of a millionaire manufacturer. To describe her as plump, frumpy, and much bedded, would be an understatement. Her vast fortune enabled her to go through the stud stables of the capitals of the world. What she wanted most of all, aside from the required nightly services of a well-paid partner, was a title. This she got by marrying and bailing out the decaying fortunes of a titled and penniless Roman, Count Carlo Dentici di Frasso.

What finally lured this oversexed matron back to Hollywood from her Roman villa was her embarrassing infatuation with the rising young film star, Gary Cooper. Cooper had been a guest at one of her notorious parties in the Eternal City. The Countess's sex antennae began to vibrate when she first caught sight of the lanky cowboy. She had also heard rumors from both gay and straight friends of his enormous "talent," which did not include acting. When Cooper returned to Hollywood, the convivial countess boarded the next ocean liner, determined to bed ambitious Cooper.

The invitation from Goulding included a handwritten note. He needed Ray's special knowledge of costumes and makeup to help him prepare for the ball. A week later, Ray arrived at the writer's residence with an armload of wigs, frocks, and other drag accoutrement. He had decided not to wear a feminine costume, as there would be more than enough cross-dressers at an event like this. He donned his best tuxedo, carefully pomaded his thick dark hair, and "butched-it-up" in his best theatrical manner. He hoped to corner some influential agent or executive and boost his future in films.

There was little hope of transforming the unlikely Goulding into a believable woman. He would have to go for the comedic look. Inspired by the comic dames from his music hall days, Ray decked out the already drunken Goulding in an oversized puffy bonnet with a chin strap, long brown sausage curls, starched apron, and an ankle-length white matronly dress. Turning the pasty faced scriptwriter to face the full-length mirror, Bourbon snickered at his creation, the perfect English nursemaid. All that was lacking was a perambulator.

The ball was a top cream event, sprinkled with the usual assortment of odd characters that always managed to wangle invitations to such obvious opportunities for advancement, whether in bed or at the box office.

The already inebriated Goulding was helped by Ray through the grand double doors of the Countess di Frasso's faux Regency town house. As soon as the butler relieved him of his topcoat, he uncoupled himself from the unsteady Goulding and headed straight for the powder room.

He was very surprised to see the square-jawed profile of now famous Cary Grant reflected in the ornate ormolu mirror, adjusting the lapels of his elegant tuxedo. Lounging next to him, suggestively spread-eagled on the basin counter top, was the impressive figure of actor Randolph Scott. Grant and Scott gave each other knowing looks, as Ray smoothed an arched eyebrow with his pinky. Ray had heard many rumors of the cozy arrangement the two impossibly handsome boys had in their Hollywood Hills home. This confirmed it.

As the trio exited the water closet, they were quickly cornered by the ever-circulating Countess di Frasso. Slightly potty, she firmly guided them to the bar.

The party was in full flight and bodies were three deep waiting to refresh their cocktails. Scott and Grant disappeared from the line and the tentacles of the Countess. Ray managed to melt into the crowd, hoping to see a familiar face.

Eavesdropping on the conversation next to him, Ray heard a rumor that Grant had become the replacement for Gary Cooper, who was occupied elsewhere. "Grant must have the goods," Ray surmised, knowing the Countess's insatiable sex hunger. That the former Archie Leach of Ray's Greenwich Village days, now the suave and sophisticated Cary Grant, was able to service both the Countess and Scott left a lasting impression on Ray.

Ray was aware of the enormous boost Mae West had given to Grant's early lackluster career. With the exception of *Blonde Venus* (1932) with Marlena Dietrich, most of the work he had done in the eight films in which he appeared prior to his "discovery" by Mae was forgettable. Grant had also utilized his charms with several middle-aged women of means to mount an expensive and aggressive career agenda.

Success brought with it the sudden glare of the publicity spotlight that shone into corners of Grant's personal life that the studio wanted to hide. His agent was having trouble answering the questions in the film magazines about Grant's and Scott's cozy little hacienda. The studio found it necessary to plant publicity stories about Grant's many "romances" with several starlets.

The unfortunate participant in one of these studio-generated tall tales was actress Virginia Cherrill, well-known only for her role as the blind girl in Charlie Chaplin's *City Lights* (1931). This naïve actress fell for the saccharine dialogue delivered by the gossip rags concerning her romance with Cary, a romance that had supposedly blossomed during the many photo-op dates arranged by the studio.

Grant was under extreme pressure from the studio to butch it up and get married. He was well-aware of the fate of stars that refused to play the studio game.

Despite repeated warnings from Ray's old friend from his Greenwich Village days, the film costume designer Orry-Kelly, Virginia got married with the switch-hitting Grant.

When they moved to the picture-perfect love nest conveniently provided by Paramount, ever-present Scott moved in next door. Whenever Virginia was away, the boys would play. The simple Mrs. Grant soon dropped her deer-in-the-headlights expression. She returned home early one day to find the Adonis duo butt naked on the pool house floor. Exit Mrs. Grant.

In an attempt to give credence to his dramatic grief over his spouse's departure, Grant faked a suicide with sleeping tablets.

The ever-reliable gossip hag, Louella Parsons, seems to have gotten the scoop even before Cary was rescued by the medics. At the studio's bidding, Lolly, as she was affectionately called, ran a patently fake article, recounting Grant's Romeo-like suicide attempt over his departed Juliet.

Grant and Scott quickly resumed their amorous alliance.

More important than the banal gossip that swirled through the Di Frasso mansion that night of the party was a genuine offer that Ray received from one of the Countess's guests.

Ray McCarey, a minor director, younger brother of director Leo McCarey, entered the film business in the mid-1920s, working up from prop boy to assistant director, screenwriter and then director. He was about to cast a series of low-budget comedies. In spite of Ray's attempt at a manly image, McCarey immediately recognized the naturally feminine side to Ray's nature. He told him this was exactly what he was looking for, an obvious gay man who thought himself to be otherwise. He described the character he was offering Ray, that of a highly effeminate but very successful designer of ladies underwear.

Ray had developed a sizeable body of work in movies, but always as a stunt double, extra, or a walk-on. This was a chance to play a second lead.

He listened raptly, as McCarey elaborated on his plans for the film. Just as he was about to outline the contract details, a petite brunette made a splashy but unsteady entrance.

Diminutive Mexican star Lupe Velez stood in the doorway. Her tiny but voluptuous figure was clearly outlined in a sheer dress that left nothing to the imagination. She never wore underwear and all her famous assets were on display. Obviously inebriated, she called out in a loud voice to Ray, "What the hell are you doing here? I bet you weren't invited either!"

McCarey and Ray stepped forward to help the unsteady star, as she teetered forward on six-inch platform shoes.

Ray had become friends with Velez when he worked on one of her first films, *Where East Is East*. He had also been the stunt double for Velez' co-star, Estelle Taylor, a unique position he would hold through many of Taylor's subsequent films.

Ray and Velez had formed an immediate connection with their love of the night life and particularly their appreciation of handsome men.

Velez had bedded a lengthy list of Hollywood's finest, and was never shy about bragging about her conquests. Her very detailed accounts of her sex life amused Ray. He was always on the lookout for naughty true-life tales to include in his act. Lupe never seemed to mind if he recounted her amorous adventures as part of his monologue.

Ray was a frequent guest at Velez' notorious parties. She told him he made her laugh like no one else. He held court, spewing out endless monologues laced with the latest Hollywood gossip. Velez' "casita," as she dubbed her modest Hollywood home, was always bathed in floodlights, as her colorful cast of partygoers arrived.

Lupe particularly loved giving costume parties, a favorite entertainment of the film colony in the 1930s. The more outrageous the guest's disguise the better. Like the ancient ritual of Carnivale in Venice, the masquerade disguises led to some outlandish sexual behavior. Velez was never reticent about expressing her sexual desire for a man. This attitude manifested itself in her real life and on screen. She was also very quick in her frank assessments of her many lovers.

Ray remembered one particularly raucous evening, when Velez, well past the legal limit, began to catalogue the attributes and shortcomings of her numerous paramours. At that time, it was rumored that she was a frequent visitor to Gary Cooper's bed. Ray finally asked the question that was on everyone's mind. So how is Gary in the sack?

Chugging back another double tequila, Velez laughed and shook her massive mane of jet curls. "He has the biggest organ in Hollywood, but not the ass to push it in well."

After a moment of stunned silence, the gathering erupted in howls.

Velez suddenly feigned surprise and cast her great luminous dark eyes downward in a maidenly fashion. "You know me. In la iglesia, I wear a halo. When I am out, I am a perfect lady, but in mi casita, I am el Diablo! I do as I wish, yell, scream, stand on my head with no panties. I am la Lupe in my own casa!"

The ever-vigilant Countess stopped in her tracks, when she spotted Velez and Ray engaged in an intimate conversation. She fixed a beady eye on the beautiful brunette star and demanded to see her invitation. Through clenched teeth, Velez hissed that she didn't need one. The two women were mortal enemies. Velez had crashed the party, purposely hoping to create an ugly situation.

Words were quickly exchanged. Ray realized that the hot-blooded Velez, dubbed "The Mexican Spitfire," could be physically dangerous. She was known to attack co-workers who had offended her.

The drunken Countess made the mistake of hurling a racial slur at her, screaming, "You dirty little spic!"

Despite her tiny stature, the enraged Velez leapt at the insult, sending the rotund Countess crashing into the furniture. Ray grabbed Velez's arm, preventing her from smashing a heavy Chinoiserie vase over the screaming Countess' head.

As the fight escalated, the entire room watched in horrified fascination. Velez's fury knew no bounds. She leaned threateningly over the hysterically sobbing Countess. "You lecherous old nympho, you have been fucking Mussolini. The FBI is after you! You run a spy ring in Mexico City. I am going to testify against you!"

With the help of several guests, Ray was able to propel Velez to the door, now fearing for her safety. It was well-known that the Countess employed several henchmen to protect her person, and they had inflicted serious harm on more than one of her detractors.

Velez was still shaking, as Ray guided her to her car. She gladly accepted his offer to take the wheel until she regained her composure.

He pressed the lever that retracted the top of the luxurious Continental convertible. Through the rear view mirror, he could see the comic figure of the disheveled Countess racing down the driveway, still screaming invectives as they drove off into the cool California night.

At first, Velez was uncommonly silent until he congratulated her on her one-two punch that had temporarily silenced their hostess. He turned to see her enormous dark eyes flashing, her profuse black hair whipped into a Medusa-like headdress by the damp wind.

In a nonstop volley, Velez recounted all she knew of the Countess' criminal activities. She was under investigation by the FBI for her associations, both sexual and political, with Italian dictator Benito Mussolini. She was also suspected of funneling money to the Communist Party.

After Velez was spent from her intemperate tirade, Ray tried to turn the conversation around. His good news of the promise of a leading part in a McCarey film only seemed to intensify the depression Velez felt about her own dead end career.

She said in a tear-choked voice that she was locked into the typical hot-blooded Latina image, hopelessly type cast by a system that had the worst kind of tunnel vision when it came to ethnicity. She said she felt there was comic parallel in their two careers. Ray would always be an old queen and she would always be an old, "hot tamale," a term she despised. Her rage spent, she managed a weak smile and put her head on Ray's shoulder.

They gently hugged, promising to stay connected, as he exited her car in front of his house. He could still smell her overpowering gardenia scent on his tux, as he watched her disappear into the early morning fog.

Ray saw Velez for the last time years later at a party celebrating her new film, *Naná* (1944). It received critical acclaim and promised a fresh start for the actress.

At the behest of Velez, he escorted Estelle Taylor, for whom Ray was had been a regular stunt double over the years. Taylor and Velez were the best of friends, despite their very different personalities and images.

An unusually colorful mix of characters jammed Velez's small Art Deco bungalow, all noisily inebriated and enjoying the rich buffet of Mexican dishes that their hostess had prepared with her own beautifully manicured hands.

During a brief lull in the hubbub, Velez banged a knife on an empty champagne bottle, bringing the clamorous festivities to a halt. With a painful smile, she made the startling announcement that she was going to have a baby. It was common knowledge she was unmarried and a very devout Catholic. Abortion was not an option.

This put a damper on the party mood and the little house was soon empty except for Ray and Taylor. Velez sat opposite them, tears streaming from her great brown eyes.

Both Ray and Taylor embraced her as she sobbingly told them, "I am afraid of life itself . . . I'm so tired of it all. I don't know what to do. I would rather kill myself."

Those chilling words were soon realized. In the middle of the night after the last guest had staggered home, she downed an entire bottle of barbiturates and a quart of tequila.

In the morning, she was found by her maid, face down in the toilet. The combination of a spicy meal and the mixture of drugs and booze had sent her sprawling into the bathroom, where she attempted to throw up the lethal mix. She died with her beautiful head submerged in the pink porcelain latrine, her magnificent hair floating like some exotic black jungle flower.

Ray was among the thousands who attended Velez's funeral at Forest Lawn. He found it sad that this enormous outpouring of love for the troubled actress was exactly what she had needed in life.

He vowed then and there to try and give the little things that matter the most to those he loved while they were still alive.

Ray welcomed the distraction of his next film project and the opportunity to work with his new director, McCarey. This rising figure in the film world had begun his career with the *Our Gang* series and The Three Stooges. His work might have been considered by some people as low-brow, but the director had a successful proven track record. Ray's co-starring role in *Hip Zip Hooray* (1933), a two-reel, RKO comedy short that was directed by McCarey and Edward Eliscu, held the promise of a possible upturn in his long history in film.

The film was released in April 1933 along with the studio's feature films as part of a standard program of features and shorts.

Hip Zip Hooray is a fast-moving, 17 · minute comedic farce involving a mix-up between patrons of an elegant fashion house, Zip Zip Salon, where Ray, as Leroy, serves as a flamboyant fashion designer. Leroy's periodic, scene-stealing appearances—only seconds-long—showcase his stage presence as a dame, with stereotypically feminine, "gay" mannerisms.

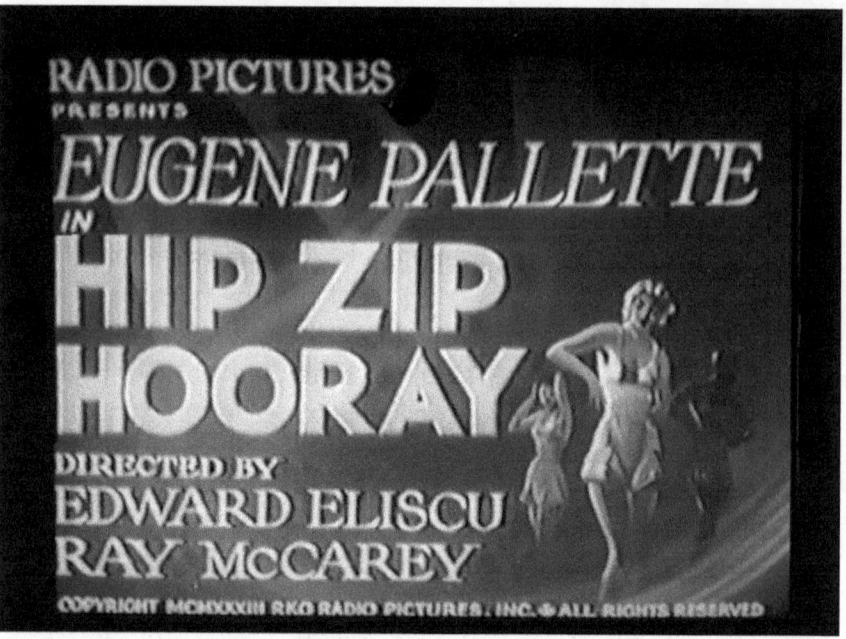

Title from Hip Zip Hooray (1933).

Opening credits from Hip Zip Hooray (1933).

A classic example from Hip Zip Hooray (1933) *of Ray's comedic body language, something he expertly applied even in his sixties when the author knew him.*

Ray displays his mastery of the understated swish in Hip Zip Hooray (1933).

This handsome profile shot from Hip Zip Hooray *(1933) clearly demonstrates why Ray was able to successfully play either gender.*

Ray possessed an ability to infuse a character with a style that he made his own. Much of it was learned from his youth in London's music halls. Hip Zip Hooray *(1933).*

Ray, seen here with character actor Eugene Pallette, concludes Hip Zip Hooray (1933) *with a burst of slapstick.*

McCarey was impressed with Ray's performances in both films and used his influence to get Ray a part in the much more important big-budget *Gold Diggers of 1937* (1936). This was a sequel to the enormously successful series, *Gold Diggers of Broadway* (1929), *Gold Diggers of 1933* (1933), and *Gold Diggers of 1935* (1935).

Over the top choreography by Busby Berkley was on board once again for the 1937 sequel. Hailed as a genius, he was also a bizarre and bullying individual. Because Ray had a long resume as a chorus boy, he landed a part in a dancing sequence under the dance director's dictatorial eye.

An elaborate number choreographed to "Speaking of the Weather" (music by Harold Arlen and lyrics by E. Y. Harburg) was staged on the tennis court of a socialite mansion during a formal dress ball. This sequence was not in the usually mechanized style of earlier Berkley extravaganzas. The guests danced freely in the style of the day, interrupted only by a solo tap number with one of the principals.

The bosses wanted Berkley to update his style, make it more natural. He balked, but had no choice. It made him testy and tyrannical.

He was finally allowed to include one of his signature-style musical sequences. The gigantic number utilized endless rocking chairs, cannons, and dozens of dancers. The massive chorus line sang:

> "The battle field's a rocking chair,
> look out, look out,
> for all is fair in love and war."

Ray was beginning to dislike working as a chorus boy, due in no small part to his advancing years. The camera kept a decent distance most of the time in these big extravaganzas, and he preferred it that way.

At the climax of the endlessly repetitive number Ray and the chorus sang of the dangers of love and marriage:

> "She marches you to the City Hall,
> and leads you through the door
> And then the deed is done,

Her victory is won,
For love is just like war."

Though unaccredited, Ray can be seen in *Gold Diggers of 1937* in the Art Deco cocktail lounge of a streamliner train. He looked very dapper in the latest fashions, a handsome fedora hat, bow tie, vest, and tailored suit. His mustache, penciled to perfection, gave him a slightly fey and cynical look.

The scene called for one of the film's stars, Glenda Farrell, to sit opposite Ray. Her character is an obvious flirt and she quickly turns her attention to the mostly male occupants of the bar. She looks around disinterestedly at the other men in the lounge, finally returning her gaze to Ray.

She bats her lashes and looks him up and down, sizing up his possibilities. For a moment, they exchange the usual pleasantries.

When the conversation turns too suggestive, Ray freezes her with a glacial stare. Farrell has misread her prospective paramour's natty appearance, not realizing his gay persuasion.

Completely taken aback by her bold insinuations he snubs her in the most imperious manner. His disdain is met by Farrell's scathing retort, a thinly-veiled insult to his gender orientation. He draws himself up in his most grand attitude, adjusts his vest and tie and swishes out the door.

What remains of the scene in the finished film is only the visual exchange between them. Both actors are clearly gifted enough to indicate their feelings by expression only. Unfortunately, the bitchy dialogue that was the specialty of both Farrell and Ray ended up on the cutting room floor.

Farrell was a good match for the hard humor and cutting delivery that was Ray's trademark. This was also a missed chance to preserve his unique vocal delivery on film.

15
Command Performance, Controversy, Cabaret

For several years, Ray had longed to return to the scene of his roots in show business. He was now financially secure enough to take some well-deserved time off.

He had maintained sporadic contact with several of his British pals over the years, but sadly, most had passed away. A retired dame from the days of his music hall career was still living in London. A series of letters led to an offer of lodging should Ray come over.

Transatlantic travel was still by ship, except for the well-heeled who could afford the astronomical air fares. Most ocean liners sailed from New York, so Ray boarded a train from Los Angeles and began the long trek to the Big Apple.

This time, he crossed the Atlantic with a modicum of style aboard the aged but still elegant *Aquitania*. His tiny second-class cabin could barely contain the mountain of luggage that accompanied him. The second-class accommodations numbered over 600 cabins with first-class nearly equal in number. The unfortunates who were relegated to third class, such as his poor mother had endured when she came to America, numbered nearly 2,000.

Due to Ray's claustrophobic nature, he spent very little time in his cramped quarters, preferring to roam the vast decks of the gigantic ship. As with any cruise experience, new friendships were formed, however fleeting.

Ray frequented one of the smaller cocktail lounges on his deck, a shrimp-colored round room that bore the fading remnants of a once elegant past. He struck up a relationship with another frequent habitué of the bar, who joined him in a martini marathon every afternoon. This led to exchanges of personal information and possibly more.

His shipmate invited him to dinner one night in the first-class dining room. His new friend introduced his travelling companion who was ensconced in one of the grand first-class suites. When Ray inquired as to why he wasn't also travelling first-class he discovered the truth. His drinking buddy was also travelling in posh quarters. He liked to pop into the bar on Ray's second-class deck because he fancied one of the bartenders. The atmosphere was also more relaxed than that of the first-class watering holes.

That night at dinner, Ray was surrounded by an atmosphere reminiscent of the grand homes of England. On the silk covered walls were portraits of Royalty and English seaports. The service staff treated everyone as if they were titled, bringing forth course after course of sumptuous and at times unidentifiable platters piled high with every manner of food: roast duckling, oyster cocktails, prawns, and creamed and sauced vegetables.

He seldom ate like this and ended up merely picking at his plate. His friends pretended not to notice, suggesting they adjourn to the smoking room, a majestic oak-paneled lounge, where a steady stream of drinks continued to appear, carefully balanced on silver servers.

The three sat cozily on a spacious settee in front of the great marble fireplace, the effect of the drinks and the radiating heat inducing a dream-like state in Ray's mind. All around was a feeling of restfulness and dignity. The conversation, however, became more sexually charged as the hour progressed.

Ray suspected that his two companions had something else in mind other than dinner and drinks. When the cat jumped out of the bag, it presented an invitation to a ménage. Embarrassed, Ray stalled for time. He said his bed was far too small for the three of them. He then discovered it would not be just three, but four. The bartender, who had caught the eye of his host, would be joining them in his capacious first-class suite.

As the three rose to leave, Ray suddenly decided he wanted no part of the planned orgy. He professed to be suffering from nausea and began to make retching noises. Pretending to be sea sick, he grabbed unsteadily for the marble mantelpiece. Those around him, including his hosts, quickly moved away, fearing the worst. He waved them off with more feigned faintness.

In his best stage manner, he staggered out of the lounge and down the grand staircase. When he was sure he was out of sight, he bolted for the second-class deck. After that, he carefully avoided the cocktail lounge where this had all begun and confined himself to his room.

Despite her age, the *Aquitania* was still one of the fastest liners. She glided regally into the great pier at Southampton, located in the central part of the south coast of England, almost four hours ahead of schedule. After descending the great gangplank, closely followed by a steward loaded down with luggage, Ray hailed a taxi to the train station for the eighty-mile rail trip to London.

After a series of calls from the London station to his host, Ray finally connected and was given directions to his flat. Upon arrival, he was met with a generous embrace.

The tiny flat was a jumble of overstuffed furniture, tables laden with photographs, and mementos of long forgotten music hall performers, and every available wall space was hung with autographed reminders of another time.

They spent the first few hours hashing over old times and old friends, including Ray's mentor, the professor who had been instrumental in his music hall career.

He was saddened to hear of his passing many years earlier. Most of the impersonators who had inspired young Ray were either residents of the elder care homes or had passed through that big proscenium in the sky. Only one still held forth at an occasional venue, having been the same age as Ray when he began.

The tiny flat of Ray's host became the scene of a constant parade of visitors over the first few weeks. An amazing assortment of types came and went. Each new visitor triggered another trip to the flat's tiny kitchen for a fresh pot of tea or another plate of biscuits. Ray enjoyed most the impressive gin doubles that appeared after tea time, but they had to be sipped in lieu of the diluting ice cubes he was used to back home.

Everyone wanted to meet this colorful American drag queen that began as a dame. They imagined a more glamorous life for this visitor than was the whole truth, but Ray never contradicted their impressions of him. Most were show business types, aspiring actors, writers, directors, etc.

One in particular, a young classical pianist, came back several times wanting to hear more stories of the old days. He insisted that Ray give an impromptu performance. To his surprise, he learned that he had packed most of his arrangements along with several stage costumes.

Ray's new fan was from a socially connected family. His lineage claimed a Baronet and several Lords and Ladies. He was the frequent entertainment at some of the smartest soirees in the best homes, and was also was a favorite of King Edward VIII.

Though classically trained, the young prodigy told Ray he quickly learned from King Edward VIII's bored expression that the King's tastes ran in another direction. A segue into a current show tune with a catchy melody would plant a smile on the Royal kisser. What particularly amused King Edward VIII were songs with clever, but suggestive lyrics.

Ray delighted in the gossipy tales of the rich and titled that were the stuff of conversation whenever the theatre crowd gathered at the flat. He learned that King Edward VIII was easily bored with the attentions of the beautiful but conventional women who constantly threw themselves in his path.

"Perhaps the king wanted to be queen," Ray offered.

Everyone snickered, but apparently that wasn't King Edward VIII's problem. Lately, he had fallen under the spell of an American divorcee named Wallis Warfield Simpson. Simpson was neither beautiful nor conventionally charming. She hailed from an ordinary background and had steadily clawed her way up the social ladder.

This unlikely couple, King Edward VIII and divorced American courtesan, was creating great alarm among the Royal watchers in England and providing delicious fodder for the gossip rags that had always been a staple of British journalism.

Ray was astonished, when his new friend handed him a monogrammed invitation one evening. The classic parchment contained the three Royal feathers at the top and was an invitation to perform at a Royal gathering to be held at historic Fort Belvedere, the part-time residence of King Edward VIII.

One week later, Ray, his accompanist, and several of the invited performers motored up the long tree-lined gravel drive to the

Royal residence. Ray's immediate impression was that Belvedere looked like neither fort nor castle. He was told it had originally been constructed in 1730 as a fortress and the only thing the remaining cannons banking the entrance were ever used for was to fire a salute on Royal birthdays.

Nestled on the edge of the Windsor Great Park, the oddly-configured building was a collection of unrelated architectural styles. Nowhere was there to be seen the British flag, but rather several odd-looking banners that Ray didn't recognize. He learned from his traveling companions that these were the flags of the Duchy of Cornwall, King Edward VIII's personal favorite. Belvedere was handsomely nestled in a very secluded wood, surrounded by massive old trees and a veritable riot of flowers.

The entertainers were the first to arrive. They were quickly escorted to the rear quarters of the Fort and instructed to remain in the pantry of the large kitchen until summoned.

It was obvious that they were just a step above the vast array of servants that scurried about the house in preparation for the evening's gathering. Ray stood apart, watching the bustle of the butler, maids, and liveried footmen. It reminded him of one of those dizzy social comedies that Hollywood ground out on a regular basis in the 1930s.

Far too garrulous to remain silent for long, Ray struck up a conversation with a particularly handsome bartender. He was stocking a series of elaborate gold carts with the evening's cocktail ingredients. Well-versed in the intricacies of mixed drinks, Ray commented on several of the cart's spirituous liquors. They joked and flirted for a few minutes until Ray decided it was safe to introduce the controversial subject of the King and Simpson.

Looking nervously about, the young man cautioned Ray in a conspiratorial tone that Simpson was tonight's hostess, and was indeed a permanent resident of the Fort.

From the general demeanor, Ray could tell that this American woman was no favorite among the staff. They found her impossibly demanding. She insisted on total formality at all times, as if Belvedere was a Royal court. No person could exit the room with their back to King Edward VIII, and most ridiculous of all, Simpson demanded the same pretentious behavior for herself. Those who served in the formal dining room were required to wear satin breeches and silk stockings, garb from an age long past.

Ray had heard numerous rumors that Simpson had her eye on the British throne. She certainly gave the impression amongst the household that she fancied herself already crowned. He couldn't help asking just what the bartender thought this American adventuress aspired.

"She's got a trick to handle his prick, but never lays hands on his scepter," was the hilarious reply. Ray had to bite his hand to keep from laughing.

Simpson was considered by many of her newly acquired society friends to be a superb hostess. Perfection was her goal, and woe to those who stepped on her ambitious toes. Ray would see when he entered the main part of the house that Simpson did indeed manage a very stately mini-chateau.

A small gong sounded, and the major domo waved the entertainers into the main chambers to await the guests and His Majesty. Here, they were instructed to remain, until called, in an anteroom adjacent the main hall.

The great doors to the Fort swung open and a steady stream of guests were announced according to their rank and then left to wander through the elegantly appointed rooms. Soon, everyone was drinking, smoking, and chattering, as the staff offered unending trays of cocktails and a tantalizing array of edibles.

A hush fell over the guests, as the major domo held up a gloved hand to announce the arrival of King Edward VIII. He entered the room in a remarkably casual manner, his arm tightly holding Simpson's.

He was a small man with a pleasant though not handsome countenance. Bright blue eyes in an already lined face looked adoringly at Simpson, as they made the rounds of the guests. He was smartly turned out in a navy blue suit that was expertly cut to his little frame. Simpson was in a fitted ankle-length black dinner dress embroidered with a veritable garden of multicolored glass flowers. The unyielding outline of the gown revealed a boyish figure with no hint of softness.

Soon, she managed to break free of King Edward VIII's hold. Once on her own, she became increasingly animated. Ray noticed from his vantage point that she was unusually plain, despite her reed-thin figure and immaculate costume and coiffure. She was wearing a spectacular tiara that echoed the colors on her dress. She reminded him of a French female-impersonator he had known many years ago.

Her tightly coiffed hair was tinted too dark, making a harsh contrast to her large bony head and face. Her features were like those of a man. Her mouth, when not artificially smiling, was small and strongly outlined in a blood-red lipstick. Thinly penciled brows rose in an imperious manner whenever she spotted a detail that was not to her liking. The rest of her makeup matched the calculated look of her entire costume.

Yapping constantly at her feet was a six-month-old Cairn Terrier. The Prince called the dog repeatedly by the name of Slipper. Simpson gathered up the tiny ball of fur and cradled him in her arms, smothering him with kisses and calling him her "naughty Loo." When queried by a guest as to why King Edward VIII called the dog Slipper and she called him Loo, Simpson let fly a raucous laugh, "Because he pisses all over everything!"

As the party grew in volume, so did Simpson's animation. She began to wave her large ugly hands, constantly directing the servants with a loud voice. She never seemed to stop talking. If she wasn't trying to impress King Edward VIII's guests, she was giving dirty looks to the staff.

King Edward VIII seemed to take no notice of her un-queenly behavior. His lust knew no bounds for this dominant woman.

Ray would later learn what he already suspected: King Edward VIII was sexually dysfunctional. Simpson, trained in the more bizarre sexual arts while visiting brothels in Shanghai, was one of the few who could satisfy the infantile needs of the Monarch.

Her mastery of Fang Chung, a particularly intense erotic art, involved hot oils, nipple massage, and intense manipulation of the main nerve centers to arouse even the most flaccid of men. Even the techniques she had learned in the Orient failed to entirely address King Edward VIII's feeble virility.

The brilliant playwright, Noel Coward, spilled the Royal beans after King Edward VIII married Simpson. His caustically bitchy comments flowed through the gay underground like mercury on a mirror.

'I like Wallis; she is a fag hag to end all fag hags. Edward . . . well, although he pretends not to hate me, he does because I'm queer and he's queer . . . unlike him I don't pretend not to be."

One of the typically eccentric guests that night was Osbert Sitwell, a poet and Baronet. Sitwell was neither a fan of King Edward VIII nor Simpson. He had written previously about the pair in a clever but decidedly unflattering way. He particularly disliked the American contingency that was part of Simpson's entourage. He strongly suspected they were hoping to ride in on Simpson's coronation train, should she manage to ascend the throne alongside King Edward VIII.

In an article that appeared weeks after the party, he wrote condescendingly: "They were a wise cracking team of semi-millionaires, with loud voices and continual loud laughs bottled in alcohol."

Among the wildly divergent crowd that evening, one figure stood out. Beautifully dressed in what appeared to be an almost operetta-style uniform was a darkly handsome middle-aged man standing alone quietly surveying the crowd.

As Ray was not an invited guest, he knew he could never work up the nerve to introduce himself to this tantalizing figure. He turned instead to the gossipy bartender, who was now serving cocktails to the sequestered performers. The story he related was like something from a Russian novel. In fact, it was.

This was the exiled nobleman, Prince Felix Youssoupov, the drink server related in a stage whisper. He had escaped the slaughter of many of his noble relatives following the collapse of the Russian monarchy. The collapse had been brought upon, in part, by the interference of a particularly evil zealot. Ray immediately recognized the name Rasputin, the mad monk, who had brainwashed the Russian Empress and triggered the downfall of the Romanov dynasty.

Prince Youssoupov's part in murdering this monster was well-known. What was also well-known was his gender orientation. Though married to a member of the Royal household, he was a practicing transvestite. This tickled Ray's curiosity even more.

The colorful story of the pansy Prince rolled quickly off the bartender's talented tongue. The art of any good bar-keep must include the proverbial gift of gab.

As a very young man, Prince Youssoupov stole gowns from the vast armoires of his mother, the Duchess. Decked out in her opulent jewels, elaborate wigs, and sumptuous furs, he prowled Moscow's infamous nightspots. He flirted with all the handsome young men, who were nearly always fooled by his naturally feminine features and manners. He was wise enough to escape their advances if they became too bold.

Apparently, Prince Youssoupov had also established a bizarre sexual relationship with Rasputin. Rumor had it that the monk, when inebriated, would have sex with anyone available. Prince Youssoupov arranged a meeting with Rasputin at a secret hideaway, plied him with vodka from the Royal cellars, and seduced him. The vodka had been laced with enough poison to kill a dozen men.

Rasputin was not an ordinary man. It took Prince Youssoupov and three co-conspirators to shoot, bludgeon, and then drown the Mad Monk in an ice-filled river before they were sure he was dead.

The murder brought on the wrath of the peasants in the form of a frightening insurrection. Prince Youssoupov and his wife fled to England with only their smuggled jewelry to sustain them. When this ran out, they were dependent on the kindness of English Royalty, who were willing to help fellow nobility.

When things looked bleakest, their fortunes changed. A canny lawyer urged them to bring a lawsuit against MGM.

Ray remembered the story of the Russian nobleman who had sued the studio for producing the film, *Rasputin and the Empress* (1932), starring John, Ethel, and Lionel Barrymore. While it was thoroughly disparaged by the critics, it also stirred up a great deal of controvery worldwide.

Prince Youssoupov considered the movie slanderous and libelous. He found MGM's portrayal of him to be unflattering and untrue. He won an enormous settlement from the studio, the largest up to that time for a libel case.

Ray felt that King Edward VIII and Prince Youssoupov had several things in common, including a certain physical resemblance.

They both seemed trapped in a timeless void, reflected in their expressions, as if gazing in memories of ages past.

King Edward VIII and Simpson gave the impression they were holding court. The household staff looked as if they were costumed from another century, silently bowing and scraping to the imperious Simpson.

Suddenly, the scandalous tale of Prince Youssoupov was interrupted with an announcement that the evening's entertainment was about to begin.

Since there was only time for a single number from each performer, due to the many entertainers on the menu, it was decided against including one of Ray's standard but decidedly American songs. His accompanist feared this might not appeal to the English ear or to that peculiarly British sense of humor. Instead, there was a new number that had been rehearsed the previous week. Ray would perform this new song, backed by the wildly popular English group The Crazy Gang. This outlandish act was a favorite of the pianist.

The zany sextet drew their hilarious antics from quick-fire crosstalk, slapstick, and a blatant disregard for social and cultural hierarchies. What Ray did not anticipate was the reaction the song they had taught him would elicit from King Edward VIII and Simpson.

Stepping into an ornate powder room, Ray quickly changed into the outfit given him by The Crazy Gang. Looking into the Venetian mirror, he saw a bizarre image: a tall cone-shaped hat covered in tiny feathers and a shimmery white metallic dress with several long trains falling from the shoulder and the waist. He wondered how his was going to manage to maneuver in this outlandish garb.

He discovered after the performance that this was The Crazy Gang's politically incorrect, scathing satirical comment on London dowager fashion. Their views on society and politics veered close to anarchy.

Gathering up the multiple trains of the gown, Ray managed to get to the piano and took his place in the center with The Crazy Gang on each side looking like bizarre bookends. Their evening wear appeared to have been fished from a dust bin, their ties askew, sleeves and trousers too short. He felt as if he were surrounded by Charlie Chaplin clones.

Drawing in a deep breath, followed by a wave of his six-inch red faux nails in the direction of the accompanist, he began:

> "Run Adolf, run Adolf
> Run, run, run
> Now that the fun has
> Begun, gun, gun
> P'raps you'll just allow
> Us to explain,
> What we did once, -we
> Can do again
> We're making shells by
> The ton, ton, ton
> We've got the men and
> The mon, mon, mon
> Poor old soul, -you'll
> Need a rabbit hole,-
> So, run Adolf, run Adolf,
> Run, run, run!"

The Crazy Gang joined the second chorus, adlibbing dance steps and taking turns whirling the taller Ray around the floor in a parody of a German polka. He quickly became entangled in the trains of his gown and nearly landed in the lap of the glowering Simpson. The thoroughly blitzed crowd joined the merriment, clapping in time just as the brief number ended.

Regaining his composure, but still breathless, Ray joined hands with his partners and bowed deeply in the direction of the throne-like chairs of King Edward VIII and Simpson. Their hands were making the motion of polite applause but their faces were set in stone.

He was bewildered by the cold reception from his Royal but remote hosts. He later learned that both King Edward VIII and Simpson were sympathetic Nazi supporters.

He had been bamboozled by The Crazy Gang into participating in a bold, politically incorrect song, incorrect in the eyes of the misguided King Edward VIII and his mistress. The song they performed was an obvious slam against the rising power of the insane Adolph Hitler.

He later discovered that his accompanist was also in on the farce. He, too, disliked King Edward VIII's treasonous politics.

When all the performances were finished, the entertainers were invited to mingle among the guests. Those who attended King Edward VIII's unusual social soirees were often described by his critics as "café society flotsam."

One of the most outlandish guests that evening was Lady Emerald Cunard, the steamship heiress. This obscenely privileged and pampered woman was nearly incoherent from the effects of cocaine. Her oddly-shaped face was far from beautiful, with a tiny bird-like mouth and thinly drawn brows. Her specialty was to pit friend against friend, inciting them with her acid wit and stinging tongue. Enormously wealthy and socially prominent, she continued to bait and insult those around her until a verbal battle to the death ensued. At her side was Sir Oswald Mosley, an ugly man, who was the head of the British Fascists organization. His decidedly anti-British sentiments had earned him a large band of detractors.

Ray watched in amazement, as Lady Cunard turned and signaled to the fascinating Russian Prince Youssoupov standing opposite her. With an imperious sweep of her hand, she said to those around her,

"Let me introduce you to the man who killed Rasputin."

There was gasp from the guests followed by an awkward silence. Prince Youssoupov stiffened, fixed Lady Cunard with a fiery stare, and turned on his heels and left.

As the party wore on, King Edward VIII became more garrulous, his tongue loosened by a quantity of the finest single malt scotch, which he chugged neat. A great lover of the German language and style, he announced he would now entertain the entertainers with a selection of songs.

The off-key bellowing that ensued drew embarrassed glances, followed by polite applause in deference to his Royal station, but neither for talent nor from political tolerance.

Finally, the hardnosed Simpson interrupted with a call for coffee in the drawing room, a signal that the evening's farce was over.

Afterward, as The Crazy Gang and Ray were being driven to their London lodgings, one of the happily inebriated performers in the next Rolls Royce rolled down the window and serenaded passersby with, "Hark The Herald Angels sing, Mrs. Simpson stole our King!"

King Edward VIII was the only English sovereign to resign the crown voluntarily. He abdicated in 1936, having ruled for less than twelve months, in order to marry Simpson. He and his lady were personas non grata until 1967, when they were finally invited to attend an official public ceremony with other members of the Royal family. This did not, of course, include Queen Elizabeth, who never forgave King Edward VIII for his abdication.

The Royal Command Performance at Fort Belvedere before King Edward VIII and Simpson became comedic fodder for Ray's live act throughout his entire career.

"I want to tell you about those Windsors," he cackled, adding some new bit of gossip or scandal over the years. He often referred to Princess Margaret as "the dyke," and Prince Phillip as, "the randy Regent."

Audiences seemed to respond to these extreme stories. He was saying what so many of them were unable to express during a time when social etiquette was rigid and unforgiving. He was giving them over-the-top satire, and they loved it.

While European nations began to stiffen their military stances and global troubles expanded, Mae's fan base was expanding as fast as her famous figure. The late 1930s saw the full-figured star adding even more curves. These bonus bulges were emphasized by the merciless eye of the camera. Mae's favorite couturier, Edith Head, had trouble lassoing in the famous hourglass figure. Special corsets were designed with extra tight lacing up the back, but, eventually, all those pretty pounds had to go somewhere, usually spilling out over the top of that already expanded décolleté. The camera added at least an extra ten pounds, and that was a lot for Mae's short frame.

The bosses at Paramount subtly suggested a diet was in order. Mae did not believe in diets, saying she needed the nutrition to maintain her level of energy, both in front of the camera lens and in her infamous mirrored bedchamber.

Added to Mae's weight woes was the pressure to add yet another film to her credit. The studio had made a handsome profit on *Goin' to Town* (1935), and they wanted to rush her into another production, fearing that this lucky streak might end.

Mae partially solved her size problem on her new film, *Klondike Annie* (1936), by casting one of the leads with the gargantuan Victor McLaglen. Standing next to his bulky tall frame gave the illusion that she was svelte.

Paramount must have had a premonition about Mae's lucky streak. Though the next film, *Go West Young Man* (1936), seemed more than appropriate for the star, there was little to recommend it. Neither the critics nor the public took to this tale of a Hollywood screen siren with a disagreeable personality. There was little humor or spice in the story, and even a veteran like Mae was hard put to make much of the skinny script.

Unfortunately, the costuming was contemporary, which did not allow for the waist-crushing corsets used in her usual period costumes. Worst of all, there were no glamorous stage numbers to showcase Mae's suggestive songs. This certainly was not the Mae West the masses knew.

Paramount did cast Randolph Scott, Cary Grant's then current love interest, in the role of a brilliant inventor. The role was a stretch for the handsome but stoic actor. Scott was young and terrific in tight pants. This made Mae look a bit like a cradle robber.

Many years later, Mae, in an obviously delusional state of mind, commented that Scott was in heat for her. This gives a glimpse into her very self-centered outlook on life, one that even she would admit was necessary to maintain that other person she had created, Mae West.

July 1937 brought home the old Mae marriage rumor to roost. She had adamantly denied for years that she had married at seventeen when she was touring as a duo with Frank Wallace.

In May 1935, a nosy clerk in Milwaukee's Registrar Office had unearthed a marriage card that attested to their wedding. Nobody remembered who Wallace was, but Mae West was certainly on the tip of everyone's tongue that had ever been to the movies. The newspapers across the country ran with the headline.

Quietly retired in Manhattan, Frank Wallace nearly choked on his coffee as he read the morning May 6 edition of his paper. A call to his lawyer set the wheels in motion and the dollar signs ran round and round in his head. The newspapers were very interested to hear what he had to say, and he was more than happy to sell his story.

Even more interesting was what Mae had to say.

"I've gotten a lot of bunnies on Easter. This is the first time I've ever received a husband. Never heard of the fellow. I'm a spinster, and you've got my age wrong. I was a child in 1911 and have never been in Milwaukee. Let this alleged Mr. Mae West come up and see my lawyer sometime!"

This seems to have been another part of the self-invented lore that Mae was fond of spreading. She actually did appear in Milwaukee before 1920. She did agree to marry Wallace at the last hour. She possibly feared she was pregnant. She was under age, so legally the marriage was null and void.

It appears in light of the New York Supreme Court documents discovered later that Mae's only real husband was Guido Deiro. Again, this was a name she never acknowledged until she wrote her memoirs years later, and even then she referred to him simply as "Mr. G."

$3,000,000 was Mae's net worth at the time of the embarrassing Wallace snafu. According to California law, half of all Mae's worth was the property of Frank Wallace.

Mae finally admitted they had been married, but never lived together as man and wife. She offered the retired hoofer a paltry $30,000 to disappear. His lawyers began to file an injunction to tie-up all of Mae's property. Her lawyers countered with a proviso in the law that states a separated wife's earnings are her own. An undisclosed settlement whitewashed the whole troubling incident. Typically, what bothered Mae the most was the revelation of her true age.

This temporary distraction hardly seemed to slow the steam roller of the Mae West career. Taking a break from filming, Mae accepted a lucrative offer to do a radio skit on the very popular *The Chase and Sanborn Hour*.

She agreed to star in a comedy scene featuring the voice of ventriloquist Edgar Bergen. Bergen's partner was a wooden dummy named Charlie McCarthy. The idea that appearing on a half-hour radio show was a new career move never entered her mind. She was merely planning to use it to promote her next Paramount picture, *Every Day's a Holiday* (1938). The end result was more publicity than she could ever have imagined.

The show involved Mae, the dummy, and a second-string film actor named Don Ameche in a comedic version of Adam and Eve. The title was, "What Might Have Happened in the Garden of Eden."

Mae was surprised when the producers suggested she write her own material. She wasn't so surprised when they wanted to review it. It came back to her with their seal of approval. To double check the acceptability of the script, the executives insisted the cast do two complete rehearsals. The three actors read their lines just as written and got the go ahead.

The night of the broadcast, Mae read her lines without changing a word. What she did change was her delivery and the tone of her voice. Without even seeing the famous face, listeners were left with no doubt as to what Eve/Mae was up to in that Biblical Garden of Eden.

On the evening of December 12, 1937, millions of Americans gathered around their radio sets, anxiously awaiting the latest *The Chase and Sanborn Hour* program, a weekly event that had captured the imagination of the American public. After the first half of the program, where Mae appeared as herself, using her familiar brand of humor heavily laced with sexual innuendoes, the announcer intoned in a sonorous voice, "We've come to the event itself on tonight's broadcast, the presence of Mae West herself . . . she turns back time and steps into the Garden of Eden, and into the character of the most fascinatin' woman of them all, Eve."

Eve: "Listen, Adam. I tell you you've gotta get me out of this place. You've gotta break the lease."

Adam: "But what for, this is Eden. Everything is perfect, quiet, and safe."

Eve: "That's the trouble, it's too safe. That's disgustin'. Adam, you don't know a thing about women."

Adam: "Oh, you apparently forgot, you were one of my old ribs."

Eve: "Yeah, a rib once, and now I'm beefin'!"

Adam: "Me, I know everything about women"

Eve: "That's coverin' a lot of territory. Listen, long, lazy, and lukewarm, you think I wanna stay in this place all my life? Now tell me the lowdown truth, ain't there anyway you can break the lease?"

Adam: "Well, yes there is. I know all about the tree."

Eve: "What tree, what tree?"

Adam: "That apple tree, in the middle of the garden. The lease says if we eat any of the fruit we get thrown out of here. I tell you, one bite of those apples and we get dispossessed."

Eve: "Ummmm, how fascinatin'. What are we gonna do now?"

Adam. "I think I'll go fishin'. I'll be back."

Eve: "So that's the trouble. So it's the tree. Hello tree. How'd you like to do a little lease breakin' for a woman with ideas? Hmm, not room enough to squeeze through the fence for a woman with my personality. Now if I only knew someone skinny enough."

Snake: "Salutations, Mrs. Eve."

Eve: "Oh, if it isn't Mr. Snake. Hello, dark, long, and slinky."

Snake: "Why are you standing by that tree?"

Eve: "Stop wrigglin' and I'll tell you. You think with the proper provocation you can squeeze through the fence around the tree? Wouldn't you like to have this whole paradise to yourself, you palpitatin' python?"

Snake: "Certainly."

Eve: "Pick me a handful of fruit. Adam and I will eat it, and the Garden of Eden is all yours."

Snake: "Sounds alright to me. I'll do it."

Eve: "Now, get me a BIG one. I feel like doin' a big apple!"

Adam returns.

Adam: "How about supper? Don't tell me we've got fig stew again."

Eve: "Oh no, somethin' new."

Adam: "What is it?"

Eve: "A new kind of sauce. It's good for you. Just to prove it's 100 proof, I'll have a demitasse of it myself. Eat your sauce big boy, and hold your hat, if you've got one!"

There is a tremendous clap of thunder.

Adam: "Oh my head! What happened?"

Eve: "We've been disposed."

Adam: "But why?"

Eve: "Forbidden applesauce!"

Adam: "Oh Eve, what have you done?"

Eve: "I've made a little history. I'm the first woman to have her own way, and a snake who'll take the wrap for it!"

Adam suddenly sees Eve in a different light and begins to make love to her.

Adam: "Oh Eve, what was that?"

Eve: "That was the Original Kiss!"

Mae had made a volcanic mountain out a literary mole hill. The switchboards at the broadcasting station lit up like a Christmas tree. All the blue-haired bon-bon eaters across the country were outraged. The Bible had been mocked, morals had been endangered, and worst of all their husbands, sons, and grandfathers had laughed out loud at what that daughter of the Devil had insinuated to millions out there in radio land.

Ironically, it was the largest audience *The Chase and Sanborn Hour* had ever had, or ever would have. The result was that Mae was banned from that particular broadcast company for ten years.

The timing of the release of *Every Day's a Holiday* (1938) couldn't have been worse. It opened only three days after the radio broadcast.

Church groups, religious lunatics, and the pious everywhere demanded Mae's head on a platter. Even the critics, fearing the boycott of the general public, got on the bandwagon. Mae's once enthusiastic and supportive audiences stayed home.

What was so strange was that the earlier films of Mae West contained much more scurrilous material than *Every Day's A Holiday*. Rather than admit she was beaten, Mae offered Paramount a new project. This one had been percolating in her mind for years.

She had always loved the story of the Empress of Russia, Catherine the Great. Catherine was a brilliant, independent ruler with a voracious appetite for men. Mae couldn't imagine a woman she admired more or who was more like her. She had been working on a script for several years and now seemed the right time to present the big boys in the front office with her masterpiece.

Paramount informed Mae that they had made the same story five years earlier with the glamorous but bloodless Marlene Dietrich. The Dietrich film had been a stinker at the box office and the studio did not want a repeat.

A very heated scene ensued in the offices of Ernst Lubitsch, Paramount's Production Manager. Mae and Lubitsch were never soul mates, and this latest rebuff from the imperious producer finally released her pent-up fury. She told him what he could do with his studio and where he could stick it.

She vowed to anyone within ear shot, as she stormed off the Paramount lot, climbing into her waiting limousine, "This is one picture I *am* going to make!"

Her plan was to independently produce the picture, with the financial aid of an admirer in San Francisco. Her plan never saw the light of day, as production cost estimates skyrocketed.

Mae, used to the abundant resources available at Paramount, wanted the top set designers, costume makers, and co-stars. When her sole prospective backer added up the tally, he sheepishly backed out.

The Brooklyn-bred star never admitted defeat. As a result of the personal appearances Mae had made at the behest of Paramount when they were promoting *Every Day's a Holiday*, she realized people still flocked to see her in person. Why not put together a new stage show and tour the country.

The resultant sexy concoction consisted of some of her most famous songs, delivered in a sensational wardrobe and backed by six very handsome dancers. Her faithful fans turned out in record numbers everywhere the act booked.

Mae harbored a secret resentment for those who found her frankness and groundbreaking treatment of sex as something "vulgar." Despite her many supporters, the naysayers were beginning to gradually erode her hard-earned image and career. She told *Picturegoer* magazine: "Sex is not vulgar, except in the minds of those who are vulgar. Why do they feel it necessary to weep and moan over what is only natural."

Another annoying subject that reporters seemed to harp on was Mae's single status. In 1935, she clearly stated her views to *Movie Classic* magazine: "I can marry anytime. I've got to hold onto fame as long I got it ... can't let anything interfere. I've got to live for my public and I don't regret it."

When the tour ended, Mae parted company with Paramount Pictures. She returned to Hollywood with a new contract in hand from another studio.

Universal Studios offered Mae a co-starring role in a comedy with Vaudeville veteran W. C. Fields. The two well-seasoned stars were to be united for the first time onscreen in *My Little Chickadee* (1940). They had frequently shared billing in their Vaudeville days.

Universal Studios had enjoyed an enormous success with *Destry Rides Again* (1930), which starred the laconic James Stewart and the synthetic Marlene Dietrich, a film star who was all about camera angles and costumes. She had been voted "Box Office Poison" and her career was in the cinematic doldrums. This latest picture had temporarily returned a bit of luster to her fading star. The studio hoped for a reprise of this successful formula by coupling an even odder pair, Mae and Fields.

Fields enthusiastically approached Mae privately at her Ravenswood residence. He was sure they could spark a career revival with this new project. He presented Mae with a screenplay he had hastily written.

When Mae read the title out loud, *December and Mae*, she gave the bulbous nosed comic a withering look. She told him that at least he had gotten the first part right, the last cold month of the year. The title gave her name second billing, and if he thought that was going to happen he must be more drunk than usual. After abruptly ending their conversation, she had Fields ushered unceremoniously out the door. She took a seat at her Louis XIV desk and began to type a suitable script, one that showcased her way with words.

The resulting script was actually two: one written by Fields and one by Mae. Even the best director would have found it impossible to make a cohesive whole out of this ego-driven mix. The finished product shows neither Fields nor Mae at their best, but it is the film most people now associate with the two stars.

In retrospect, Fields got the lion's share of humor. His sometimes dubious dialogue managed to escape the censor's snips, but Mae, ever the target of the righteous, came under much closer scrutiny.

Her only song in the film, "Willy of the Valley," had the single, double-entendre line removed after the initial screening. Mae originally sang, "I said he was a good man, and I ought to know," which became, "I said he was a good man, he should have hung around."

The first version was delivered with all of the veteran actress's famous tricks, the undulating hips, and the knowing look in the scimitar eyes. The finished product eventually projected on theatre screens was as harmless as a cup of cocoa.

As soon as the cameras began to roll, discord pervaded the set. Fields was jealous of all the attention Mae was receiving, and insultingly called her the "poor man's Cleopatra." Mae had a poor impression of Fields' lack of professionalism. He was a notorious alcoholic, and she intensely disliked hard drinking. Mae made sure there was a clause written into Fields' contract that forbade him to be drunk at any time during the filming of the picture.

As Mae would soon learn, Fields was as wily as she when it came to getting what he wanted, and he wanted to drink. In fact, he found it difficult to face a camera without "a snoot full," as he would exclaim.

To ensure he stuck to his word, Mae bribed a studio guard to follow Fields when he wasn't filming. He would suddenly disappear for a supposed trip to the "terlet" as Mae mangled the word in her heavy Brooklyn accent. Despite her vigilance, she was unable to keep Fields sober for very long.

Growing increasingly impatient with the expensive delays Fields' insobriety caused, Mae decided to see just what he was getting up to between breaks. While Fields was excused for a bathroom break between takes one day, Mae crept behind his dressing room trailer and waited until he went inside. Peering through the venetian blinds, she couldn't see Fields doing anything out of the ordinary. About to return to the set in disgust, she noticed the comic was on his third trip to the large water cooler next to his dressing table. *How unusual for someone who claimed "to never drink the stuff."*

Mae appeared at the open door of Fields' trailer saying she had a message from the director. Before he could stop her, Mae crossed the room and filled a paper cup from the cooler. Gingerly sampling the clear contents, she quickly spat out the aromatic liquid. "Gin!" she said triumphantly.

The next day, the chastised comedian was back on the set, compliant and sober.

Mae neither smoked nor drank, not because of moral values, but she was convinced it would make her less attractive.

Once Field's well-known thirst was temporarily held in check, the filming progressed normally.

My Little Chickadee was a tale of the Old West done in an almost Burlesque style. Mae portrays the well-stacked Flower Belle Lee. In the opening scene, she shocks the townspeople. A local busy body, brilliantly played by Margaret Hamilton, best-known for her role the following year as Miss Gulch/The Wicked Witch of the West in *The Wizard of Oz* (1939), catches Flower Belle with her bloomers down while entertaining a masked bandit in her bedroom. The righteous ride her out of town on the rails. On board the train, Flower Belle meets Cuthbert J. Twillie (Fields). Always digging for gold, the avaricious Flower Belle is duped by the crafty Cuthbert into thinking he is wealthy. She accepts the smitten boob's immediate proposal of marriage. The ceremony is performed by a travelling salesman that Flower Belle cons into posing as a minister.

The newlyweds arrive in the town of Greasewood, where Cuthbert is strong armed by the local crooks into becoming the new sheriff; the previous dozen had all been murdered. The comedy comes in fits and starts, yet never really takes off. The director had the impossible task of melding the two stars very divergent styles, each having written a different script.

Halfway through the filming, things came to a head. Fueled by a liquor-laced pot of java, Fields attempted to direct Mae's movements in a pivotal scene. Suddenly, there was a deadly silence on the set. "No one can tell me what to do. I have a certain look, a walk, a talk . . . the others have to move around me."

Mae preferred to work in the afternoon, Fields in the morning. Mae eventually won the battle.

To ensure that the aging actress would be seen to best effect, Mae insisted on her own lighting man. She had learned that brilliant lighting with a special filter, shot head on, would erase most of what time had etched on her face. Fields, like most drunks, hated bright lights. Mae won again.

Mae soon learned that Fields could never stick to a script, so she wisely allowed him to ad-lib his lines. This was the best way to get Fields to be spontaneously funny. He had been weaned on Vaudeville and Burlesque and would always play it that way.

She had seen his unique brand of comedy many times on the stage. They had shared more than one Vaudeville circuit. Her studied style seemed at odds with the bumbling comic and the result was not cohesive.

Despite the at-odds relationship the two comics shared, Mae had to laugh to herself at some of Field's impromptu antics.

The moment that brought spontaneous laughter from the usually self-contained actress was the honeymoon scene that required several takes, not usual for the letter-perfect performer.

The bumbling groom was literally all a twitter at the prospect of climbing into bed with the desirable but distant Flower Belle. The reluctant bride substitutes a goat under the covers while Cuthbert is in the powder room preparing his toilette for the promised marital bliss.

The script called for the anxious groom to quickly slip under the sheets, turn to the camera with a look of surprise, and then cut away.

This was the perfect moment for a Field's off-the-cuff comment. The odoriferous goat squirmed beneath the covers as Fields wriggled his bulbous nose, sniffed the air vigorously, and delivered the perfect bon mot, "Darling, have you changed your perfume?"

Typical of the reined-in dialogue that the censors demanded of the unmanageable Mae, is the following scene. Riding in a buggy on a country road with a prospective suitor, Flower Belle gives the guy the once over with those steely blue eyes. "I see you're a man with ideals. I guess I better be going while you still got them." What she had written in her original script the censor's quickly removed. This watering down of the Mae West witticisms soon eviscerated her once sensational film persona.

Mae was forced to compromise on several issues to insure her return to the screen. Though she wouldn't admit it, her career needed another big hit like the ones from her early Paramount days.

She was willing to take a substantial cut in salary with a proviso added to her contract that she receive a large percentage of the film's eventual profits. She walked away with a six-figure check that equaled her top earning years, and reinforced, in her mind at least, her vision of eternal stardom. The Hollywood film colony didn't agree.

Critics didn't agree either. Mae defended herself by explaining that the studio cut her scenes too closely, not allowing her the usual slower pace that was a trademark of her style. Universal offered Mae two more films with Fields, but she didn't hesitate to turn them down.

While Mae, now in her early fifties, pondered her next career move, Ray was still in London, enjoying all the sights he had missed as an impoverished youth.

He kept remembering how the manly Mrs. Wallis Simpson looked so much like his friend in Paris, the impersonator, Monique Maphrodite. Both were hard and artificial. Monique played her look as part of her act. Simpson was what she appeared to be.

Bored at last with the charms of jolly old England, Ray decided it was time to look up Monique and see what Paris had to offer.

His London host made inquiries among the gay theatre crowd he knew from the French capitol and presented Ray with several letters of introduction that might help in finding lodging, and possibly work.

Bidding the foggy town on the Thames goodbye, he packed his bags and got his reservation. He sailed from the white cliffs of Dover to the port of Calais. A short train trip ended with the spectacular sight of the night lights of Paris.

Arriving after midnight at the first address on his list, he was quickly invited to bunk on a stylish but stiff love seat. A colorful group of characters were spread about the rooms in various states of dress and inebriation. As the liquor dwindled and then disappeared, so did the guests. There remained only two with the arrival of the French dawn. The rest had been party crashers at what turned out to be an almost perpetual open house, replete with drinks, shared memories, and shared beds.

The ever-changing crowd was fascinated with Ray's theatre history and his unique life story. After a singularly gin-soaked evening of merriment, he realized that this was too seductive a lifestyle with no safe landing in sight.

He began to cast about, hoping to connect with Monique, who might lead him to a job. He still couldn't find her and none of his new friends even remembered her.

Bemoaning his lack of work one night to the ever-present house guests he was told of auditions to be held the next morning at the legendary *Follies Bergère*. The star of the *Follies Bergère* was the equally legendary Josephine Baker, a former chorus girl that Ray had worked with many years before. He jotted down the address and the name of the stage manager. The gray Parisian dawn found him hoofing it in search of a taxi.

The tiny Citroen cab lurched to a halt in front of the theatre. Ray had arrived even before the stage doors were open, leaving him to wander around the building's façade, taking in the architectural details. There was no sign of activity, so he went into an adjoining bistro for a coffee. On the table was a day-old copy of the newspaper *Candide*. Thumbing through the arts section, he found a review of Josephine Baker's *Follies Bergère* performance:

"Much has been written about Miss Baker. Some people have gone back six times to see her show . . . others slam the theatre doors . . . 'a disgrace, anarchy, pandering to the base instincts', they mutter. The Revue begins each night at ten fifteen . . . Paris society crowds the auditorium . . . then a curious figure dashes on stage . . . sagging at the knees, wearing a pair of the briefest shorts, looking like a cross between a boxing kangaroo and a racing cyclist . . . it's Josephine Baker!"

He was hoping that Josephine would remember him from the old days of Vaudeville in New York. He had known the controversial star when she was just a chorus girl in the sold-out Broadway musical, *Blackbirds* (1928). He and Josephine were part of a hard-partying theatre crowd that burned up the night life in Manhattan. As long as someone was entertaining, Josephine loved them, and Ray and his gay entourage kept the ebony chanteuse amused. He remembered her as a skinny little Black girl with outsized ambition and an even bigger talent.

From his vantage point at the front window, he saw the doors to the *Follies Bergère* lobby swing open. Rather than enter through the usual stage entrance, he proceeded confidently into the lobby, inquiring about the location of the stage manager's office. The office was unoccupied, so he followed the noise he heard coming from the stage in the main auditorium.

Backtracking through the lobby, his attention focused on a spectacular painted frieze of the *Follies Bergère*'s current star, the bizarrely beautiful Josephine Baker. The larger than life figure was swathed in furs, jewels, and little else. He had heard the many tales that swirled around the Cinderella story of this stunning Black performer. She had conquered the world of cabaret, film, and recordings.

The real Josephine Baker had a life that few of her adoring fans could have guessed. Born Freda Josephine Carson in St. Louis, Missouri, she first saw the light of day in a laundress's basket. Her mother scrubbed clothes for the wealthy. Josephine herself became a laundress, maid, babysitter, and anything else that put food in her mouth. She auditioned when she was only thirteen for a group called The Dixie Steppers. She got the job, doing comic bits, eventually moving up to a starring spot.

Later, she joined with a dancing partner, Joe Alex, and they traveled to Europe, finally settling in Paris. Together, they created a wildly primitive routine called the Danse Sauvage. Baker appeared clad only in a tiny skirt made of feathers. The sophisticated Parisians went mad for this new vision of a natural woman, exotic, uninhibited, and unbound by clothing. Soon, she was the top-paid entertainer on the continent. In addition to her stage work, she starred in two feature films.

With his long history of auditioning, Ray knew the routine. There were dozens of hopefuls on stage and in the wings, each nervously stretching, trying out their vocal chords, and checking their make-up for improvement. He took a spot next to an attractive young dancer, hoping to learn what the director might be looking for. In a dialectal French and fractured English, the young man told him the director was a "batard" and was usually looking to get laid, but with women only.

Just as the next artist was called stage front and center, Baker arrived with a great flourish, surrounded by a chattering entourage. She was swathed in a long coat of black monkey fur over a simple tight frock. Her hair was covered by a turban of cerise silk with a spray of sparkling stones dropping from her ears. She wore no makeup and bore little resemblance to the glamorous creature Ray had just seen in the lobby poster. Her smile was wide and genuine, as she happily greeted those on stage. Handing the shivering little Terrier she carried to the director, she took a front row seat.

Ray was next. He stepped forward and flashed his considerable smile in Baker's direction. She pointed to him, leaning over to the director, as Ray handed his sheet music to the pianist. He had chosen "Suppose," an old song in the Vaudeville/music hall style. It contained a spoken introduction and he rendered it in the half sung and half spoken style that had become his own. It worked for him both in and out of drag.

He finished with a little impromptu waltz step at the end of the song, holding out an imaginary skirt.

Baker was still huddled with the director, as Ray stood waiting for the verdict. The star walked onstage and greeted Ray with an embrace. She had remembered him. In a heavily accented voice, she told the director to find Ray a spot in the show. Rehearsals began two days later.

This turned out to be one of the most physically demanding shows that Ray had ever been involved with. He was featured in three numbers that required a lot of singing, dancing, and endless posing.

The first was an elaborate jungle theme. In this, he was a chorus girl in a fiery orange costume made of silk panels and an enormous feathered headdress. He was onstage during the entire lengthy scene singing in fractured French, constantly dancing, and all the while trying to keep the weighty headdress from toppling.

Next was a gypsy theme. This time, he shed his plumes and donned the costume of a Gitano dancer, furiously dancing the Flamenco to the fiery gypsy music. The simple plot had Baker playing the mother of a child who had been kidnapped by gypsies. She steals into their camp and manages to rescue her child. In between, there was a great deal of dancing by Baker in various states of undress. At the spectacular climax, she sets the camp on fire.

The Flamenco, a style Ray had little experience with, required a great deal of stamping and clapping. He wasn't used to such exuberant dancing in high heels. Every night, he found himself soaking his bruised feet after the performance in a hot tub of Epsom salts laced with gin, which he alternately swigged and splashed into the bucket. Baker danced bare footed and in the barest of costumes. How he wished he was a woman at times.

The theme of the show might be described as *le grand tour de l'amour*. Each act featured the theme of love in a different exotic location around the world.

For the finale, the stage was transformed into the Arctic. Ray was totally unrecognizable dressed as an Eskimo in a fur parka and seal skin boots. Ten minutes of exuberant dancing and singing under the hot stage lights gave Ray's costume an aroma not unlike a wet dog.

The climax of the show was as spectacular as anything he had ever seen. Heralded by brass fanfare, Baker was transported onstage in an enormous golden sled pulled by a team of dogs howling in tune to the trumpet accompaniment. Baker descended from the sled wrapped in a twenty foot cape of white ostrich feathers. With the wave of a skinny ebony arm, she whipped the coat aside, revealing a costume that consisted of three strategically placed snowflakes and nothing else.

On opening night, pandemonium reigned throughout the 2,000-seat theatre. Baker was feted and fawned over backstage by luminaries from every walk of life.

Reminiscing many years later, Ray recalled one of Baker's numbers:

> "Josephine Baker was the most sensational thing I'd seen in years . . . she came down a wide Baroque staircase . . . wrapped in white fur coat, dragging at least six feet behind her. Even the sleeves of the coat dragged as much as the coat did . . . center stage she opened the coat . . . all she had on was a tiny jeweled crotch cover, jeweled pasties, and jeweled high heels. On her head were black jewels and white feathers spraying out of a cone. The ovation was thunderous!"

Over the long run of the show, Ray was drawn ever-closer to the inner circle of Baker's closest friends. She had a special place in her heart for her gay performers and great empathy for anyone she felt was persecuted. She knew all too well the enormous pain that discrimination and bigotry can bring.

Her sympathetic nature stemmed from her humble beginnings as a maid and waitress in St. Louis. A youth spent in extreme poverty and suffering belied the exalted status she now held with the French public.

Her very special gifts and eventual star status were never given the respect they deserved in her birth country. Despite her obvious talents, she experienced the racist attitude that permeated every corner of the American entertainment world. She could perform to standing ovations in the best theatres, but when it came time to dine or seek a hotel, she was turned away.

"No Negroes here," was the phrase she came to hate with all her heart. Later, despite her enormous success in Europe, a return to America as the star of the *Ziegfeld Follies* proved to be a complete disaster. She had gained an air of sophistication and chic that made White audiences very uncomfortable. Previously, she had amused them with her safe and unthreatening assumption of a clumsy, shuffling servant. She rolled her eyes and feigned a fawning attitude. Now, when she appeared onstage, her elegant head held high and boldly displaying her spectacular figure, she received scathing reviews.

The *New York Times* called her a "Negro wench." She returned, brokenhearted, to her adopted home in Paris.

She was now a regular fixture at the *Follies Bergère*. Her audiences adored her exotic and shocking beauty. Her dancing consisted of improvisational abandon. No matter how hard her choreographer tried to get her to stick to the routine he had created for her, the excitement of performing always inspired her to improvise.

Ray found the line up at the *Follies Bergère* to be very like that of the English music halls. In addition to the mix of sketches, serious and comic songs, and even circus acts, the French added a very non-British element. Spice and sex was the life of the French and a long line up of statuesque bare-breasted chorus girls was integral to each show.

Ray was one of fifty cast members, and a stage crew twice that size, not to mention the dozen dressers and makeup artists and hair dressers. Out front, there was an orchestra as large as some symphonies. The *Follies Bergère* was the most spectacular show he had ever accompanied.

He loved the fun of being involved in something so beautiful, but again he was just a tiny cog in the show machine. He was also bit homesick.

His little California hacienda was calling. The rumblings of war were on the horizon with Germany again threatening neighboring countries. Putting as much space as possible between himself and the horrible Huns seemed like the only choice.

Back home safely, Ray quickly set to work on a new project, the aptly titled *Don't Call Me Madam*. There is an interesting back story to the show's title. In 1933, Mae West was at the beginning of her remarkable film career. *She Done Him Wrong* (1933) had just opened with a box office that Hollywood had not seen in a long time. Paramount decided to rush their hot new star into another movie.

In typical Mae West fashion, none of the scripts offered met her standards. There was something called *Rings On Her Fingers, The Golden Soubrette,* and finally *Don't Call Me Madame.* This last title was something Mae had always liked, but not the story.

Mae often reminisced with Ray on the phone about the good old days on Broadway and Vaudeville and their pasts in the movie industry. When she told him of *Don't Call Me Madame* and how she liked the title, Ray agreed. He said he might use that title someday, and Mae, too, thought it a good idea. From that conversation sprang the idea for one of Ray's most successful ventures.

Don't Call Me Madam was an expanded one-man-show that was different than anything he had attempted. It was more for the stage than the cabaret, and far more elaborately structured than the typical nightclub acts he often performed.

With constant pressure on good friends in high places to open certain financial doors, *Don't Call Me Madam* opened at Carnegie Hall to a sold out crowd. It then toured the country, receiving full media coverage, although critics still couldn't resist being just a little condescending when reviewing anything this lavender.

From the Carnegie Hall performance, a reporter sniped:

> "Odd Fellows Meet. On Sunday night you could hardly claw your way through a mob of very spectacular characters who bought out Carnegie Recital Hall. They turned out, one and all, for the gayest recital of the season. They all came, The Tall Ones, the Short Ones, the Old Ones, the Little Ones. It was obvious, just from watching them, that the recital was to be something special.
>
> "Now what, you may ask, could happen in Carnegie Recital Hall? Was it to be a showing of lost Picassos? No, No. a forum on the atom bomb? Dearie me, no! A heart to heart talk with Dr. Kinsey? Don't be silly. It was a one-man recital by Rae Bourbon of Mae West's 'Diamond Lil' fame, and if

there were any doubt about the general artistic appeal the recital was titled 'Don't Call Me Madam.'

"Well, it sold out, with standees, and there has been nothing like it since the days of the great ballet premieres. Even Bourbon, who at one point wore a costume which made one think of Spivy riding sidesaddle, admonished the audience at intermission,

"Go out and gossip on the stairs. Don't go in the street. They watch this joint closely. Mr. Bourbon is booked for a series of these evenings."

16

I've Been Famous Wicked Women Before; I Can Be the Woman I've Always Wanted to Be

The winds of war were reaching the American shores. The country was gearing up for the conflict to come. Society was changing, as well. Audiences were interested in youth and a quick laugh, a style that reflected the changing face of America.

Mae West was well into her fifties, no longer able to fool the camera. Yet she insisted that she was as ageless and as desirable to men as ever. In her defense, she was far ahead of her time in insisting that a woman could be sexy at any age. Studios still offered her scripts, but these were stories that were not suitable for the institution Mae had created. A Mae West film was about Mae surrounded by adoring men, lots of men, but never just Mae and one man. No "happily ever after" for her. That would never be her style.

The months passed and Mae was becoming more of a legend, but a legend with no current image on America's movie screens. Several film offers arrived, but these were always in secondary or cameo roles, and none allowed Mae to pen her own dialogue, an absolute requisite in any Mae West performance.

One March afternoon in 1944, Mae had an appointment with a pair of up and coming filmmakers, who suggested they had a movie offer that she would definitely be interested. Two stocky and rather overdressed men were buzzed into Mae's penthouse. Mae's butler seated the pair in the formal front room. The carpet under their expensive Italian shoes was as plush as fur and as white as a Polar bear. Everywhere they looked were reminders of the mistress of this ornate love nest. An enormous portrait of the star, nude and rather amusingly featured with a monkey, dominated the room. The pale cream walls served as backdrop for the enormous white grand piano, covered with all sizes of photographs of Mae. French gilt antiques filled the rather small space. Everywhere were vases filled with artificial flowers, adding the only touches of color to this Arctic color scheme. They sat silently staring at the nude statues and paintings of Mae while the crafty star stalled for a fashionable fifteen minutes prior to making her entrance.

Finally, she appeared in the doorway and paused for a theatrical moment, letting them take in the image she had carefully crafted: a form-fitting long afternoon dress covered by a sheer open coat. Mae made an entrance worthy of any star.

Her guests got up simultaneously and introduced themselves as the King brothers, Morrie and Frank. The chunkier of the two, Frank, cigar clenched firmly between gold-filled teeth, spoke first.

He had an offer for Mae that he felt would definitely be a smart career move. The two visitors had an aura and style that Mae understood. These were tough guys, who were obviously self-made and definitely aware of their worth.

She had known men like them all her life. It was never the subtle man of manners and handsome features that interested her. A burly guy with a sense of self-assurance always caught her roaming eye.

She motioned to them to take a seat in one of several white silk Louis XIV gilt chairs scattered around her parlor.

Planting his muscular butt gingerly on the edge of the fragile-looking furniture, Frank King began, "I don't want to say things in a boosting way, but in my short life, whatever me and my brother have been in, we have both gone right to the top, just like you. You will learn when you talk to my brother he is one of the smartest mugs in Hollywood. To understand how smart he is, he brings me at least five magazine stories a week that will make good movies. You see, we make movies. We just bought one of these magazine stories for a measly 300 smackaroos. After we got it, we were offered $65,000 for it by another studio. Morrie is very artistic in finding good material, ya see. So far we've made seven pictures, and everyone made a profit. We've had such stars as John Carradine, Ricardo Cortez, Edmund Lowe, Victor Jory, Simone."

Mae knew all of these names, and had even worked with a few. She still didn't get the angle they were trying to pitch her. Frank, lighting another expensive Havana cigar, continued, "We do our projects on short money, unlike the big studios, who only waste time and dough. Maybe you remember *Paper Bullets*. This picture put the unknown Alan Ladd on the map. We keep expenses low and profits high. We rent a sound stage at Monogram Pictures. I know what you're gonna say, that is poverty row in picture lingo. We don't care. We rent space there and there are no charges until we actually begin filming. We make sure we use good sound men, engineers, technicians, and writers. Our hairdressers and makeup department are among the best."

Mae stopped him there to remind the brothers she always had the final say about hair, costumes, and contracts. She used her own people for her gowns and makeup and told them when she was Paramount's top box office draw that her exclusive contract included all her demands.

Morrie, the younger of the two, interjected, "We don't do long-term contracts with big names, and yours is certainly the biggest. It would be a one-off picture. After the first project my brother and I would decide if we wanted a repeat. It ain't necessary to squander [$1 million] to make a movie, wasting time and money when it can be done quickly. While we shoot one scene, we rehearse the actors for the next one right next door. Our overhead is almost nothing. We had problems at first getting good actors to come on board. We make B pictures, a bad word to some former stars or those on the way up."

Mae silently bristled at the suggestion she might be a "former star." As to whether "we would want a repeat," that was a blatant insult as far as she was concerned. She rose slowly in her most imperious manner and extended a jewel-encrusted hand. The interview was over for now. She would consider their offer and her agent would be in touch she told the slightly stunned pair as she rang for her man servant to let them out.

She investigated "the King," a.k.a. the Kozinsky, brothers, and their reputation through some of her contacts in the underworld. She discovered they had begun as slot machine distributors. They bankrolled this into the juke box racket, a notoriously shady business, and were soon millionaires. Besides movie making, they also owned a race horse stable.

All of this appealed to Mae's taste in men, self-made entrepreneurs with a slightly dangerous style. She owned race horses and was frequently seen on the arm of a natty escort at the track. What did not appeal to her was the attitude they took concerning her current status in Hollywood.

She decided to attend a matinee of one of their films to see just how good these bargain basement efforts looked. Tricked out in a short, black wig, sunglasses, and a church lady suit, Mae blended in with the rest of the bored housewives who frequented neighborhood movie houses during the day.

After the usual *Pathé* newsreel, two Daffy Duck cartoons, and a re-release of *Watch on the Rhine* (1943), the King brothers film played the second half of the bill. The boys were telling the truth. It was a B picture. This was a genre of movie that always played the second half of a double feature. A few of these could be first-rate in style.

What Mae saw that afternoon was not first-rate, nor was it up to her standards. The physical trappings, lighting, makeup, and script were nothing she would ever consider being a part. If she never made another film, she wouldn't consider a King brothers movie and risk tarnishing a reputation she had worked decades to achieve.

Unfortunately, years later at the end of her iconic career, she would be seduced into movies that would make the King brothers' efforts look like Academy Award winners in comparison, such as *Myra Breckenridge* (1970) and *Sextette* (1978). She never admitted to mistakes, but she would not get over the disaster that had marked the final film of her first Hollywood career in 1943, *The Heat's On*. She was deceived into appearing in this unworthy debacle by an actor from her past.

The Russian character actor, Gregory Ratoff, had appeared in a featured role in Mae's *I'm No Angel* (1933). They had maintained a friendship since first working together. Ratoff, now a producer, came bearing the tantalizing offer of a starring role in a film tentatively titled, *Tropicana*. This promised to be an oasis in the desert of Mae's stalled career.

Ratoff would produce and direct, and Mae would star, with her name above the title. Ratoff said he had the rights to a successful Broadway musical, and the story he wove ensnared usually wary Mae. Unfortunately, this Russian's tale was all cobwebs and moonlight.

The Mae of the old days would never have been seduced by a sales pitch without hard copy proof before her. There was no finished script, the persuasive Ratoff admitted; but, he had read the outline and knew instinctively it was perfect for Mae.

He returned again and again to Mae's gilded apartment, contract-in-hand. With no other offers to consider, she penned her signature with a diamond-laden hand.

Ratoff rushed Mae off to the studio, where he convinced her to film two very expensively-mounted musical numbers. Beautifully gowned, coiffed, and photographed, Mae was impressed, even though she still had not seen the actual story. She looked better and younger than she had in years, and with the promise of total script control, there were visions of a comeback dancing in her head.

Weeks later, the promised script arrived. To Mae's horror, it was so ordinary and unimaginative that she was tempted to chuck it in the trash. It also contained only 25-minutes of actual scenes with Mae. Just a few years earlier, this would have brought an automatic refusal from the self-absorbed star. Time had changed all that. There was also the question of money.

She knew that Ratoff had already invested a lot of his own money in the sets and music for the picture, and had only been able to secure further bank loans because Mae was the promised collateral. When she expressed serious doubts about the whole idea, Ratoff promised she could write her own material. Mae mistakenly imagined that that alone could salvage the project.

Mae states in her biography that she "tried to get a release from my contract . . . against my better judgment, I made the picture . . . I did manage to write the only good scenes for myself that I had in the picture . . . but there wasn't enough time to make it into a good picture."

The film was released, but *The New York Times* felt "the heat is definitely off." The same paper didn't lay the entire blame at Mae's door. Mae's 25-minute contribution to a film that ran for over 80-minutes was not enough to save the day.

She vowed never to film again unless she had total control of her part. Little did she realize that it would be more than twenty-five years before she again appeared on the silver screen.

The theatre and her plays had been good to her, and so she returned to her typewriter. The finishing touches were added to her play, *Catherine The Great*. The revised version was destined for the legitimate stage, a medium that Mae knew inside-out.

The Schubert Brothers were producers who had been a big part of Mae's Broadway past. A long distance call to their New York offices produced an immediate response. They were sending a dynamic new producer to work with Mae on her beloved *Catherine The Great*.

Mae had worked with producers, good, bad, and indifferent. Nothing prepared her for the personality of the young genius the Schubert Brothers dispatched. Mike Todd was a short, swarthy, cigar chomping dynamo. In later years, he would be one of Elizabeth Taylor's many husbands.

Todd came on like the most important man in show business, and knew just how to push Mae's buttons. He flattered her, kissed her hand, and was not the least bit shy about making it apparent that he knew just how to please the ladies. Mae was fascinated, but not interested in sampling his charms, and wasted no time in setting Todd straight. "Strictly business," was her last word.

Todd's first suggestion was to make the title a little more comedic. *Catherine the Great* became *Catherine Was Great*. He wanted the play to be a satire of the Empress, played in Mae's broad comedic style. This is how he knew Mae from all her past incarnations on screen. He never guessed she thought of herself as a serious actress who would offer an evening of the historic Catherine.

Mae was going to play it relatively straight as if she was channeling the spirit of the monarch. She felt that she, too, had been a statesman, surviving the conflicting politics and schemes of the movie studios, just as Catherine had navigated the troubled waters of the Russian Royal Court. Reincarnation had long been a fascination for Mae. Some said she believed she was the reincarnation of Catherine.

The Schubert organization initially invested $150,000 on the costumes and sets for the play, a very large amount for the time. Mae's contract allowed her to select the important players. A young Gene Barry, who went on to movie and theatre fame, was cast as the handsome Lieutenant Bunin. (Barry would receive a Tony nomination for his role in the original, *Le Cage Aux Folles* (1978), forty-three years later.)

Mae told Todd she had written a special part with a certain someone in mind. She could not imagine anyone other than Ray playing the part of her French dressmaker, Florian. She had her agent contact him just as he was returning from Paris.

Ray almost missed this golden opportunity by making a detour to Cuba. A good friend had just opened a club in Havana and offered a lucrative, month-long engagement as part of the grand opening, but the atmosphere of drugs, violence, and mob influence thoroughly frightened him. He returned after only a short run in Havana to California.

Waiting for Ray in his tiny entry hall was a mound of mail. Among the past-due bills and a couple of offers from his agent was a contract from Mike Todd Productions offering him a co-starring role in *Catherine Was Great*.

Ray wasted no time re-packing. With the country heavily involved in World War II, civilian transportation was tough. Most of the available seats went to the military. Flying was expensive and limited. Even squeezing onto a train required dogged persistence. After a week in transit, with several days wasted on layovers, Ray arrived while the play was already in rehearsal.

Mae's opus was already being booked without all the parts completely cast. There was a constant tug-of-war between Mae and Michel Todd. He wanted everything bigger than life and played for maximum laughs. Mae had her own ideas. She wasn't hesitant to throw them back at Todd when he criticized her approach.

Catherine was Mae's favorite subject of all the plays she had written. Mae respected Catherine immensely and felt a common bond with this powerful autocrat. The fact that Catherine was also a notorious man eater only increased the fascination of the like-minded Mae.

Mae insisted on inspecting every single male who was to be cast, regardless of the importance of the role. They all had to be tall, broad shouldered, reasonably handsome, and obviously masculine.

The two exceptions were Catherine's dress maker, Florian, and his assistant. Ray was tailor-made for the role of the swishy couturier. The assistant was harder to find. Mae didn't want two identical types of queens. She finally settled on a newcomer named Dick Ellis, as effeminate as Ray, but lacking his sense of comedy and stage élan.

Eventually, the role of the assistant was cut from the show. During a dress rehearsal, Ellis tripped over a foot stool and crashed into Mae. Already a little unsteady in her 75-pound costume and towering tiara, Catherine the Great toppled backwards and landed on her well-padded royal butt. Ray rushed to help Mae to her feet. Straightening her headpiece and smoothing her dignity, she extricated herself from her heavy train. She turned in the direction of the cowering Ellis, "Don't make the same mistake twice, unless it pays. Unfortunately for you, it doesn't. You're fired!" Dick Ellis, who started out life as "Richard Selzer," then as a juvenile actor was known as either "Richard Selzer," "Dick Selzer," or "Dick Ellis," would later become a famous fashion designer and an even more infamous fashion critic. He eventually assumed the name Mr. Blackwell, creator of the dreaded, "Worst Dressed List." He placed Mae at the top of the list in 1970.

The War had a strange effect on the country's economy. Those that did not go off to fight had more disposable income to spend. Everyone that was not drafted was somehow involved in the war effort. Workers pulled double shifts in factories and took home large paychecks.

Movies thrived as did live entertainment. Broadway was no exception. Todd was not only onboard with *Catherine Was Great*, but he was involved with two other major productions that year. Box offices reported record ticket sales and most shows sold out. In this climate of plenty, Mae knew she had a hit despite the critics who warned she was over the hill.

Never one to be told what to do and how to do it, Mae presented her Catherine as she imagined her. She had jumbled up the historic time sequence of the play, but she was clear on how the audience should see this important Russian empress. She wanted to emphasize the power and strength of this ruler in a land that had always required an iron fist, but this time, it was a woman's fist.

When Todd dared to disagree with her too literal portrayal of the Empress, Mae shot back, "I'm the regal type—that not a posture you learn in school, dearie. It's the way you look at the world."

There were brief moments of levity scattered throughout the play, but Catherine's historical importance was first and foremost to Mae.

When the play had run just over a week, Mae began to admit that it wasn't quite the reception she had hoped. Fans loved seeing her live and put their hands together to prove it each night at her entrance. She had expected a little more fervor during the remaining scenes.

Todd knew this was the perfect moment to step in and revive the spirit of the Mae West he knew from movies. A terrific battle of wills ensued. Todd was a bulldog of a fighter and never backed down. Finally, Mae decided to try it his way.

The revision in the tone of the play produced an entirely different reception. Catherine now strutted and stalked the stage, tossing off her lines in that insinuating voice while manipulating the billows of her 75-pound jewel-encrusted cape. Her delivery now sounded as if it had come straight from a house of Burlesque. This was the Mae the world knew and loved.

What audiences failed to notice was that every scene was structured almost the same way. In each act, Mae had a prospective officer ushered into the throne room, questioned him in her most provocative manner, her knowing gaze looking him up and down. Finally, those effervescent eyes stopped and lingered on his crotch.

Mae made sure that all the soldiers' costumes showed a nice bulge, and if the occupant of the pants didn't have the stuff, she saw that the costume designer added it. Every male on stage, except Ray's character, was broad-shouldered, big in the box, and very athletic.

Only a few of the critics found serious fault with Mae's good-humored take on the Russian empress. Columnist Ed Sullivan wrote:

"If you doubt the box office appeal of Mae West, ponder that she converted *Catherine Was Great* into a hit. I know no other star strong enough with an audience to have accomplished this!"

After every performance, Mae acknowledged the enthusiastic applause with her signature smile and a set curtain speech: "I'm glad you liked my Catherine. I liked her, too. She ruled 30 million people and had 300 lovers. I do the best I can in three hours. Fourteen was all I could manage to squeeze into the three acts of the play."

Ray had the time of his theatrical life. He had never experienced such a rush. At last, he had arrived in a major production alongside a friend who was also an icon. His Florian was quick, comic, and oh-so-queer. He delighted in his elaborate costumes, a brocaded blue jacket, satin breeches, white silk hose, and patent dress shoes with two inch heels and grosgrain bows. His fluffy white powdered wig with the bow tied tail completed the elegant look of a Russian courtier.

Ray instinctively folded all those years of stage work and experience into this soufflé of a role and he drew delicious laughs as a reward. His timing was flawless and his lines were word perfect.

Even his famous cackle came into play by accident one night. Though it had become part of his delivery in all his nightclub work, he was careful never to use it as it was not indicated anywhere in the script. He was sure Mae would be furious over this unintentional adlib. "Leave it in," she said with a wink, as they took their curtain calls.

Mae was an absolute stickler for perfection for herself and those around her. She rewarded Ray for his excellent work with an invitation to tour with the show when it finished on Broadway. Several of the other cast members did not get the same invitation, having somehow annoyed the demanding Mae West during the New York run.

During the run of the play, Ray declared bankruptcy. The following article appeared in *Billboard*, November 18, 1944:

"Ray Bourbon Goes 'Clean-Up' Route
"A voluntary petition of bankruptcy was filed Wednesday (8) in Federal Court by Ray Bourbon, actor, currently

of the cast of Catherine Was Great. Petition stated that Bourbon has been with the show for five months and gives his address as Hotel Lincoln. Liabilities are listed at $62,904, which figure includes a $50,000 damage action pending in California for personal injuries in 1939. Twenty-two unsecured creditors are named in the petition, which include debts for advertising, commissions and publicity services. His assets amount to approximately $350, which will be entirely dissipated by payments for clothing. Also listed is a harp, valued at $495 but which is rented from the Sherman Clay Company, of California, at $7.50 a month. Bourbon stated that he was known also under the names of Richard F. Mann and Hal Waddell. He listed his earnings in 1942 at $2,510 and for 1943 at $5,465."

Catherine Was Great did a booming business for almost 200 nights, with matinees added as ticket demand increased. The producers and the star then decided to take a slightly scaled down version on a nationwide tour.

Ray was touring again, this time in a sure-fire hit with an important part. It was grueling, but troupers like Mae and Ray had cut their baby teeth on this sort of schedule. Baltimore, St. Louis, Cleveland, Chicago, Des Moines, Memphis, Wichita, and many other cities turned out to cheer the legendary Mae West. They sold out nearly every night.

Along the way, Ray had the chance to visit many of the clubs he had played in the past, contacting old friends and establishing new contacts for future engagements.

Catherine Was Great was a success despite the fact that very few critics found the play worthwhile. Many were puzzled by the enthusiastic audiences. What they didn't seem to realize was that Mae West was now a beloved American institution, part of the National conscience. Mae knew that touring *Catherine Was Great* was a given. The audiences she played to in smaller cities could have cared less for the standards by which the elite New York reviewers, and, in fact, almost any critic, judged a play.

A typical review touted Mae's talent, but trashed her material:

"Any talented actress can take a good play ... a supporting cast and staging to match, and make a success of it. But the star is rare who, equipped with a script that would flunk a student out of a freshman course in dramaturgy, can make a hit by virtue of her own magnetic personality. Mae West has shown that she has the hips to swing this unusual feat by opening on Broadway in a play of her own conception, Catherine Was Great, and doing a turn away business despite as fancy a panning in the press as any recent production has received. Audiences thronged the theatre, gave Miss West show stopping ovations at her regal entrance scene, and called her back for curtain after curtain."

The drama critic from *Time* magazine had other ideas:

"Catherine Was Great is an opulent and incredible fancy un-dress affair in which the queen of all the sirens essays the Empress of All the Russians. 'Catherine" said Mae West in a first night curtain speech, 'had 300 lovers. I did the best I could in two hours.' For a while, her best was reasonably good; she seemed to make Lords of the Bedchamber of the whole Russian court and boudoir-warriors of half the Russian army. As she followed her hips about the stage in a solemn slink, as she languidly drew shameless innuendos from her husky throat, actress West caught some of the aplomb, humor, and matchless vulgarity of her 'Come up and see me some time,' but pretty soon her unvaried role began to pall and so, soon after, did her unvarying way of playing it.

"Worse yet, the man-eater Catherine was not enough actress West. She insisted on encompassing the Empress as well, and far from spoofing the imperial manner, tried to outdo it. When a courtier reminded her that 'They also serve who only stand and wait', she replied, 'prone, I presume'. She had sponged up enough history to soak her play with wars, uprisings and palace intrigues. But the excitement was conveyed in dialogue that had the specific gravity of lead, and the results, when not merely sedative, were often crushing."

Undaunted by the critics and encouraged at every performance by her enthusiastic audiences, Mae told a reporter:

"Virtue has its own reward, but has no sale at the box office. I tried to write as many legitimate laughs as possible, while sticking close to the spirit of Catherine. I didn't want too much comedy, for it lowers the tone of the play. The public has come to expect a certain characterization from me, and anyway Catherine is a lot like the character I have been playing for a long time. I've been famous wicked women before, including Cleopatra and that Borgia woman. I did them when I starred in Shubert Revues years ago."

When the national tour of *Catherine Was Great* ended, Ray was sorry to leave, but this time he was not at loose ends. Several significant contacts had been made along the road. The most important was an offer to play the legendary Finnochio's, located at 506 Broadway in San Francisco. This was one of the first nightclubs in the world dedicated to presenting only female impersonators.

Named after the owner, Joseph Finnochio, the club opened its doors in 1936. Vaudeville was breathing its last and there were very few options for drag performers. Joseph's father owned a speakeasy in San Francisco. It was nothing fancy, but on weekends offered an open stage, where anyone with nerve and a couple of belts of bathtub gin could try out their talents.

One night, Joseph saw an uproarious performance by an impersonator, who was a dead ringer for the "Last of the Red Hot Mamas," Sophie Tucker. Talking to the talented Tucker clone after the show, Joseph learned that finding work was becoming increasingly difficult for the local drag queens.

That evening, the concept of Finnochio's was born. A great deal of money was poured into the physical aspects of the venue.

Unlike so many clubs, where drags played from tiny stages to smoky, noisy crowds, Finnochio's was world-class; it was a true cabaret. The seating was all tabled, elevating gradually to the rear of the club. Soft lighting and tasteful fixtures completed the picture of sophistication. The audience was made up primarily of straight tourists with a sprinkling of gays. Prices were commensurate with any entertainment on this level in San Francisco.

Ray arrived a week prior to his engagement, an open-ended contract in hand. He could work as long as the management was happy with his performances and his ability to draw an audience. Unlike the limited scope of so many of the impersonators whom Ray knew in the business, his long background on the stage gave him a large variety of characters and numbers from which to choose.

On the first day of rehearsal, he was surprised to see his old friend, Lucien Phelps. This was the same impersonator who had inspired Joseph Finnochio to create this unique theatre. Phelps, now known as "The Male Sophie Tucker," was still doing his famous impersonation of the rough and raunchy song belter. Both Tucker and Phelps were Junoesque figures, ample in all the right and wrong places. Phelps was always beautifully costumed in expensive white furs, gorgeous long gowns, enormous jewels, and elegant white Egret feathers in his towering wigs. Many of the accoutrement had been purchased from the legendary singer he was impersonating.

Unlike the real Sophie Tucker, who had a voice like an over the road trucker, Phelps had an almost operatic vocal range, reaching the dizzying heights of an E above high C, something many opera divas would envy. Joseph Finnochio was mad for anything operatic, particularly Italian, and begged Phelps to include something along this line in his act. Knowing that the real Tucker would never attempt anything remotely like an aria, Phelps stuck to the ribald songs the audiences knew and loved.

Opening night, Ray introduced a new number he had been working on for several weeks. It was an old song done in a jazzy 1920s flapper style. As "Rae," he wore a dropped waist dress, beaded in silver, with a short skirt of sparkling fringe. Long white evening gloves, accented with an armload of glittering bracelets and a ten-foot-long black ostrich boa, completed the ensemble. His wig was a copy of a heavily-waved Mae West coiffure, with a diamond-encrusted head band.

The tinny band played the introduction, and Rae came on in a swirl of feathers, kicking in rhythm to the syncopated tune:

> "Hey, hey, women are going mad today
> Hey, hey, fellows are just as bad today
> Go anywhere, just stand and stare
> You'll say they're fops when you look at the clothes they wear
> Masculine women, feminine men
> Which is the rooster, which is the hen?
> It's hard to tell them apart today, I say
> Sister's busy learning to shave
> Brother is loving his permanent wave
> It's hard to tell 'em apart today, hey, hey
> Girls were girls and boys were boys, when I was a tot
> Now we don't know who is who, or even what's what
> Knickers and trousers, baggy and wide
> Nobody knows who's walking inside
> Those masculine women and feminine men
> You say hello, to your Uncle Joe
> Then look again, and you'll find it's your Auntie Flo
> Those masculine women and feminine men
> You go in to give your girl a kiss in the hall
> But instead you find you're kissing her brother Paul
> Ma's got a man's suit up to her chin
> Pa's got a girdle holding him in
> Those masculine women and feminine men
> Since the Prince of Wales in ladies dresses was seen
> What does he intend to be, the King or the Queen
> Those masculine women and feminine men!"

Delighted with the reception that audiences gave Ray, Finnochio's extended his run for several months. He played strongly to the fact that he had just come off a very successful Broadway show with the legendary Mae West. Mae hade even graciously allowed him to use the only song from *Catherine Was Great*, "Strong, Solid, and Sensational."

For this number, Ray did a full-out imitation of Mae as he had seen her during the run of the play. To add an extra touch, he made sure one of the waiters would pretend to heckle him from the audience. Ray, in an effort to replicate the Westian silhouette, made his figure even more abundant in the bosom by adding extra padding. He wore a floor length, heavily beaded black gown. An enormous white feather boa trailed behind him as he made his entrance.

"Hello boys, how ya doin'?
My, the joints lousy with sailors tonight."

From the heckler:
'I never saw you before little sister.'

Rae as Mae shoots back:

'I never saw you before either big brother.'

And again from the audience:
'You work around here?'

Hand on hip, Rae, as Mae, drones in that nasal Brooklyn accent:

'Yes, I'm workin' it with a double beat. Why don't you come over some time?'

The response comes:
'What kind of a man do you like?'

Swiveling in the direction of the band, Rae, as Mae croons:
'Leader man, tell him.'

To a honky tonk beat Rae, as Mae, begins:
'His lips curled in an ironic smile,
the years of Burlesque, Vaudeville,

and seedy clubs written across his face.
He must be strong, solid, and sensational,
And be able to fill my samovar with tea.
But let me tell you brother,
If you're going to be the kind of lover,
Who leaves me wanting another,
No, you're not for me. Oh no, you're not for me.
Now when a butcher slices my meat,
And he cuts too far from the bone.
I'm not the one to say butcher,
Put your knife to the hone.
But when it comes to slicin' meat,
Of that I'm not too sure.
But when it comes to love, I'm a connoisseur.
He must be strong, solid, and sensational,
He must be able to keep in time with the music's beat.
Now he can be a peasant from the old Ukraine,
Don't have to make love with your brain.
But if I notice the slightest strain,
No, you're not for me. Oh no, you're not for me.
Now when a baker kneads his dough too loose,
And his pastry falls apart.
I'm not the one to say, baker, you make a lousy tart.
For when it comes to makin' tarts,
it's there my knowledge is low.
But when it comes to makin' love,
that I undoubtedly know.
He must be strong, solid, and sensational,
Not to mention a dash of hot virility.
Now if you're a handsome man to whom I'll give a title.
I'll do for you what Catherine did for Peter the Third.
But if you mention a single word,
No, you're not for me, No you're not for me.
He must be strong, solid, and sensational!'"

Just as Ray came offstage to sustained applause, he noticed all the queens buzzing in the wings. A waiter stood surrounded by the excited group. Through the curtains, he pointed out a glamorous celebrity just being seated at a front row table. The legendary Tallulah Bankhead was in the audience. The petite star wore a simple black jacket and pants topped by an eight foot sable stole thrown dramatically across her shoulders.

The initial flurry of recognition among the cast was followed by a sudden panic. The next number to go on consisted of a routine that included a scathing satire of the husky-voiced actress sitting front and center, an actress who had a well-deserved reputation for hard drinking, and indiscriminate sex with both genders, coupled with a total lack of inhibition. Bankhead attracted, repelled, fascinated, and shocked almost everyone who ever saw her. Either despite or because of this, she had a legion of fans and admirers. The impersonator played heavily on her deliciously scandalizing traits and was now faced with this formidable subject of his cutting-edge humor staring back at him from the audience.

Backstage, the Bankhead imitator was in a panic, pacing up and down and chain smoking. Fortified with a straight gin double and physically propelled into the spotlight, he managed to go on.

The high point of the Bankhead imitation came when she told the story of the first time she worked with Marlon Brando in a play, *The Eagle Has Two Heads* (1947). Because of Brando's unprofessionalism, the actress said the play should have been called *The Eagle Lays an Egg*. She described one scene where she had a monologue that lasted nearly twenty minutes. Brando was notorious for his inability to stand still. All during Bankhead's important speech, he grabbed at his crotch, picked his nose, cleared his throat, flirted with the audience, and ignored her while he leered at a handsome offstage actor.

By the end of the mimic's number, the real Bankhead was chortling in her distinctive baritone voice and wildly applauding with the rest of the audience.

There were bravos all around, as the cast crowded into the noisy smoke-filled dressing room after the last act. The rumpus was interrupted as the door flew open and there stood Bankhead, hardcore chic in basic black, clutching her sables. In her best throaty growl, she cried out, "Daaahlings!"

She was immediately surrounded by the entire cast in a great group hug, completely encircled by a mass of padded bras, lacquered wigs, and the smell of masculine sweat.

She froze. The petite star had a notorious aversion to being touched, but this time she didn't let on. She insisted the entire troupe join her at her hotel suite for a party. Turning to Ray, she singled him out with praise for his imitation of Mae West.

When the Finnochio cast arrived at Bankhead's posh digs they found a lavish spread of canapés and a fully stocked bar. Ray thought he had seen major drinkers in his life, but Bankhead topped them all, man or woman. In addition to the booze, the dramatic star was also sniffing something up her nose, a pastime Ray never approved of even in his wildest moments.

As the night wore on, everyone sat on the floor, a captive audience for the dissolute but always dramatic actress. She told one hilarious story after another. Ray later learned she suffered from insomnia and often held all-night soirees, regaling her guests with witticisms and tales from her lengthy and scandalous career.

She told of her sudden departure from London where she had been a famous but controversial stage star. She darkly hinted that the British authorities were behind her departure. It seems they didn't approve of her cocaine habit, or her habit of suddenly appearing at her own parties completely nude.

"Not addictive at all, daaahling! Why, it's been my steady companion for years! And as for my penchant for disrobing at my own parties, it's my house, but I keep it simple and quick because I loathe underpants!"

She continued to talk in an erratic fashion, constantly changing subjects. From her ongoing flood of gab, Ray learned they had several things in common. She had begun her film career at the age of sixteen in several silent movies, including *Thirty a Week* (1918), produced at a studio in Astoria, Long Island, where he too had many years earlier. When she finally made it to Hollywood, she had rented his good friend, William Haine's, house after the blacklisted star's career had taken a nose dive.

From Hollywood, her narrative ricocheted to Broadway, where she had a series of stage disasters, including Shakespeare's *Antony and Cleopatra* (1937). She seemed to take great pleasure in quoting a particularly scathing review in her inimitable cloudy croak. "Last night Miss Bankhead barged down the Nile and sank!"

When Ray mentioned he had worked with Mae West on Broadway, Bankhead took up the thread. "But, daaahling, I know that old broad. We both worked Las Vegas. Mae was bumping and grinding with her naked muscle boys. Most of them were queer as $2 bills. I was starring in *Ziegfeld Follies* next door. I, too, was surrounded by queer chorus boys, but they had their clothes on. Can you believe it? I sang and danced, with this voice!"

Everyone laughed, as the actress paused for a breath, and then suddenly said she was hungry. The silver platters that had been laden with hors d'oeuvres had been licked clean. Bankhead picked up the phone, and, within minutes, a waiter appeared with a cart overflowing with refills. She nonchalantly pulled out a $100 bill from her brassiere and stuffed it down the front of the startled server's trousers. Greedily munching on the rich offerings, she continued her tale of Las Vegas between noisy mouthfuls.

"Can you imagine, my chauffer pulls up in front of the theatre and I see my name is not at the top of the bill, so I go storming down the aisle of the theatre screaming at the director, Jack Entratter. How dare you, darling! This simply will not do! My name *always* comes at the top of any bill. It must read 'Tallulah Bankhead starring in the Jack Entratter Production of *Ziegfeld Follies!*' I personally went outside to help hold the ladder while the maintenance boys climbed up to give Tallulah top billing."

The conversations became more animated, as everyone drank and Bankhead continued to snort. Thoroughly engrossed in a story Ray was telling about his music hall days, she suddenly stood up. "I've got to take a little pee. Do not finish that story until I have answered nature's call, daaahlings!"

With that, she turned around and headed down the hall to the bathroom, walking backwards all the way and still talking, reminding everyone to wait until she returned. To make sure she wasn't left out, she dropped her ensemble to her ankles, sat on the throne with the door wide open, and continued a non-stop dialogue with the startled guests who watched in disbelief. She couldn't help but notice the looks of incredulity. "And I suppose you think Greta Garbo pisses champagne!"

What everyone loved about their hostess was her brilliant and edgy delivery of the simplest line. She could match double entendres with the best, including Ray, who modestly attributed his ability to turn-a-phrase to the many years he had worked with Mae West.

Bankhead asked Ray if he had heard any of Mae's recordings. It seemed everyone in the room had, and they loved them. Apparently, this brought out the competitor in Bankhead. She leapt-up and crossed the room to the big blonde Crosley® record player, popping on one of her own long-playing vinyl discs. She told the party she had just signed with Columbia Records to do a series of comedy recordings.

Everyone laughed politely as the turntable spun and applauded at the end of the recording. The material was mildly amusing, but everyone told her it didn't compare to the real Tallulah Bankhead in person. She explained that a label like Columbia simply wouldn't allow her to record anything really off-color.

Lucien Phelps turned to Ray, suggesting he favor everyone with one of the routines he had recorded for U.T.C.

"U.T.C." croaked Bankhead, "What the hell is that, Mary?"

Ray replied that it stood for "Under the Counter," explaining that his material was considered too hot and a little too lavender to be sold over the counter. His records were kept out of sight under the counter until a customer requested a title.

He protested he couldn't perform unless someone would accompany him. Spotting the rather battered baby grand in the corner of the suite, Phelps curtsied and went to the piano. He had heard Ray's recordings and seen his act many times.

"What's it gonna be?" he asked.

"When I Said 'No' to Joe," Ray replied, referring to the half-sung, half-spoken monologue that was a staple in his repertoire.

Ray grabbed the luxurious white fox furs that Phelps had carelessly thrown on his chair and draped them across his own shoulders.

Since Phelps didn't have the actual sheet music for the number, he tinkled the ivories in the generic manner of many cocktail lounge pianists, taking his rhythmic cue from Ray's snapping fingers.

Borrowing the long, black cigarette holder from Bankhead's ashtray, Ray as "Rae" struck an exaggerated pose and began:

"Now I've turned down fortunes
And I've done it with a smile
I've unsigned movie contracts
I've dumped within my file
I've nixed plenty of offers
For those cruises across the sea
And delicious propositions coyly made to me
These treats were never tough to shun
My dear I know just what to forego
But the hardest thing I've ever done
Was when I said no to Joe
Now Joe was very hung and handsome
The answer to a maiden's prayer
My friends all thought me quite insane
When I gave Joe the air
I'd always planned that we would marry
But those plans got quite a blow
When I caught him using my mascara
That's when I said no to Joe
He he, ha ha!
Oh, I've turned down posh apartments
A Rolls, chauffer and maid
Ermine wraps, Schaparelli gowns
Those gifts I can evade
I've spurned big rocks and other things
The very things you bitches wish
I've shook my head with calm disdain
Declined those trinkets with a swish
I had my heart all set for a sweet old fashioned beau
So the hardest thing I've ever done is just say no to Joe
Oh Joe was every drag's ideal
Those pecs, that bulge, that buff behind
He had his share of sex appeal, but not for the right kind
My dates with him became a fixture

> My girlfriends knew he was my beau
> But when I caught him kissing Clark Gable's picture
> That's when I said, oh no, not you too Joe
> And I meant it girls!"

There were bravos as Ray returned to the little hassock next to Tallulah.

Their conversation turned to movies. Ray recounted his early years in silent films in Long Island and later working for Paramount. She was fascinated with his stories of Valentino and Swanson.

When he mentioned William Haines, she broke into fits of laughter. She had rented Haines beautiful home when she worked in Hollywood, including all the very expensive furnishings and accessories, but found the bill for damages to be phenomenal.

Sensing his befuddlement, Bankhead explained that whenever she gave large parties she removed Haines priceless antique glassware from the bar shelves and smashed them—Russian fashion—in the fireplace. She enjoyed the noise and the shocked looks of her guests. What she remembered most was what she overheard Greta Garbo say to a guest during one of these wild evenings. "That's a girl to keep away from," mimicked Bankhead, in a dead ringer for Garbo's husky voice.

The party continued well into the morning until Bankhead finally fell asleep, mouth agape, still sprawled cock-legged on the chaise.

The guests, wigs askew, and mascara running from hours of laughing until they cried, tiptoed out of the hotel into the damp and silent San Francisco dawn.

At fifty-eight years of age, Mae was reconfirming her reputation as an ageless and tireless trouper by taking to the road again in another of her self-written plays, *Come On Up* (1946). She was as vigorous as ever, but the material was not. Critics found her as entertaining, but called the play "pure corn." Again, she was the center of attention, with a motley assortment of males on stage for the sole purpose of adoring her. It was all a little too familiar.

A year later, she took, *Diamond Lil* (1928; resurrected in 1947) out of mothballs and set sail for England. The British only knew Mae from her many films, and were a little surprised that she was actually petite and not nearly as raucous as she appeared to be on screen. They press quickly developed a genuine affection for her, and she was feted on several occasions by Lords and Ladies and other Royal members, anxious to get a close-up of this unique sex symbol. Once they spent an evening with this at times shy and alternately hilariously outspoken actress, they were captivated. Mae tried to explain herself to her hosts.

"My basic style has never changed. I couldn't change it if I wanted to. I am a captive of myself. It, or I, created a Mae West, and neither of us could let the other go, or would want to."

One of the most unusual evenings Mae experienced while touring England was at a party hosted by the eccentric Sitwells, a British family of ancient lineage. Their 600-year history had produced a long line of unique and colorful characters. The present tribe included the siblings, Osbert, Sacheverell, and the Egret-like Edith Sitwell. The family home, Renishaw Hall, was one of the oldest residences in England. Set in an enormous estate of lakes, gardens, and parks, the main house is an endless ramble of rooms from several centuries. The family prided itself on their unconventional nature, and entertained very much in that vein.

The evening's party was presided over by the Baronet, an intellectual and charming man. Mae was introduced around to the Sitwell's guests, most of whom meant nothing to her. Suddenly a vision, in what appeared to be a gray shroud, appeared grandly at the door to the ballroom. Edith Sitwell stood a good six feet tall, reed thin, with a face like a predatory bird. She crossed the room in great loping strides, propelled by large feet shod in what appeared to be men's loafers. She made directly for Mae, towering over her like a curious ostrich looking at a plump-breasted little pigeon.

Mae suddenly recalled seeing Sitwell's photograph in the Hollywood papers when Sitwell was touring the United States promoting her books and poetry. There had been some sort of a scandal, but Mae couldn't recall exactly what. Feeling slightly uncomfortable and at a loss for words, she gazed up at the strange arrangement of gray fur bands wrapped around Sitwell's long bony head. During an awkward lull in the conversation, she inquired, "Is that your hair, or are you wearing a hat."

Those who knew her well were expecting a sharp retort from the bizarre poetess. Instead, they were amazed to see the towering figure wrap a long arm around the well-stuffed figure of the screen star, ushering her gently around the great hall, introducing her to the literati and titled members of the Sitwell circle.

Sitwell whispered little bits of information in Mae's ear prior to presenting her to certain guests. When they approached the Duchess of Kent, she suggested that Mae execute a little curtsy. When the moment of introduction arrived, rather than bending at the knee, Mae stuck out her own bejeweled hand to be acknowledged. She was, after all, Hollywood royalty.

Over the course of the evening, Mae began to relax, enjoying the wisdom, obvious independence, sparkling wit, and satirical gifts of her hostess. A more unlikely duo could not be imagined.

Returning from the Derbyshire home of the Sitwells, Mae made a stop in London at the world-famous Wax Museum of Madame Tussaud to have her likeness immortalized in wax. After a long sitting at Tussaud's, Mae boarded a Pan American Stratocruiser for an overnight flight to the United States. A revival of that old chestnut, *Diamond Lil,* awaited her.

The giant aircraft touched down at La Guardia Airport. As the plane shuddered to a halt at the gate, Mae was the first to appear at the top of the landing stairs, looking fit and refreshed. She had spent the night in one of the luxurious first-class sleeping compartments made available by PanAm to well-heeled passengers. At the foot of the staircase was a contingency sent to personally escort the star, enabling her to side step the long lines of immigration and quickly escort her to the customs inspector.

Like most inspectors, this one seemed detached and very matter-of-fact. He quickly eyed every piece of Mae's extensive luggage, passing them off with a shrug. He paused when he saw the alligator case Mae was clutching to her ample bosom. His attitude suddenly changed when he inquired what it was. Mae replied it was her beauty case and she had, "Nothing to declare!"

The agent insisted she place the case on the counter and open it. Mae stalled, fumbling in the pockets of her fur jacket as she searched for the luggage keys.

Growing increasingly impatient, the agent called over another inspector. When Mae realized she had met her match, she produced the right key. There was an audible gasp when those around her saw the contents.

The shiny brown case was overflowing with jewels: rings, bracelets, necklaces of every length, brooches, all glowing from the bright overhead lights. It was a veritable salad of diamonds, interspersed with a smattering of rubies, emeralds, and other colored stones. This was mixed in with tubes of makeup, a leaky powder box, and several sets of Mae's false lashes.

Suddenly realizing who he was inspecting, the agent thanked Mae with a great show of graciousness and indicated the inspection was over. She was free to go.

Ray was appearing in a club in Los Angeles, when he received a call from Mae. She needed him to come to New York to join the cast of *Diamond Lil*. He was to play another comedic role, this time in drag, as Bowery Rose. He quickly cancelled several upcoming engagements and headed for Broadway.

This time, the reviews were good, the audiences terrific, and Mae and Ray were doing what they knew best, keeping them laughing.

Ray's character, Bowery Rose, was a bedraggled charwoman that frequented a seedy saloon in New York's infamous Bowery section. (He would borrow the character of Rose in years to come for his night club act.)

On the opening night of *Diamond Lil*, the police were required to handle the large unruly crowds outside the theatre.

The play enjoyed a successful revival at the Plymouth Theatre. An excellent review of Ray's performance and career appeared after opening night:

> "Mr. Bourbon is as popular in the chic boites throughout the country as he is on the stage. He has combined stage, screen, radio television and records into a one-man parlay that has paid off and established him as a first-rate all-around entertainer. He last appeared with Miss West in her New York production of "Catherine Was Great," in which he played an important role and won personal ac-

claim from press and public alike. His amusing records are "collectors' items" and in one of New York's leading record shops he ranks with such popular recording stars as Beatrice Lillie. Wherever Mr. Bourbon appears, whether it be stage, screen, radio, TV or night clubs, he is sure to be followed by the leading stars of the entertainment world."

Mae received the best reviews of her career for this revival. *The New York Times* esteemed Brook Atkins outdid himself:

"Gallantly supported by four handsome muscular leading men, Mae West has brought Diamond Lil back to New York, where it began its renowned career 21-years-ago. She wriggled through it, attired in some of the gaudiest finery of the century, the femme fatale of the Bowery, bowling her leading men over one by one with her classical Burlesque of a story book strumpet.

"But she is a fabulous performer and her saloon singer is an incredible creation-a triumph of nostalgic vulgarity. She is always in motion, the snaky walk, the torso wiggle, the stealthy eyes, the frozen smile, the flat condescending voice . . . even in the clinches she is monumentally disinterested and she concludes her love scenes with a devastating wisecrack . . . Miss West is the goddess of sex, but she scrupulously keeps sex out of her acting by invariably withdrawing from anything but the briefest encounters."

During the run of *Diamond Lil,* Ray got to see a side of Mae that he hadn't encountered. Though reportedly very wealthy, Mae could be a penny pincher.

After a Sunday matinee performance, the cast was relaxing backstage. Ray was standing in the hall outside of Mae's dressing room, trying to chat up one of the hunky stage hands. Through the door, he could hear the voices of a man and Mae discussing something about a recording. At first, the conversation was barely audible, but as tempers increased so did the volume.

"We have never received a penny in royalties for the recording... 'My Man Friday' was written exclusively for you, and you have interpolated it in *Diamond Lil*. My lawyer has requested a minimal payment of $25 weekly royalty for the song. We also haven't been able to trace the distributors of the recording you made of our song."

Mae's unmistakable voice replied flatly, "That's funny. I have no idea who distributed it."

When Ray told the story to members of the cast, they repeated similar scenarios. Apparently, Mae had more than one reason for one of her oft repeated witticism, "Every day is Mae's Day!"

It looked as if *Diamond Lil* was set for a long run, as advance ticket sales poured in. One of those unforeseen little incidents in life changed the whole plan. Mae slipped one night in her dressing room, catching her shoe on a throw rug. Her foot, already unstable in her six-inch platforms, turned under her and she heard the sickening crunch of a bone breaking. Her ankle was shattered. She had no understudy to assume her role, and if she had, people wanted Mae West, and not another actress. As she was carried from backstage to the ambulance, she was greeted by reporters in the alley. Turning on the charm, she smiled and said in her best stage voice, "There's a rumor goin' round that I broke this thing stumbling over a pile of men."

Ray returned to his club commitments, waiting to see what would become of the play.

Mae returned home. During her convalescence, she quickly grew bored and decided to hold a press conference in her bedroom. She was artfully arranged on her famous gold bed, made in the shape of a giant swan. Immaculately coiffed and made up, she peered out from the fronds of her film lashes. "I'm playing for the first time in my life, a bedroom act I don't like. My doctor tells me I have to stay in bed for several days. What's worse is the 'No Visitors Allowed' sign on my door."

While still abed, she received a film offer from director Billy Wilder. He had a script he felt was tailor-made for Mae West. It was a dark tale of a former silent movie star, who attempts a comeback, aided by a younger lover. It all seemed to fit Wilder's idea of the real Mae West. Not only was Mae not interested, she was insulted.

She informed him she had never played in silent movies, and would certainly not play something she was not, an aging actress.

The role finally fell to Gloria Swanson, who had begun in silent films, including *Beyond the Rocks* (1922), the film that Ray had a small part in decades before. Swanson's portrayal of the exotic Norma Desmond in *Sunset Boulevard* (1950), drew rave reviews and an Oscar nomination.

Mae received a number of choice film role offers, but nixed them all. Her insistence on being the absolute focus of any film made it almost impossible for any script not personally penned by the egocentric actress to meet with her approval.

Pal Joey was a case in point. The character she was offered ends up being taken advantage of by the title character, Pal Joey. It was either Mae triumphant, or nothing. This plum role went to the stunning Rita Hayworth.

The determined diva made a speedy recovery from her injury and was soon wowing audiences everywhere. Ray was invited to reprise his character, Bowery Rose, in the national tour of *Diamond Lil,* a cross-country odyssey that would last for almost three years.

The first stop was in the former mining town of Central City, Colorado. It had become the center of a summer arts festival, staging plays, concerts, and opera. What had been planned as a few performances ended up being a full month's run of the play, during which time Mae revealed yet another fascinating side of her personality.

Ray was living in a boarding house with several other members of the cast. One night, he was awakened by the disturbing feeling that something or someone was in his room. Rubbing his eyes, he thought he saw a blurry figure reflected in a mirror on the door. When he sat up and spoke, it moved toward the foot of his bed. As he pulled the covers up around his face, the vision disappeared. Over the next few nights, the scene repeated itself. At breakfast, he related the incident to some of his fellow players.

Later, Mae overheard a conversation among the cast that questioned Ray's mental stability. She called him to her dressing room. She had never done this before, and he was a little nervous. She assured him there was no problem with his work. She just wanted to discuss a subject they might share in common.

Seating herself at her dressing table, she motioned to Ray to take a seat on the chaise lounge next to her. As Mae applied her heavy stage makeup, she watched the fidgety Ray through her mirror.

"I was initially interested in spiritualism a number of years ago. I had achieved stardom in films, written plays, headlined in Vaudeville, but it wasn't enough. 'Is there a hereafter?' I have asked of religious leaders. I wasn't satisfied with their answers. That there might be a hereafter has always fascinated me."

Ray finally relaxed a little and warmed to the subject. He looked up, as Mae's sapphire-blue eyes met his gaze.

She continued. "I found the answer at a spiritualist meeting in Hollywood one year. I realized I couldn't attend the gathering without creating too much of a distraction, so I sent my assistant. There was a famous medium conducting the program, who took questions from the audience. My assistant didn't have the nerve to question the man, but the medium pointed to my assistant and revealed something about him that was impossible for him to know. He asked him if his father had not died under mysterious circumstances, his body being found in a river. He also knew the father's surname. I was so impressed with what I heard that I arranged to meet this medium at a private séance. My closest friends, along with my sister Beverly, attended that night. To insure that there was no trickery involved, I wrote several questions and placed each in a sealed envelope. Each pertained to matters of national importance. America had not yet entered the Second World War. No one believed him when he said American forces would soon be attacked in Hawaii, President Roosevelt would die during his fourth term, and America would win this war, a war we were not even involved in yet."

As she paused to re-glue an eyelash, she turned and took Ray's hand in hers. It was as soft as a young girls and he felt her tighten her grip just slightly as she finished the story. "He also told Beverly things about family matters that only she and I had ever known. Sensing my deep interest, he referred me to a spiritual teacher in

Hollywood, who, over the next year, would guide me, to hear my inner voice, and to contact people from the 'other side'."

Mae grew pensive for just a moment, looking beyond Ray as if she was seeing something or someone. "I don't live in the past, but I like t'see people from then. I used to always figure when you're dead you're dead, but I wanted to know the truth. One day a few years ago I walked into a room and there was a departed loved one sittin' right there. I screamed for my maid who runs in, and the vision vanished. I don't kid myself or have mystical illusions. You know I never drink or take anything."

Mae then confessed the reason for their little conversation. She had heard cast members discussing Ray's story of the nightly visitor in his room. This she was sure was someone from the "other side." She counseled him to ignore any dubious reactions he may have received from his fellow players. What mattered was that she believed him.

Later, she gave him several books on ghosts, spiritualism, and séances. Several years later, Ray was invited to her home for dinner and was not surprised that she held a séance after the meal.

It was that evening that Ray finally grasped the intense interest his sultry friend had in the afterlife. One of her favorite activities was to organize a séance. Mae revealed that she had become involved on a serious level with Lily Dale, a discreet community that embraced the religion of Spiritualism. It was from this group that Mae learned many of the secrets of holding a proper assembly to contact the dearly departed.

One of her favorite targets to contact from the beyond was Rudolph Valentino. Having only met Valentino once at her friend, Texas Guinan's, speakeasy, she was very much taken with the dark lover. When he died unexpectedly soon after their meeting, Mae and Guinan arranged for a séance. Mae, often prone to conspiracy theories, was convinced Valentino had been poisoned by a screen rival.

Mae heard the voice of Valentino warn her of impending danger, "Mae, you have a lot of enemies and don't trust any of them."

She replied in earnest, "No, I won't."

Ray learned that Mae's ongoing interest in speaking to the dead had some strange consequences. She told him that she once had a Filipino chauffer, Benny Blanco, who had no idea what a séance was. She decided to invite him to one of her frequent get-togethers.

As the evening progressed, Mae carried on conversations with her deceased mother, Tillie, and her father. She also claimed to see a group of handsome muscle men. When she extended her hand to them, she claimed they suddenly disappeared. When Blanco realized what Mae's group was up to, he became terrified, fled the room, leaving a hastily scribbled note that he was quitting his job and leaving Hollywood.

When Ray said farewell to Mae and *Diamond Lil*, the tour had exceeded anyone's expectations for longevity. The impetus it gave his career lasted for a time, but, like all publicity, it, too, faded. By the mid-1950s, steady engagements were increasingly hard to find.

The once fine fortune bequeathed by his mother had dwindled into nothing. A mound of out of date designer furs, jewelry that was worth little of the original value, and a small home were the remnants of ill-spent monies.

Ray's old nemesis, reporter Walter Winchell, got wind of his financial difficulties and in his typical mean-spirited fashion now gave more attention to what he wore onstage than to his performance: "Rae Bourbon, femme mimic at Deuces Wild Club, wears a white Hindu broadtail mink jacket rumored to have a $4,000 price tag, as well as an even more expensive white mink Eton designer wrap."

Winchell also hinted at the impersonator's growing reputation as an eccentric, when he reported in his column: "Those delicious appetizers Rae Bourbon served at his cocktail soiree the other evening following a performance were reported to be made from dog food."

It seemed as if the editorial tide was taking a turn for the worse. *Variety* now viewed his act through an unflattering lavender tinted lens: "The Torch Club is dipping into dangerous waters for its pulling power. The lavender scented policy might work as a penny-catcher once word gets around the soprano-hipped circles that new camping grounds have been established. On opening night, the joint was jammed with ambiguous characters."

In an attempt to reverse his fortunes, Ray decided to create a new format. He made the rounds of the better clubs and selected several promising young impersonators and comics to join him in a modern revue. He managed to interest several wealthy gay backers in putting up the necessary monies. "Rae" would head a lineup of several well-known acts and a sizeable cast. The venue for this slightly avant garde entertainment was the 400-seat Ivar Theatre.

On opening night, less than half of the seats had been sold, despite desperate last minute efforts to hock the tickets at half price. Ignoring the half-filled house, the cast struggled valiantly to put on a first-class entertainment. The emptiness of the theatre contributed to the seemingly lukewarm reception, and, as the show drug on, the performers began to lose their nerve.

Rae's final number in the show was not only decidedly downbeat but its autobiographical nature revealed things about his career the audience probably didn't get: the opening reference in the monologue to his appearance in a porno film and attempts by the Johnson Office to censor such material; his work as a film extra at poverty row studios on Gower Street; and his inevitable rejection by an industry that feeds on the image of youth.

For the last scene, the stage was blacked out as all the house lights dimmed. Suddenly, a tiny pin spot focused just on his face, then gradually increased to reveal Rae in a sparkling black tulle gown, his bare shoulders draped with the last of the expensive furs he had squandered so much on. A short piano arpeggio introduced the song:

> "Now if all my films that are in the can
> Had only photographed just my once lovely pan
> Then the Johnson Office wouldn't raise that damned ban
> You can see what I've had to fight
> On Gower Street where the doormen leap
> And has-been actors their vigil keep
> And taxi drivers do nothing but sleep
> I pass by most every night
> Oh, once I was youthful, so fresh and fair
> Once had the most lovely coral hair
> I was every college boy's obvious snare
> The best thing at the bottom of the bill."

He continued, slowly crossing the stage with a pink follow spot, a gloved hand to his aging throat:

> "Ah well, those days have past
> And I've lost my allure at last
> I'm Tessy, the messy old extra
> Calling every studio each day
> Fixing my face, and hope just in case
> While shouting my voice away
> I've been living in sin
> My funds are quite thin
> It's a shame, but I don't want to show it
> Oh, the failure I've been in the past several years
> Each producer I phone must have wool in his ears
> But if a director phoned me, I'd give him three cheers
> I'm well on the skids and I know it."

Those that had remained in the audience after the intermission didn't know what to make of the song. There was a prolonged awkward silence before a smattering of applause began. The rest of the cast stepped in front to the curtain for their bows, but Ray was already on his way to the dressing room. Stopping just outside the door, he heard angry voices. He recognized his disgruntled backers heatedly discussing their lost investments. Still in his fur and gown, he bolted for the stage door and hailed a taxi. For the next several months, he made himself scarce until the heat died down.

Audiences were now more youth oriented. Many impersonator clubs featured performers who invested far more in their gowns, hair, and accessories than in experience. What they did on stage was little more than strike a pose and move their overly lip-lined mouths in sync to a popular recording. The long-playing record, the reel-to-reel tape, and high fidelity ushered in a new era in sound. This made the lip synching by impersonators much more believable.

In the past, entertainers had sung with their own voices, danced with professional style, or held the stage as an amusing stand-up comedian. Now, any queen with a little nerve could put on his sister's formal, pop on a cheap wig from Frederick's of Hollywood, and flutter a pair of dime store eyelashes in a pale attempt at impersonation.

Alcohol and even a few experiments with drugs did little to solve the increasing depression that Ray was experiencing. He had seen many cohorts from the nether world of female impersonation head down this dead-end road of booze and barbiturates. He didn't want to join them. He might be only a novelty from a glamorous and fading past, but he wasn't quite ready to throw in the proverbial makeup towel, not just yet. Standing in front of his dressing table, he laced up his bustier, snapped on his garter belt, and straightened his stocking seams. He still had a lot of living to do.

There was a new medical procedure that was causing a worldwide stir and making headlines for those that had undergone it.

Ray first investigated the idea of a sex-change (hereafter referred to as gender reassignment) at the respected Johns Hopkins Hospital. They had a Psyco-Hormonal Research Unit and Gender Identity Clinic dating as far back as 1915. They would eventually pioneer genital reconstructive surgery. The very first of these was performed in 1925. The woman in this case was changed from a Francis to a truck driving John. By 1951, plastic surgery had become an addition to this new field of gender reassignment. Soon, the office of the Chief of Staff was besieged with transgender individuals seeking this life-altering procedure. This involved the removal of the male genitalia, and the construction of a vagina.

Ray hoped that this clinic could do the same for him. After the initial exam, they told him it would be impossible.

After months of searching, he read about Dr. Emerick Szekely, who had a clinic in Juarez, Mexico. The doctor was a refugee from Hungary, driven out of his homeland by the Nazis. He ended up in Mexico and opened one of the first clinics specializing in gender reassignment. After consulting with Dr. Szekely, and spending a fortnight in Juarez, Ray returned to the United States. He immediately contacted everyone he knew in the theatrical press and began his publicity campaign to tout his new gender.

In an interview he gave to George Capozzi, Jr. of the *New York Journal-American*, Ray's explosive claim became a featured article:

"Female Impersonator Needn't Fake Again—Says Surgery Made Him a Her. Now a buxom Rae: Operated OnIn Mexico, female impersonator Rae Bourbon, who wore dresses when he performed with Mae West on the Broadway stage, has undergone sex transformation surgery and today can wear dresses all the time. "Yes, it's true, 'I am now a woman.'"

"According to Rae, who talked with the N.Y. Journal American over the long-distance phone from El-Paso, Tex, the operation was performed last September by a Hungarian doctor in Juarez, Mexico.

"'I was the first one on the North American Continent,' said Rae. 'The other sex transformations of American men were done in Denmark.'

"The 54-year-old nightclub performer, whose forte has been risqué songs and impressions of women, said he is returning to show business shortly with a new act.

"'I don't know why I shouldn't,' explained Rae. 'I've always had a good following when I worked in a tuxedo. I should triple it in gowns. Besides, I'm a lot prettier as a dowager than I was as a man.'

SHE'LL SLIM DOWN

"The 6 foot Rae, who feels like he is a bit overweight at 175 pounds said she will slim down for her return as a femme.

"Concerning the operation, Rae said:

'Psychologically I think I am going to be happier than I have ever been in my entire life. Now, I am what I always wanted to be.'

"Rae decided to become a woman a year ago when he went to Juarez and found Dr. Emerick Szekely, a woman's doctor who had fled Hungary during the Nazi purge.

COMPLETE CHANGE

"Rae said Dr. Szekely found ovarian tissues during the surgery. Then on May 2, Dr. Szekely performed a "corrective" operation. The doctor also gave Rae a certificate that reads in part, "Bourbon is now more woman than man."

"'And there's no doubt about it,' Rae asserted, 'My hair is thicker, my voice is higher, and my shape is like a woman's- a big woman's. I measure 44-36-40. That beats Mae West, doesn't it?'

"Rae played Mae West's French hairdresser from the Court of Louis XV in "Catherine Was Great" at the Royal Theatre in 1945, and wore dresses as Bowery Rose in "Diamond Lil" for several years."

The resulting publicity from Ray's claim to have been a successful patient of Dr. Szekely spurred newspaper interest in his story. It also renewed an interest in his career. He had learned a great deal about the power of the press from Mae.

Another much discussed medical procedure around the time of Ray's purported gender reassignment was the use of glands from monkeys to bolster youthfulness and lagging libido. Everyone from aging movie Lotharios to the Pope was rumored to be benefitting from this radical and controversial procedure.

Ray often penned his song lyrics. He decided that this medical monkey procedure was hot topical material that might tie-in with his own sensational claim to have altered his gender.

The result was, "New Glands," a number he used for several years, and was eventually released as a recording on the label, *Bourbana*:

"Now here's advice for young women
And here's advice for young men
And for you young unwed mothers, and such
Tell me who gives a damn for a broken down old man
Why they won't even give him a crutch
Now, any old putz whose spirit is willing
And whose flesh is, shall we say, pliant
Can be a real Brigham Young
With a gland operation
Ha ha ha ha
Hooray for surgical triumphs
Ain't science wonderful

Ain't science grand
It certainly is the nuts
If the date on your can has faded
You don't have to be an old futz
Now a washed up Casanova, who could only stand and leer
Was given a new set of monkey glands
That made him act quite queer
And now he is known as Pappy Tarzan
While he dives from the glass chandelier
Don't be a chump, prime your pump
Get a brand new set of glands
Ain't times wonderful
Ain't times grand
It'll make worn out libidos live again
By grafting on brand new glands
Now a certain worn out bachelor
Who had gone from frail to frailer
Discovered no stevedore's glands were in stock
So, they gave him a ladies tailor's
And now he's camping at the beach
And making passes at all of the sailors
Ha, ha, ha
If you've lost it, get defrosted
All you need is new glands
Now if you're as low as a submarine
And your periscope just won't stand
And you torpedo will not fire
It's a sign that you need new glands
Now a cowboy who once fought Indians
Was feeling sad because
His pistol was as good as new
But the damned thing wouldn't draw
Now once more he's chasing Indians
And has his eye on the squaws
Ha, ha, ha
Don't sit and pine for auld lang syne
Bessie, go get some new glands

> Now surgery is wonderful
> It gives an old guy new hope
> You too can ring the bell once more
> Providing you still have the rope
> Now you all have heard of Custer
> And that poor boy's last stand
> Well, with new glands he'd still be standing
> With his situation well-in-hand
> But instead of that he went to bat
> And history said he's damned
> Poor ignition is a sorry condition
> That definitely calls for new glands
> So you'd better get some!"

Ray's new nightclub billing read, "Not a Female Impersonator." For several months, this worked well, guaranteeing a full house each night. The problem was it was just a bit of a freak show. Those who came might laugh at some of the standard Rae Bourbon fare, but they had really come hoping to see what a sex change looked like. At that time, he looked like any middle aged female impersonator. His chin sagged, his eyes drooped, and his figure had spread.

The sensational nature of his claim to have been sexually altered led to a new audience, and with that audience came a lot of uncomfortable moments.

Often, there were insults shouted out accompanying the applause. A particularly inebriated young man screamed one evening, "Show me your tits!"

Rae shot back, *"Show me your willy and I'll show you my tits!"*

He knew that most hecklers were cowards and took this opportunity to turn the tables and win the audience over to his side.

Coming to the front of the stage, he pointed to the perpetrator and insisted that he join him onstage. Usually, the embarrassing heckler nearly disappeared under the table.

Then, Rae closed the subject. *"Alright audience, he's afraid to show his short comings!"*

Undaunted by the sometimes hostile tone of the audience, he opened each night with a song he composed about his new "condition." Note the clever reference to Mae West:

> "To all of you who know me,
> You probably saw it coming,
> So this will be no surprise.
> Everyone asks me, how does it feel
> Well, it feels just fine to me
> I can be the woman I've always wanted to be
> For the change, I went South of the Border
> It took me just days to pack
> I arrived there with excess baggage
> But, I had a lot less coming back
> There's been a change in the gender
> A big change in me
> From R-A-Y I've changed to R-A-E
> So, if anyone should ask you
> Just feel free to say
> There's been a change in Ray
> Oy Vey! There's been a change in Rae
> Now I can do many things as a woman
> I could never do as I was
> I've been dropped from The Man of Distinction ads
> So, I'm dickering with Maiden Form Bras
> Now, all that fuss about Marilyn Monroe
> And her ever shifting gears
> The poor little girl has stopped only one bus
> But I've been lousing up traffic for years
> Of course, I could star in a show in Las Vegas
> Dressed like Mae West, all net and allure
> In her case, they knew what was caught in the net
> In my case, they'd never be quite sure!"

The whole cleverly-wrapped package began to come undone one night in 1956 at a jammed club in West Hollywood. In the middle of "There's Been a Change in Rae," six police officers accompanied by members of the Vice Squad jumped onstage. Ray was read his rights and arrested in front of a stunned audience who heard the charge, "Impersonating a female." One Los Angeles publication carried the detailed report:

> "The age old injunction to change his act led Rae Bourbon into court yesterday and posed a legal problem that may call for a modern Solomon. It all began when a long time female impersonator underwent a sex change in Mexico. He now billed himself Miss Rae Bourbon. Under this new gender designation he was booked into the Melody Room on Sunset Strip. Seated at ringside Monday night for the first show were three uproarious gentlemen, one attired in a flaming red sport jacket, laughing, applauding, pounding on the table for more. When the show was over, they followed (Miss) Bourbon into his . . . her dressing room and flashed their badges. Sheriff's deputies. Ray/Rae was charged with impersonating a woman."

The *Los Angeles Examiner* described the same scene that night:

> "Wearing a black and white nylon dress, false eyelashes, heavy perfume and a five o'clock shadow, Ray (or Rae) actor/actress/ Bourbon enters Beverly Hills Municipal Court on August 1st, to deny he (or she) was guilty of impersonating a woman. He produced a certificate from a Mexican doctor changing his sex. The entertainer and 14 dogs live in a Venice trailer court."

The mention of the "14 dogs" and the "trailer court" is an indication of the lifestyle to which Ray had been reduced. It was also the first mention of his growing predilection to hoard animals, a habit that would eventually have tragic consequences.

He was released to stand trial, and subsequently convicted. He continued, undaunted, to bill himself in the same way. As long as clubs were willing to hire him, he was willing to take the chance. Most of the time, there was no trouble. Only three locations, El

Paso, Seattle, and New Orleans, charged him with a crime, and those never stuck.

Ironically, in Miami he was arrested for "impersonating a man." He was working in a straight club as a man, doing his stand-up comedy dressed in a tuxedo. Someone had tipped the cops off that Ray was now a woman. The outcome became a legal jumble and the charges were quickly dismissed.

Perhaps the best explanation for this controversial period in his life may come from his own words:

> "Some background to the stories circulating about my 'change' may be in order. When asked by friends about my new existence, I hardly know where to begin. An 'in between' at birth, I first saw the light of day on our family ranch on the Mexican border. I've been a border case ever since! Sent to school in England I used to darken the stage doors of Music Halls and an endless array of little entertainment clubs. Since I can remember there has been an urge to act and the theatre in all its many-sided glories has been my fascination. I guess the most important thing I do is make people laugh. I never did think I could sing, but for years other people have, and I have made many so-called 'straight' records from blues to ballads. They say to succeed in show business you have to be different or beautiful or surprising. I'm different. With Broadway shows I've toured the globe. I've appeared in the best big spots and some of the damndest [sic] little spots you can think of. What are my plans now? My house trailer and jalopy make the entire country my home. My twelve Cocker Spaniels, one Boxer, and one 'you name it', I think of them as my kids, travel with me. There are always new people to perform for, and who knows, perhaps that man in my life is just around the next corner. Meanwhile you can know, I'm not cutting corners!"

It was at this time that Ray got in on the ground floor of America's fascination with comedy records, specifically risqué platters.

The advent of the long-playing vinyl record saw an explosion in the comedy genre, particularly the "party record," usually adult material with a warning printed on the album cover.

Backed by two friends, Irving Kratka and James Gardner, Ray entered into a contract with their new record label, Under the Counter (UTC), and apt name for records that were, indeed, sold just that way. They were carried by many legitimate vendors, but had to be specifically requested by customers. The clerk would then reach under the counter and produce what would eventually amount to a dozen of such albums by Ray. This was far more than any other comedy artist at that time had in their catalogue. These seemingly impromptu-recorded performances were appreciated for not only their humor but their satirical comments on mainstream culture. He deplored hypocrisy and had little tolerance for the self-important. He could laugh at others, but took greater pleasure in laughing at himself. Years later, his record producers would reminisce:

> "Rae went all over the country. Certainly, no other gay performer has had the effect on America's gay community that Bourbon did. People remember him... he would walk in a room, gauge the audience and figure out what they could stand. Then he would push it ten percent above what they could take. There is little doubt that Rae's remarkably long stage career was a contributing factor in his sixth sense when it came to an audience."

17
TAKING *IT* ON TOUR

The 1950s was also a time of change for Mae West. Television was the new entertainment medium, and the movies were feeling the crunch. Families now gathered around small black-and-white screens watching a menu of variety shows, Westerns, and cops and robbers. You didn't have to get dressed or even put on your shoes. You could kick back, swill a beer and gobble popcorn, and eventually even have a selection of more than one station to watch. Many performers that had experienced a decline in their careers in film, due to age or changing tastes, cast their nets upon the television waters and hoped to restore their fading images.

Mae decided to stick a well-manicured toe into the television waters, but quickly drew it back. She had been offered a chance to star in a series called *It's Not History, It's Her Story*. The hastily-conceived project was stillborn. Mae was to have portrayed an important historical female figure every week. The network, remembering the infamous Charlie McCarthy radio broadcast, soon considered withdrawing their offer.

When they heard a rehearsal tape of Mae discussing one the historical characters she was to portray, Betsy Ross, they decided to pull the plug. "Good women are no fun. The only good woman I can recall in history was Betsy Ross, and all she ever made was a flag."

Mae's first significant appearance on television was for the largest audience she had ever played, The Oscars of the Academy of Motion Picture Arts and Sciences, at the Pantages Theatre in Hollywood. Millions tuned in to watch the blonde cougar and her prey perform.

Mae sang "Baby It's Cold Outside," with the current young film heartthrob, Rock Hudson. She, of course, insisted on changing the lyrics to suit her style. The network caved-in to her demands, and the ratings went through the roof when word leaked of the highly improbable pairing.

The former Paramount film star personally staged the entire number, just as she had always done in the days when she was top box office.

On the night of the broadcast, the camera pans in to discover the swivel-hipped siren reclining on a silver chaise lounge. Mae slowly rises, bats her impossibly long eyelashes, and encircles the slightly bewildered Rock Hudson like a sequined boa constrictor. The darkly handsome young actor is completely overcome by the satirical sixty-something sex bomb. In response, the star-packed audience roared in delight. Mae was discovered by a whole new generation.

The Examiner ran the headlines the next morning:

> "Mae West and Rock Hudson stopped the show cold. Mae, appearing in a black spangled gown, white fur, and a white plume headdress, and singing "Baby, It's Cold Outside" with Rock, brought down the house!"

It was during the negotiations with the network executives that Mae lost her longtime manager and friend, James Timony. He had been her strong right arm since her Vaudeville career. After years of battling obesity and heart trouble, he succumbed.

Many years before, he had hoped to inspire a permanent romance in Mae's fickle heart, but foregoing that, he quietly guided her through the rough and tumble world of show business. One of the last important contributions he made to Mae's career was to introduce her to the burgeoning vacation destination of Las Vegas.

One thing most entertainers who played the posh stages of Las Vegas had in common was a backup of beautiful and nearly nude young showgirls. The "parade queens," as Mae recalled Ray describing them, seemed to do just that: walk slowly around the stage, knockers-up, and arms extended.

Timony constantly reminded Mae that she was as famous as Coca Cola®. Why shouldn't her brand be on display in one of the better Nevada nightspots? After he made several discreet inquiries, he signed her to open at what was then the top salary ever paid a Las Vegas star.

In July 1954, Mae stepped on stage in the elegant surroundings of the Congo Room of the Sahara Hotel. Not about to suffer a comparison to the usual Las Vegas bevy of buxom beauties, Mae had a titillating concept. If randy men can ogle firm young flesh for high dollar, why can't the ladies be treated to succulent slabs of beefcake? She hired seven top specimens of male beauty to be her back up boys, all clad in very brief loincloths. "It's not the men in my life that counts," she told the audience, "It's the life in my men."

While she crooned such lascivious songs to the assembled studs as, "I'd Like to Do All Day What I Do All Night," the women in the audience sat mesmerized. Their male escorts had mixed feelings, particularly when they compared themselves to the Adonis lineup.

The Congo Room immediately sold out for every performance. The hotel was so impressed they had her return for the all-important Christmas season. They also raised her salary from $25,000 to $30,000 a week.

In sharp contrast to her obvious money-making abilities, Mae could be notoriously tight fisted. She wore the same black gown for the entire run of both engagements. It had been used in one of her early films, and had to be let out several times to accommodate her increasing curves. This was at a time when female performers in Las Vegas spent a fortune on costumes with dozens of changes.

One possible explanation for Mae's miserly habits was her family. She was the sole support for her sister, Beverly, a sad alcoholic, and her seldom employed brother, John.

Las Vegas afforded the still highly-sexed Mae the opportunity to cruise the stable of available men. Never mind that she was involved with a Mexican lover, who was part of her orchestra and watched her every move off stage. She insisted they not share a room when their little afternoon delight was over. This gave her the opportunity when Latin lover boy was in the land of nod to sneak in the latest challenger. Every ambitious stud in the Mae West stable wanted to claim the gold ring for staying in the saddle the longest on her merry-go-round.

Over the course of the show's run, Mae became embroiled in the sort of scandal on which tabloids fed. She made the mistake of pitting the highly competitive bodybuilders against each other in seeking her famous favors.

One of them, Mickey Hargitay, had initially attempted to bed the star, thinking it would lead to a positive boost in his publicity. Mae wasn't really interested, sensing this man's obvious ambitions. He soon turned his attention to a much younger blonde actress. This incredibly well-endowed bombshell would soon hit the silver screen. Jayne Mansfield became the apple of Hargitay's eye.

When the notoriety-crazed nymph and her muscle-bound consort entered into a public spat with Mae, she fired Hargitay. Mae was infuriated that the pair should use her fame to further their careers. She called a press conference to set the record straight.

Aware that every reporter of any importance would be present, Hargitay waited until the right moment, as he sequestered himself outside Mae's dressing room door. When he was sure all of the press was inside, he burst in.

Standing at Mae's side was her present lover, the youngest and most impressionable member of the cast. Fearing that Hargitay was going to harm Mae, he delivered a one-two punch that flattened the older bodybuilder.

In the ensuing pandemonium, the photographers captured the humiliating image of Mae caught in the melee falling to the floor, mouth agape, as she screamed, "You can't hit a legend!"

Due to the nationwide notoriety of the Las Vegas fracas, Mae was again invited to appear on television. There is no such thing as bad publicity. This time it was the very tame *Person to Person* show. The half-hour program featured Mae taking the viewers on a tour of her apartment while answering questions from the host, Charles Collingwood.

When asked about her opinion of foreign affairs, Mae replied, "Oh, I've always had a weakness for foreign affairs."

Collingwood tried to steer the conversation in a new direction, asking Mae about her opinion of men in general, to which she replied, "I generally avoid temptation, unless I can't resist it."

Her answers all seemed to have more than one meaning. She had become so used to speaking in double entendres that she didn't realize this would land her in hot water again. When the sponsors viewed the rushes, the show was shelved.

In 1954, Mae took her muscle boy parade back on the road to the top-tiered Latin Quarter, and returned by popular demand two years later. Reviewer R. Dana was on hand for the opening and reported:

> "The old belief that everything should be bigger and better, a thought most forcefully pronounced by Hollywood trailers, can be applied with forthright honesty to Mae West, who has returned to the Latin Quarter. Instead of changing her act, Miss West has embellished it. Most noteworthy, I think, is the addition of some song and dance men whose soft-shoe capers and grace provides a fair contrast to the muscle boys who are background for her boudoir comedy. They rock and they roll and Miss West demonstrates that her vocal chords are as roving as her come-hither eyes. This is the one chance for women to get back at the men who go to the Quarter to ogle the pretty dancing girls. Miss West, stretched on a chaise lounge with a plush, seductive look, allows a ringmaster of the Olympic games to trot out eight Goliaths of the day, clad in a breech cloth and sandals, with muscles seemingly built on muscles. Packaged in regal white robes, they march first toward the audience and then turn to Miss West and throw back their robes. Her expression of approval regales the customers. One of the muscle specimens is Mickey Hargitay, Mr. Universe. As before, Miss West pretends to have a bona fide romantic interest and her current candidate is Tito Coral, Mexican singer and motion picture actor. His position is shaky at best, and one notes that he isn't included when she passes out keys for the "Oh what a Night" finale."

When Mae and her men appeared at the chic Ciro's in Los Angeles, the *Daily Variety* crowed, "Those who check their inhibitions at the door will have themselves a night; an experience they won't soon forget... Miss Mae West!"

Mae and her bevy of masculine beauties toured for almost five years, helped in no small way by the sensational publicity created by the ongoing conflict between the aging Mae West and the new Hollywood sensation, Jayne Mansfield.

During breaks in the tour, she made occasional television appearances on *The Dean Martin Show* (1959), *The Red Skelton Show* (1960), and even the ridiculous sit-com, *Mr. Ed* (1965).

The muscle tour finally closed, brought on in no small part by a particularly unflattering review of Mae's appearance. It called into question her use of unusually dark stage lighting to hide her "battle with Father Time." She publicly fumed to reporters that audiences thought "she still looked great," despite what some vicious reviewer might say. At one point, she suggested breaking the writer's fingers.

She bounced back immediately with a tour of a play, *Come on Up, Ring Twice*. This was not a major production, nor were the venues top drawer. The reviews were kind, but mixed. The budget was a far cry from the good old days, and the whole cast traveled in a caravan of motor cars.

It was after a performance in Niagara Falls, New York, that Bourbon and Mae were again face to face backstage. Ray was appearing with the world-famous Jewel Box Revue in the same town. When he saw the posters for *Come on Up, Ring Twice*, he insisted that his fellow performers from the Jewel Box Revue visit Mae's new play.

There were over fifty members of the Jewel Box Revue in the audience that night, including Gita Gilmore, who did a perfect imitation of Mae West. When Mae discovered that they would be out front, she substituted Ray's name for that of a character in her play.

Ray and the rest of the Jewel Box Revue were asked to stand after Mae received a rousing ovation. They were called on-stage to join hands with the entire cast. Everyone stayed afterward for an impromptu performance by Mae, Rae, and Gita of famous one-liners and bits of scenes they had shared in their past. Afterwards, there were hugs and kisses all around.

Before Ray returned to his hotel, Mae pressed an envelope into his hand containing her personal phone number and the promise of collaboration on future projects.

In 1961, Mae bid farewell to the legitimate stage, after six decades. She bowed out in a play of her own making, *Sextette* (1961). She claimed personal authorship of the script, but it was partially purloined from a play by Charlotte Francis.

This cotton candy fantasy featured her as a famous movie star about to wed for the sixth time to a man at least half her age. It asked the audience to accept the idea of a white-gowned bride of some sixty-eight years taking on yet another husband. Added to this hash of a story are gangsters, Hungarian film directors, titled lovers, suicide, and a raft of shady characters from China Town.

The production began on a shoestring budget in Chicago, under rehearsed and unprofessionally executed. To top off the many fumbled lines during opening night, and the bad reviews, the leading man died immediately after of a heart attack.

Saddened but resilient Mae forged ahead, playing in small venues throughout the Midwest. She wrote new lines, found better actors, and by the time she reached the Coconut Grove Theatre in Miami, she was back in the saddle. At her curtain speech, she made reference to the many men in her play. "All discarded lovers should be given a second chance, but with somebody else."

Audiences cheered, but Mae wisely decided it was time to retreat to Hollywood and reconnoiter her future.

In the mid-1960s, it looked like Mae would make a much-ballyhooed return to the silver screen in *The Art of Love*, cast appropriately as a madam. Despite her dicey health problems—a mild stroke brought on by diabetes—she signed the contract. Studios then as now were forced to obtain health tests from stars before filming in order to meet insurance requirements. Mae had her well-paid physician alter her medical data. The wardrobe and screen tests were made in preparation for the filming.

Again, she had failed to thoroughly read the script in advance. She disliked the dialogue and insisted on writing her own. The studio bought out her contract. The brassy Broadway singer, Ethel

Merman, assumed the role, and the film starring James Garner, Dick Van Dyke, and Elke Sommer was released in July 1965.

Mae returned to her white-on-white Hollywood love shack, safely surrounded by mementos of her own creation, Mae West.

As Mae contemplated her next move, Ray continued to tour on-and-off with the Jewel Box Revue. The Jewel Box Revue had been founded by two dynamic entrepreneurs, Danny Brown and Doc Berner. Their financial acumen afforded the Jewel Box Revue a spectacular staging. Only the finest in their respective fields were employed. Top wigmakers from New York and Hollywood, hair stylist to the stars Jan Britton, and designs and spectacular feathers from Maison Parfain in Paris, all contributed to this world-class production.

The stylist, Jan Britton, was both backstage hairdresser and onstage star. He was featured as the classical ballet dancer of the Jewel Box Revue. He performed "on point" just as did female ballerinas. Audiences had trouble convincing themselves this was a man, so utterly feminine and sylph-like was the dancer.

One of the agonies many of the female impersonators had to endure when wearing tight dresses or dancing a strip tease was an item called a "gaff." This was an undergarment used to hide the pesky penis bump and transform it into the smoothness of a desirable vagina.

Ray had worn a gaff years before when sporting a tight gown, but soon learned to have his costumes tailored so he didn't require one. He never got used to pain they caused. The following instructions should make this readily apparent:

> "Directions: Lying down, pull gaff up to your upper thighs. The wide part should be facing the front and the thinner part is in the back. Put your testicles up into your abdominal cavity. You can do this by simply holding each testicle and gently pushing until you find the opening of the cavity. Once you have both testicles up, hold them there in front (you will be able to feel them protruding around your pubic hair) and tuck your penis between your legs and pull your gaff up. You should now have a flat appearance in the

front. If you are wearing tight fitting clothes, this method is best. If you obtain an erection using this method, it will cause extreme pain. Be careful."

The Jewel Box Revue was a magnificent feast for the eye and ear, on par with any "straight" revue, including those in Las Vegas. A type of act that Ray had not seen since his halcyon days in Greenwich Village was the "half and half."

The impersonator, Bruno, created a split body, involving one half of his body and face made up and dressed as a woman. On the other half was an elegantly-dressed man in evening wear. He carried the illusion even further by appearing to have the two different halves dance romantically with each other. It was nearly impossible to accept that there was actually only one person involved in this sexy duality.

Another member of the cast, the lovely and rather understated impersonator, Mr. Carrie Davis, was to become a longtime friend of Ray. The singer's look was soft and feminine, emphasized in part by his "baby fat." Davis, classically trained as an opera singer, had an incredible soprano voice, capable of hitting every note intended for the female voice.

Years later, as a budding author, I would include the following memory of Carrie Davis in a review of Kansas City's Jewel Box Lounge (not to be confused with the Jewel Box Revue):

"I remember Carrie always came on near the end of the program at the Jewel Box, (a show club in Kansas City, Missouri), in one of the star spots, just before Rae Bourbon did his number. Carrie was always immaculately groomed, glamorous in the tight waist, full skirted dresses of the period, often a tasteful matte gold. Her strawberry hair was smartly coiffed, but never as big or overdone as some of the other cast members, sort of Dina Merrill looking. She would do some light operetta number or a current show tune, and end up always with "Some Day My Prince Will Come." Depending on the condition of her voice by this time, she would pull out all the stops in the second verse, going for the high note at the end with all she had. You could always tell when she knew it was going to be bad, for she would give the pianist a certain look, and he would suddenly drop it an octave. When she did make it, it brought down the house."

One of the star comics with the Jewel Box Revue, Gita Gilmore, did a perfect imitation of Mae West. Unlike so many Mae West imitators, Gilmore relied as much on his flexible voice to emulate sultry Mae as he did on the copies of her gowns that he wore. Gilmore bonded quickly with Ray when he discovered that he had been Mae's protégé. He constantly pestered Ray to authenticate any new features he incorporated in his Mae West parody, including that peculiar nasal delivery that revealed Mae's Brooklyn background.

There were more impersonators in the Jewel Box Revue than any show in which Ray had ever appeared. He was not the star attraction, but he stayed viable in the eyes of Brown and Berner by the strength of his versatility. He was a veteran showman.

Ray was first assigned to the chorus, both as an impersonator and a chorus boy. The latter was a stretch for a sixty-something queen, but he still cut a decent figure in his faithful tuxedo. His full head of hair was dyed a dark brown in a valiant attempt to hide the march of time.

As the tour crossed the American landscape, stopping in Detroit, Chicago, and Baltimore, Ray was finally given a solo spot.

Comically dressed as a belly dancer, he made his entrance in front of an elaborate Egyptian backdrop painted with an image of the Sphinx and a silk tent surrounded with palm trees. The orchestra played an introduction laced with tinkling bells and tinny flutes, like those of a snake charmer:

"Now the Sahara is a desert
Famous for its sand and vamps
On my trip to Egypt
I met a follower of the camps
She was born upon a camel's back
The daughter of a prince

And around the old oasis
She's been hoppin' ever since
Ah, Sarah from Sahara
With her prayer rug on the ground
But Sarah does no praying
When the Bedouins are around
If a Bedouin is her choice, and he turns out not so grand
She merely squats upon a dune
And scratches in a bit of sand
This girl has no repression
She always gets her man
Why she even had the nerve
To top a mile-long caravan
She's the desert's fond delight
Pays not one bit of rent
And the Arabs come from miles around
To help her pitch her tent
Sarah from Sahara has patriotic flairs
And always does her duty with the Foreign Legionnaires
And if she finds a new recruit
And he turns out not so hot
She merely drops back on her rug
And does the best with what she's got
One day she met a Bedouin who played upon his flute
But she hates solo serenades and joined him with her lute
Sarah from Sahara is the pride of every sheik
They let her smoke their water pipe
They say she's got the best technique
But that is how she met her downfall, so runs the desert myth
She tried to smoke 'em too much pipe, and choked herself to death!"

18
I Damn Well Need the Dough!

The Jewel Box Revue was not immune to the changing times and tastes. America was being fed a diet of youth at every media level. It was the youth revolution, and the 1960s were happening. Many of the cast members were updating their looks and trying to emulate what was happening in the "Swinging 60s."

The press was not as cooperative with coverage of drag shows as it had been in the past. The Jewel Box Revue travelled more than any other impersonator ensemble in the country, often playing in small and medium-sized towns. This invariably led to a more confrontational or even sensationalized reporting.

During a weeklong engagement in Ohio, a particularly pesky journalist seemed to be underfoot backstage after every performance. At first, the queens smiled and played nice, giving the stock answers and tired old retorts, the kind often used when dealing with an audience heckler. On closing night, Ray returned to the communal dressing room to pack for the overnight journey to the next venue. As he wedged himself between two rather portly drags at the dressing table, he looked in the mirror to find this same reporter standing behind him. Ray brushed him off with a barrage of bitchy put downs, thinking the yokel would get the picture and leave.

Just then, one of the Jewel Box Revue's founders, Danny Brown, stuck his head in the dressing room door to remind everyone that their tour bus would be ready to board in an hour.

The reporter ignored Brown's presence and continued to harangue Ray about his chosen profession, finally stepping over the line. He suddenly pushed back the communal makeup bench, toppling the two half-dressed drag queens on either side to the floor. There was a great explosion of feathers, finery, and furs, as the three not diminutive divas tore into the startled journalist. Ray slammed him against the wall, while his two companions delivered a series of punishing kicks with their steel-heeled stilettos. Brown intervened and pulled the enraged trio off the now simpering reporter. When he had gained a modicum of composure, Brown explained that he did not witness what had just happened, and he had for the gentlemen's publication a statement that he was sure would please the editor. He also strongly suggested he print it.

Everyone calmed down and returned to their packing, as Brown explained to the hack writer a bit of the history of this art form.

"It's an old mannish custom, guys getting done up in gal's clothing. Because it's a far cry from Juliet to Hopalong Cassidy, it's hard for most of us to realize the immortal Shakespeare created his greatest feminine role, Juliet, knowing it would be portrayed not by a woman but by a young man. In the days of Elizabethan theater, all feminine roles were played by young men, and this custom prevailed until after the Reformation."

Making sure that the reporter was getting all this down, Brown paused and looked at what had been written so far.

"To continue, female impersonation—men making the ladies look to their laurels in the matter of fashion, finery, and such—has long been with us, and the Jewel Box Revue has maintained the art in its true and original sense." There was a pregnant pause and then applause from the cast.

The following weeks and months found the Jewel Box Revue struggling with a dwindling audience and several pay cuts across the board. As Ray's contribution to the Revue was gradually diminished to chorus work only, he fulfilled the last month of his contract, and quietly departed.

In 1960, Ray experienced one of the strangest incidents in his long career. This involved the FBI. That same year, there had been a serious defection by two National Security Agency (NSA) workers, who went over to the Soviet Union, carrying top secret information. This was the era of the Cold War, where America and Russia had endless confrontations, strutting, bragging, and threatening each other like mad dogs in competition for a bitch in heat. In this instance, the bitch in question was world domination.

Ray, in what appears to have been a sudden surge of patriotism, contacted the FBI by phone. He claimed to have met the two men that had defected to the Russian authorities with that important classified material. The FBI wanted all of the details, particularly how Ray knew these men.

There had been a birthday party given in Ray's honor several years earlier, when he had been appearing in a Washington, D.C., club. The two fugitives had been invited guests.

The FBI, it appeared, already had a file on Ray and considered him a "dangerous person." At that time, both gay and transgendered persons were considered "dangerous perverts," as the FBI put it. They knew that he was gay and assumed that the two guests at his birthday bash were of the same persuasion.

There was a round of phone calls made and information exchanged, finally including the names of the two suspects, Martin and Mitchell. As soon as the FBI confirmed that Ray's information was correct about the two traitors, they became increasingly aggressive in their questioning. They demanded the names of all the gays and lesbians Ray knew that worked in any capacity in Washington. When he refused, his interrogators made thinly veiled threats.

Within days, he found his car vandalized, followed by a frightening incident on the road. He was driving home from the club where he worked one evening. As he left the parking lot, someone shot out his windshield, barely missing his head.

He called the FBI the next morning, hoping they could offer him advice. The reply was terse. They couldn't help him, or protect him.

He promptly severed all ties with the agency. He never learned if he had been the target of the Russians, or the FBI. Overnight, he packed his bags and cancelled the rest of his club contract.

His two sure-fire bookings were the 100 Club in Chicago and the Jewel Box Lounge in Kansas City, Missouri (no relation to the Jewel Box Revue). There he had a faithful following who still appreciated the Rae Bourbon brand of humor, even though it seemed a bit passé. He ricocheted between the Windy City and Kansas City, picking up any short bookings he could manage in towns in between.

He was becoming a little jaded, and a bit more bitter as he watched the years pass. Some of his routines now had a decidedly sharp edge, despite his toothy smile and raucous cackle.

An almost biographical monologue, half-spoken, half-sung, was added to his routine. Kansas City was the first to hear this untypical piece that gives a telling insight into Ray's mind:

"So now, you're going to hear Rae Bourbon
They say I'm ultra urban, and I veil a bit of silk with fantasy
It's said I often traffic in subjects pornographic
And raise eyebrows with rash impunity
Now this may border on high treason
But I have a valid reason
For my actions and the things I say, you know
I'm not here for recreation, it's not my relaxation
I'm doing this because I damn well need the dough!
So when I leave these putrid portals
To hell with all mere mortals!
Nobody knows just what becomes of me
Now I have no aversion to the art they call perversion
I contend that each man's hobby is his own
You may say that I'm a sissy
In fact, an object prissy
But I have the right to change my mind when I start for home
So, while you squander sheckels
I'll take your laughs and heckles
For a bit of what you squander comes to me
I distribute it astutely and I need it quite acutely
Nobody knows where my money goes when it leaves me
And I have no aptitude for labor or a yen to flash the saber
Office routines are a as boring as can be
So while the wealthy are tycooning I'll continue my buffooning
It brings the dough, that's all that counts with me
You may think that I'm quite silly, perhaps a willy nilly
Think as you please, Mary, it's quite alright with me
I care not if you're frowning when you sit and watch my clowning
It's my business, not an idiosyncrasy
You see I've known the dolts, I've known the bores
I've known the good girls...and the whores
I've know some priests, I've known some wimps

> I've known some street wise flashy...pimps
> So time, and time alone will tell
> Some day I'll see you all in hell
> A cheer will rise and they'll all say
> Hooray, hooray for here comes Rae
> Yes all you gals and all you drunks
> And I'll skip right by you campy punks
> When I'm old and gray, and 87
> My God Mary, I'm twice that old now!
> I will have earned my place in Heaven!"

Rays final attempt at a new beginning in show business was inspired by advice from his old friend, Mae West. They had stayed in touch by mail and phone for many years. Their notes and conversations usually prattled on, filled with small talk and gossip.

This time, he candidly revealed his plight in an uncharacteristically lengthy letter. He described himself as an aging drag queen with more memories than future plans. Mae's prompt reply arrived on tuberose scented stationery.

Had he forgotten about *Sex, The Drag,* and most importantly, *Catherine Was Great?* Mae wrote plays about familiar subjects. Her literary efforts had paid-off in spades. Now, he must put pen to paper and write about the things with which he was familiar.

The end result of this wise piece of advice was the play he wrote, *Daddy Was a Lady.* Before Ray's final edit of this semi-biographical presentation was even done, he placed the following "Cast Wanted" ad in *Variety* magazine:

> "Daddy Was a Lady" to star Rae Bourbon. Available roles: male, young, must be well built, women, 18 and gorgeous, good figure; woman, mid 40s, stripper type, man, mid 40s overdressed business type. Send photo and resume c/o MMO, 17th Floor (43 W. 61st St, N.Y., N.Y)."

The results looked promising. It took several days to sort through the throng of hopefuls who lined up to audition. Ray personally supervised every element of the selection process, quickly sorting out those who met the requirements.

Through his connections with his former accompanist, now a successful composer, he found a financial backer.

Like a lot of artists, Ray felt he was a person of discriminating, even exclusive, tastes. He had seen the finished product that resulted from Mae's insistence on a certain level of quality when staging a play. This involved set design, costumes, and technicians behind the scenes. He felt his play deserved no less.

As the rehearsals rolled on, and Ray's expensive demands increased, his backer began to question the growing budget. To safeguard his investment, he decided to make a daily visit to the theatre. What he saw alarmed him.

Ray had morphed from a witty and clever theatrical type into a shrill and demanding director. He criticized every line the actors read, no matter how many times they tried it a different way. He insulted the stage designer's efforts to replicate the scenery he wanted. The constant interruptions slowed the rehearsals so much that the cast never got through a single scene. The backer decided a time-out was needed.

When he took Ray aside to calm the waters, he realized things had gone too far. Not only was the entire cast ready to walk out, they refused to read the obscene dialogue that Ray was substituting for the original. Ray had overestimated his ability to force the issue. When he threatened to walk out, the backer turned him in the direction of the stage door. He had overplayed his hand.

The show business papers quickly seized on the inflamed scenario, reporting the next day, "La Bourbon fled the rehearsal hall in a huff, accusing the producer of trying to 'castrate' the show by cleaning up the tawdry script. Bourbon felt the show would not have a chance without the vulgar element."

Ray's hissy fit seemed to parallel Mae outspoken objections decades before during the contentious rehearsals for *Sex*, her most controversial play. Unlike Ray's ill-timed exit and subsequent loss of financial backing, Mae knew the ropes and made good use of bad publicity. Mae prevailed where Ray failed.

An ominous footnote to the debacle was the dramatic exit Ray made from the show's rehearsals on the arm of baby-faced Bobby Randall Crane. Crane had been cast in a leading role, and he would later play a fatal role in Ray's life.

One of the turning points in the social revolution that had been sweeping the country all through the 1960s exploded at a little gay bar in New York City.

The Stonewall Inn at 57 Christopher Street in Greenwich Village was at the heart of a three-square-block gay community. It was there that New York experienced its first serious gay riot on June 28, 1969. The police, attempting to shut the little bar down, were met for the first time with fierce resistance. "We've had all we can take from the Gestapo," shrieked the infuriated queens. Within minutes, a huge crowd of supporters had surrounded the bar, blocking the street. When the police began to shove and push, the crowd exploded with a fury. The police backed off, dumbstruck, and called for the Tactical Patrol Force. Though the bar was permanently shuttered, the legal repercussions were felt all across the country. The Gay Rights Movement had officially begun.

Unfortunately for Ray, the new youth movement was no longer shocked by clever couplets and double entendres. They wanted to let it all hang out.

As Mae advised him, "If you put your foot in it, be sure it's your best foot." Ray just wasn't sure which foot was his best, or if it was even one in step with the times.

Like so many factors in the rapidly changing face of entertainment, drag queens had radically changed their approach to performing. The trend was to lip synch to a recording. Ray saw no value to imitating someone else, moving lips in tandem with a popular vocalist. There had been so many performers in his past that had that elusive something called charisma.

Now, impersonators all seemed canned. Like anything in a tin, he found they had very little flavor. Ray had worked a lifetime to harvest a crop of eccentric characters. His eye and ear for what made a person interesting or funny gave life to his impersonations.

"I don't want to be considered just as a man dressed as a woman," he said to those who championed the newer style of impersonation. He wanted to present his catalog of women as a symbol of the independent woman. Summing it up, he insisted, "Yes, they are outlandishly dressed up, frequently bitches, campy, and always worth imitating."

The 1960s ushered in a new term for an age-old style, "camp." Camp is really a style of acting and reacting to current social conventions. Camp relies heavily on the use of irony, humor, theatrics, and even Burlesque or ridicule. So-called normal social conventions frequently forced gay men to reconcile the contradictions they had to face between how they were expected to behave in society and how they really felt. They often did this through an expression of anger veiled in camp. Sheathed in the scabbard of humor the sword of their comicality could cut very deeply, often without the recipient of the thrust being fully aware.

Ray had always been a practitioner of the art of camp, a high priestess of the thinly-veiled insult. From the bygone era of the music hall, to the tawdry little gay clubs he was forced to play at the end, the double-edged text of his songs and patter never have a single meaning. The very same may be said of Mae. She, however, used the double entendre to sell her one message, unencumbered and uncensored sex. It is doubtful that she was consciously laughing at society, though her symbol of a strong woman in charge was decades ahead of the liberated woman of the 1960s culture.

When the craze for camp reached its zenith during the 1960s, Mae supposed it indicated that a whole new generation had discovered her—and they had—but in a less than flattering light. Her insistence that she was oblivious to the march of time made her a target of a cruel press. This was the era when most journalists referred to her as a drag queen, but not in a jesting manner. She was viewed as something grotesque and slightly unnatural. Her view of herself as an eternal sex goddess surrounded by randy young studs struck the wrong cord. It was her desperate attempt to unearth her former self, a self that required at least an approximation of a youthful appearance, which torpedoed her intentions.

Camp had become a pejorative, but Mae didn't seem to get it until it was too late. She believed too strongly in her myth, and never really understood the current meaning of camp. It wasn't the camp of the 1920s and 1930s, a more gentle poke at cultural institutions. Today's camp was often mean-spirited. Whether she realized this, in true Mae West fashion, she never let on.

Along with the change in social mores, music had dramatically changed. Rock and roll now ruled the recording industry. Mae was identified with early jazz and low down blues, such as "St. Louis Woman." She had swayed suggestively to the steady and slow accompaniments of some of the most famous jazz musicians, pouring forth her tales of stolen love and lust. She was still remarkably aware of the change in what was marketable in music. Always willing to polish her image while still keeping the things that made her Mae West, she decided to give this new sound a try.

In 1966, she entered the recording studio for the first time in years to cut an album that was rock and roll. It was aptly named *Way Out West* (1966). For the cover of the recording, she was transformed into a hip-looking woman of indeterminate age. Holding a guitar across her lap, she sported a new long hair style, and contemporary makeup. Gone was the long elaborate gown. She was in a psychedelic print dress and her legs were showing. The magic of the photography studio had created a new image, but one that was almost impossible to recreate in person.

The songs on the record were all current, with numbers by The Beatles and Bob Dylan. She displayed an affinity for this music, and surprised everyone with the strength of her voice and the solid delivery. The album sold well enough—100,000 copies—to produce two more over the next two years.

The end of the 1960s saw Mae experience a minor career revival. She was introduced to a whole new generation of followers. This came about partly because of the craze for "cult' classic films shown in coffee houses and art theatres. It was through this new awareness of the Mae West screen persona that she gained the dubious title of "Queen of Camp."

She capitalized on this as much as possible, giving interviews and making vague promises of a return to the screen. The impact of her camp crown on her own imagined image was to prove far more damaging than she could ever have imagined.

In 1971, the former queen of the Paramount lot returned to Hollywood. The brilliant author Gore Vidal had written a bestselling novel, *Myra Breckenridge*, (1968), based on a bizarre story of a man who undergoes a sex change. 20th Century Fox had purchased the film rights and needed a very established star to put across this controversial subject.

Mae was, at first, mystified that they would offer her a film in which she, the quintessential woman, should play the leading role as a transgender. They explained that the role of Myron would go to film critic Rex Reed, and the role of Myra would go to the relatively new Raquel Welch, an actress Mae pretended not to know. Mae's role would be that of a powerful Hollywood agent.

Only after Mae had extracted a promise of a $350,000 salary, total control of her script, her own designer, Edith Head, to create her gowns, did she acquiesce. As a final demand, she wanted to select certain males to play opposite her.

Remembering the long friendship that she and Ray had during the *Catherine Was Great* days, she instructed the studio to contact him. She also penned a personal letter, outlining a small role she had conceived for him. Even more importantly, she wanted his advice on the issue of transgendered people, the role Raquel Welch would be assuming.

She wasn't sure whether he had actually become a woman, even though she had heard from him first-hand when his claim of a sex-change had sparked such uproar. She felt he could give her a deeper insight into this still controversial procedure. Regardless whether his sex-change, or gender reassignment, was authentic or not, he might also have some material she could add to her script to give it more relevance. What the director had envisioned for her role was far from her idea of a starring part.

From the very beginning, the production was fraught with confusion. Mae insisted that only she could wear either all black or all white, and had this stipulation included in her contract. When Welch showed up on the set in black, the filming stopped until she was attired in another color. Mae constantly built up her own part, and changed the dialogue to suit her famous style. She soon came to hate the director, David Sarne. They clashed on every level.

When interviewed for *Playboy* magazine, Mae couldn't help making a dig at Welch, who had made a career out of undressing:

> "Let 'em wonder. I never believed in givin' 'em too much. I let the other women in Myra do that. My advice to those girls who think they have to take their clothes off to be a star: Baby once you're boned, what's to create the illusion? Never be obvious. Let both the men and the women wonder. The men for what they think they haven't got and the women for what they know they haven't got!"

Long after Mae died, Welch gave several interviews in which she assured the public that she felt that Mae was actually a man. Whether this was a publicity stunt for an actress who had little career left, or was actually an observation based on fact, will remain a mystery, just as so much of the Mae West myth remains unexplained.

Despite the rivalries and tension, Mae reveled in the attention paid to her on and off the set. Her every wish was met, just as in the old black-and-white days. She had the most luxurious dressing room of all the cast members and was delivered to the studio every day in a Rolls Royce.

Commenting on her still vaulted position, "Too much of a good thing can be wonderful." Just prior to the release of *Myra Breckenridge*, (June 1970), Mae sat down for an interview with columnist Dick Stroud:

D.S.: "The Empress of sex and wit, Mae West. At the age of seventy-six, Miss West has now returned to the screen to star in a 20th Century Fox production of Gore Vidal's *Myra Breckenridge*. . . We are in Miss West's glamorous apartment in the heart of Hollywood. May I say it is a pleasure to be here."

M.W.: "Ummmm, glad you made it."

D.S.: "This apartment is fantastic. Would you give us a brief description?"

M.W.: "Why, yes, love to. The décor is white and gold. I love anything gold. I'd like to have an apartment in Fort Knox sometime. The furniture is French. It's Louis the XIV. Even Louis would have loved it, especially in the boudoir.

D.S.: "You have so many beautiful mirrors."

M.W.: "Yes, I like to see how I'm doin'"

D.S.: "What is your definition of sex?"

M.W.: "Oh, well, sex is an emotion in motion."

There was a plethora of interviews published about Mae's return to the silver screen. Many articles looked at Mae with respect for her amazing durability in an age of fifteen minutes of fame. The one glaring exception was an article penned by the "English faggot," Cecil Beaton, as Mae's ever-faithful sister, Beverly, described him.

Beaton, a famous photographer, was to shoot scenes of Mae's apartment and include an interview for *Vanity Fair*. Mae, of course, insisted that she approve all photographs prior to publication. This was standard fare for any star. While the photograph's met with Mae's approval, what he wrote did not. He described her as having "Fat, pointed fingers ... borrowed hair ... false diamonds ... a muzzle like that of an ape." Mae was livid with Beaton's article and vowed never to agree to anything published until it received her final stamp of approval.

When *Myra Breckenridge* premiered in New York, the police had to control the crowds of fans that nearly rioted in an attempt to get close to the star. At the sneak preview of the film in San Francisco weeks before, the entire theatre stood and applauded Mae when she first appeared on the screen.

When the critics attacked the film, Mae was oblivious. As always, she drank her own bath water and believed her own publicity. This was her way of coping with what the mirrors on her ceiling must have told her. She was timeless and as self-absorbed as ever.

When Ray never arrived for his part in *Myra Breckenridge*, she brushed it aside, thinking he was too busy. Too occupied with holding together her fragile image, she never contacted him again.

The final chapter of Mae's film career closed, just as her stage career had ended, with a movie based on her play, *Sextette* (1961), which she had written many years prior. It was privately financed by a group of her wealthy fans. They fervently believed, based on all the hype created by her entourage of handlers, that Mae could still pull it off.

The ludicrous tale casts eighty-nine-year-old Mae as a twenty-eight-year-old bride. The story opens in London. The bride, a famous movie star, has just married her sixth husband. Mae's character, Marlow Manners, alights from a Rolls Royce and, supported by a horde of dancing bellhops, enters the lobby of a posh hotel.

The whole thing smacks of a poverty row musical from the 1940s. Decked out in full white bridal regalia consisting of an enormous white dress and veil, Mae levitates across the lobby of the hotel. She appears to be floating. No longer able to move at a normal pace, the studio rigged up a platform beneath the giant dress. A series of wheels with an attached wire pulled her forward. Her expression remained frozen in a perpetual half smile. Atop her head was a mound of bleached hairpieces that resembled a Dairy Queen® cone.

George Raft, the former star, who had given Mae her first film part, took a small role in *Sextette* (1978). George Hamilton and Ringo Starr were the other unlikely romantic interests of the octogenarian sex symbol.

One exception to all the negative statements that greeted the film's release was honest praise from the handsome Timothy Dalton, who played Mae's husband.

Dalton was an established star when he was offered the role. His many credentials included a starring role opposite Katherine Hepburn in *The Lion in Winter* (1968), major triumphs with the Royal Shakespeare Company, and a run as James Bond in *The Living Daylights* (1987) and *Licence to Kill* (1989). He certainly didn't need the small salary that was offered, but, like all the stars that made cameo appearances in the film, there was a feeling of respect and veneration for Mae's valiant attempt at a comeback. Dalton said:

> "I'll never forget meeting her for the first time. We went on to see Mae West at her apartment. Everything was white with gold trim on it. It was quite small, I thought, for somebody as fabulously rich as she was. It was only later that I realized she owned the entire apartment building, and the whole block. She then came in. She was wearing a white suit and a large bouffant hairstyle, and these long nails... there was a great lady. I was very curious, very fascinated by her. Not to put too fine a point on it, we were all wondering, knowing how old she was, if we were going to be able to work with her. As it happened, she was delightful. I think the most extraordinary thing about knowing her was the realization that she was a brilliant lady. When somebody is that famous, you're never quite sure whether her fame stems from the publicity hokum, but she could always come up with a line that was funnier than anybody else's. She took me aside as we were leaving her apartment that day. Squeezing my hand she said, 'Anytime you got nothing to do, and lots of time to do it, come on up!' Of course, she was a bit of a flirt. But she tried it only once with me! She had a twinkle in her eye, a nice sparkle. Oh, it is definitely an experience I wouldn't have missed for the world. The film was made as some sort of tribute to Mae, with all her old lines. But it went beyond that. It was a bizarre, extraordinary, and mad film, with Mae as a sort of centerpiece. If you took it seriously, you'd think it was grotesque. I mean here's this very old woman supposedly with six men all in love with her. I liked her. She could tell you stories about New York before the turn of the century, what Broadway was like, what life was like when there were still horses everywhere. And she was a star even then."

He went on to relate a charming anecdote of a bedroom scene the pair did in their honeymoon suite.

"She was actually ninety-one-years-old when she made *Sextette*, and she wasn't very good at remembering her lines. I remember one scene in particular. I had to come into the bridal suite with her, and I had to say, 'Oh darling, I feel like the first man who landed on the moon' and her line was something like, 'that's a small step for man and a giant leap into the boudoir,' but she could never remember it. I don't think she even knew that the Americans had landed on the moon, so there was this kind of lack of connection with this line! We did it again and again and again, and she kept forgetting, and every time we stood outside the door waiting to begin she'd tug at my sleeve and say, 'What's the line?' She'd get so annoyed with herself! One moment we walked in and I said, 'Darling, I feel like the first man who landed on the moon,' and she said, 'In a minute you're going to feel like you landed on Venus,' and into the boudoir we went!"

Sextette fared even worse than *Myra Breckenridge* at the box office. Most theatres refused to book it, and those that did, withdrew the film after a few days.

Rex Reed, who had appeared in the earlier Mae West freak show, *Myra Breckinridge* (1970), got back at the star for ignoring him during the filming. The serpent-tongued queen who wrote an important theatrical column cruelly described Mae's appearance in *Sextette*: "She looks like something they found in the basement of a pyramid."

Mae withdrew into her own world.

Ray continued to hang-on at the Jewel Box Lounge in Kansas City. I began to notice a world-weary aura hung over most of his performances, which I saw nearly every week during this period. He seemed more withdrawn and less talkative whenever I would meet him. He dwelled on his financial woes, and laughed when I told him that I, too, was cash strapped. He seemed to think because I was a hairdresser I was always flush with cash, probably based on the skimpy wad of dollar bills that were the accumulated tips of a week's work.

One night, he made a surprising suggestion. The Jewel Box Lounge, in an effort to bolster their dwindling audience, had begun a series of amateur night contests that paid the winners a grand total of $75. Despite my protestations, he told the manager, John Trujillo, that I would be a contestant the following week.

The prize money would be more than welcome, so I convinced a friend of mine, who could do drag at the drop of a hat, to join me as a duo act.

The end result was a pair of overly chic impersonators, more upper-class suburban than was the norm for a typical drag venue. Outfitted in shimmering white, pristine opera gloves, me in yards of black fox, and my friend, Phillip "Pansy" Beard, in white mink, all borrowed from our Mission Hills clients.

We chose the then wildly popular song, "The Shoop, Shoop Song (It's in His Kiss)," (1964) by Betty Everett as our number. Rehearsing in the mirror, we decided we needed something a bit raunchier to spice up our pallid girl group appearance.

On the night of the performance, as we came to the last phrase of the song, "Pansy" hiked-up his elaborate gown above his hips and dipped bow-legged up and down, a giant black furry spider attached to an elastic string bobbing wildly between his skinny legs. The audience, which we had augmented with every friend we could find, applauded and whistled wildly. The prize was ours, but we both decided that this would be our only foray into the wonderful world of performance.

It was during this time that Ray accepted an offer to appear at the Follies in Juarez, Mexico. The contract was for a month, the money was good, and the change of scenery would be welcome. The Follies was owned by a friend he had met in 1956 on his journey to Juarez when he visited the sex-change clinic.

Whenever Ray spent more than a few days away from home, he had a problem. His habit of collecting stray dogs had grown over the years. In mid-town Kansas City, which had now become home base, he rented a large space from a friend to keep the animals. It included an empty storage building with a high privacy fence in a rather derelict neighborhood. He visited the kennel each day and cared for the dogs. He couldn't ask anyone else to assume such a responsibility for so many dogs.

Whenever he travelled, his solution for the pet problem was to attach a trailer to his enormous old Ford station wagon. He fitted the trailer out with several wooden dog crates and crammed his costumes and belongings into the back of the wagon.

As he headed to Mexico, the car's wiring shorted out just North of El Paso, Texas. Within minutes, flames spread throughout the interior of the car. With the help of passing motorists, he managed to unhook the unscathed trailer from the inferno. With most of his stage wardrobe in ashes, it seemed his career was over.

In desperation, he searched his billfold for a number he might call for help. He found a stained business card with the name of a good friend in New York, composer Bob Wright. Ray had been instrumental in helping him get on at Paramount when he was working there as an extra. Wright had gone on to an award-winning Broadway career, writing such shows as *Song of Norway* and *Kismet*. Wright had always had a sympathetic ear for Ray's topsy-turvy life and career.

That afternoon, Wright wired Ray enough money to purchase a second-hand car, a well-worn Cadillac. With a new ride and the trailer intact, Ray decided to return to Kansas City. His Jewel Box Lounge contract would resume Halloween night.

The car's value proved to be short-lived, never getting the motley assemblage of trailer and tired occupant past the Texas state border. The engine blew in Big Springs, Texas. Ray had no choice but to find a kennel that would board his furry friends. He found one just outside of town. Arrangements were made with the owner, Mr. A. D. Blount, for a temporary boarding plan. With barely enough left to purchase a bus ticket, Ray crammed his remaining costumes in a battered suitcase and reluctantly returned to Kansas City to finish his contract at the Jewel Box Lounge.

He stayed in touch daily with Blount, sending payments each week from his dwindling bank account. When he had saved enough to pay off the balance, he rented a truck and set out to retrieve his pets.

Fifty miles outside of Big Springs, he called the kennel to let them know he was on his way. The reply from the other end of the line gave him a shock. He was told not to come . . . that his kind wasn't wanted around there . . . and that his dogs had been disposed of in February. Blount's way of disposing of the pets was to sell them to a medical research lab.

Ray returned on the long trip to Kansas City in a state of shock. Further trouble awaited him at his apartment. As he turned the key and opened the door, he was attacked from behind. A glancing blow inflicted a flesh wound on the back of his head. When he came to, he discovered his apartment had been ransacked. After a thorough search of the rooms, he decided not to call the police, thinking nothing of value had been stolen. Police involvement seldom resulted in a positive outcome. Gays were frequent targets of theft and mugging, and few law enforcement agents cared at that time.

The painful events of the last 72-hours were swept aside with the delivery of a registered letter the next morning from Hollywood. It was from Mae West's agent, informing Ray that his services had been requested by her for her new film. Shooting was to begin in six weeks. The film was *Myra Breckenridge* (1970), a story Ray knew from the bestselling book of the same name.

A return call to Mae's agent re-affirmed the offer. This would mean a fresh start, and the money he needed to continue his search for his beloved pets.

Feeling better than he could remember in recent memory, he decided he needed to share his good fortune. Boarding the bus, he made the short journey to his favorite watering hole, The Colony on Troost Avenue, a shabby neighbor to the Jewel Box Lounge.

The habitués of this dimly lit lounge were a mélange of humanity. Flamboyant drag queens rubbed elbows with small-time mobsters and prostitutes. In the center of the bar was an elevated stage with a piano, where amateur entertainers of every description held forth nightly.

One patron, the son of a wealthy society family, fancied himself an operatic performer. Dressed in a shiny velvet dinner jacket with a startling head of bleached hair, this combed-over queen would shriek out a series of Italian songs to an immune audience.

It wasn't hard to imagine why his mortified family, scions of the advertisement world, gave him an enormous allowance to stay away from home.

An over the hill drag with the improbable name of Barbara Lame attempted to recreate her days as a stripper. With a visage like a truck driver and the body of a turkey, this sorry sight clumped around the stage, greeted with howls of derisive laughter.

Ray never acquiesced to the patron's calls for his comedy routines. The owner offered no recompense, other than a couple of watered-down drinks.

Around the curve of the bar were perpetually seated a clutch of rich old queens from Kansas City's soignée Country Club Plaza, scanning the dark corners of the bar for young men for hire.

Decorators that plied their overpriced trade among the Mission Hill's elite mansion owners, stiffly coiffed hairdressers flashing sparkling pinky rings, closeted investment bankers carefully clothed in conservative suits, all surreptitiously shopped the "meat market" for a prize package to take home.

Cozily tucked in the embrace of one of these "Sugar Daddies" was someone Ray had known while appearing in Colorado, and later had hired for his ill-fated play, Daddy Was a Lady.

Handsome baby-faced Bobbie Randall Crain had been a one-night adventure for Ray. For Crain, it seemed that Ray must be an important show business figure, and Crain always had vague plans about being in show business. For Ray, it had meant nothing other than a quickie.

Crain joined Ray at the piano bar, holding up an empty glass in an obvious bid for a complimentary cocktail. Ray obliged, and was soon relating his tragic story of the loss of his dogs, followed by the much better news of his Hollywood offer. When Crain heard it was from no less a star than Mae West, Ray had his full attention.

That night, his guard let down after an endless series of vodka shots, Ray invited Crain to his apartment. Soon after their tryst, Crain, with help from Ray's meager bank account, rented a one-room apartment across from Ray's.

Whenever Ray was away for any length of time, Crain looked in on two elderly Chihuahuas that Ray had rescued from the animal shelter. The too trusting old queen had foolishly given the young punk a key.

Very early one morning, Ray was awakened by a knock. It was Crain, apologizing for such an early call. He was leaving town for a trip to Mexico, and wouldn't be available to baby-sit the dogs for two weeks. Ray continued the story:

> "We had coffee, and I asked him to take me shopping before he left. I needed makeup, the paper, and odds and ends. While we were out, he asked me for a $50 loan. He feared his car might not make the trip to Mexico and he'd need the extra just in case of trouble. I never carried money, only traveler's checks. We went to a Western Union, where I paid for a $50 wire to Dallas. This was his first stop on the way to Mexico and he could retrieve the money there. In a few days, he called from Dallas, affirming he had picked up the money. Several days later, he showed up at my apartment. He said he had changed his mind about the trip. I thought nothing of it."

I remember the last time I saw Ray Bourbon onstage in his "Rae" persona. It was at the Jewel Box Lounge. He appeared in a costume I had never seen before, a faded and slightly tattered jacket of blue silk brocade that barely fastened around Ray's increasing girth. Well-worn satin pants of a different shade of blue stopped just above his ankles. His wig, not the typical bouffant silver blonde affair, was a cottony white crop of curls such as worn by a liveried footman in days of old. Initially, I didn't realize the significance of this new look, nor did I suspect any other audience member that night.

Sitting on the silver stool he always used as a prop, sipping the inevitable cocktail, he began his monologue with a few familiar jokes, and then signaled the pianist to slow the tempo of the music.

> "I've been around a long, long time.
> When the man said 'Let there be light',
> I'm the bitch that threw the switch!"

Getting up slowly, he came to the edge of the stage. He indicated to the bartender to dim the house lights. A small spotlight moved uncertainly across the room, finally landing on Rae's well-lined face. The once flattering pink light now cast shadows on his lids from the enormous false eyelashes that could no longer hide the cruel march of time. The big flashy smile was still there, but there was none of the old glimmer in the tired eyes.

"Oh my dears, I'm glad you're here tonight. Don't you just love what I am wearing? This is the costume I wore when I portrayed the character of Florian at the Court of Catherine of Russia, when I was second only to the Queen in 'Catherine Was Great.' I was dressmaker to the Empress."

The tempo of the piano increased slightly as Rae began:

"I kept her buttressed in boucle
Very smart, very chic, and something very warm, for Mae
I had no trouble mixing with the ladies of the court
For I've been in and out of many of an entirely different sort
I wasn't always elegantly dressed in silks and lace
Life wasn't always Moet & Chandon, to swill or taste
I've had my lower moments, while entertaining everywhere
In dives you should remember, because most of you were there
I lead a life you read about in books they ban in Boston
I skipped around in circles even Oscar Wilde got lost in
I've been involved in stories that would smell just liked burned Crisco
I've entertained for royalty, been a gay old broad in Frisco
I've been talked about by experts, I've been slandered by the worst
What ever dirt they had on me, I always told it first
I've been mentioned in reports public, but never in 'Who's Who'
And I've never been asked to the White House
But after all, have you?
Now I've never been requested to endorse a cigarette
And there are hotels out in Hollywood I can't go back to yet
Whatever I've wanted to do, I've done
Whatever I've wanted to say, I've said it

You can laugh and leer at the life I've led
But, Mary, am I glad I've led it!"

Not long after, Ray was performing on the well-worn stage of the Jewel Box Lounge. He had done the usual songs and skits with the other cast members, "Sisters of Charity," and a bastardized version of the old chestnut, "Down on The Farm." Ray had a talent for taking the most innocuous of lyrics and turning them wrong-side-out.

"I wanna go down, I wanna go down, I wanna go down on the farm
Far away from harm, with a douche bag on my arm
I wanna be there, just to see there that certain someone full of charm
Oh how I wish again that I were in Michigan
And I'd go down on him on the farm!"

The rest of the cast cleared the stage and Rae came forward, as the house lights dimmed. He climbed on his inevitable stool and suddenly turned nostalgic.

"Some Chicago music, honey," he said to the little old lady at the piano in the pit. Like a favorite aunt telling a tale on herself he began the song, "Chicago, Chicago, that toddlin' town . . . ." and his voice trailed off into a monologue.

> "This occurred in Chicago several years ago in the 19 and 20s. I won't say what year, why should I give my age away. Not that you all don't know I'm over sixteen.
>
> "This big bitch and myself, you know her, Miss Sherry who looks exactly like a bottle with legs. Spread! Mary, when she sits down you've never seen so much in your life, all over the chair. You could cut enough off and feed the hogs for weeks.
>
> "But anyway, we were working Chicago, so to speak, and these two friends of ours were going to get married to each other. Well, in Chicago in those days you just didn't do those kinds of going on; that is not as openly as they planned on doing it.

"They decided they were going to defy convention and so they sent out 100 engraved wedding invitations to their wedding. They had planned it for an old church on the North side of Chicago, no less.

"You can check all this in the police records. It's all there, headlines and everything. So they decided on the church wedding and would have it on a Thursday.

"Well, the minister of the church had gone into the Wisconsin North woods, whatever he was going into the woods for, we may never know. And his son, twenty years old, who had been under suspicion for ages among our community, was going to preside. Well after this mess was all over, they proved the suspicions were correct.

"So, Miss Sherry and I got a hold of an engraved invitation and away we went to the church. I grabbed her arm outside and asked whether she really thought we should go in. She said she wouldn't miss it, Mary. She called me Mary for short, so we ducked into the church.

"I have never in my life seen anything like it. There were young men turning into young women right in front of my very eyes. Lipsticks, powder puffs, oh it was grand!

"So, I said to Miss Sherry that we should go back into the ante-room and say hello to the two who were getting married.

"We went back into the ante-room and said hello to all the old aunties. Then, we said hello to the two who were getting married.

"They were having a heated argument over which one was going to wear the veil! I asked them why not tear it in two and they could both wear it.

They drew straws, and decided they would tear it down the middle and share it.

"Mary, they looked lovely. I have never seen anything so grand as they came down the aisle. All of a sudden they got right up to the altar and the young man who was going to perform the ceremony was standing there looking as gay as a goose. You couldn't tell who was the bride, with her standing there.

"As she looked down at the two and said, 'Do you take . . .'"

"Before the couple could get an "I do" out, the law came busting in.

"I have never seen so many police in my life. If they had flashed their badges all at once we'd have gone blind from the reflections.

"There was such a commotion happening. The bitches were stripping off their drag. Everyone was running for cover.

"So, I told Miss Sherry this was certainly no time to run. They would catch us sure as hell. I grabbed her arm and ran for the church organ. I said we could hide in the organ and pulled her ass up the stairs behind the pipes. I shoved her into a big pipe, the G pipe, and I crawled into the A.

I cautioned her to just try and hang by her armpits, so there we hung, two scared bitches.

"We watched the exodus up the aisle, such a commotion as they ran for cover. It's the first time I ever saw faggots run down Michigan Avenue wearing stained glass halos. Voom! Right through the windows.

"We heard the wagons pull up, sirens screaming, police everywhere.

"Finally, they cleared out the church. There were lipsticks and powder puffs, bras and girdles everywhere. It looked like someone had thrown a hand grenade in Elizabeth Arden's.

"I panicked and said we had to get out of this damned organ and get away. I pulled out of the A pipe, but Miss Sherry couldn't get out of G. I ran down and turned the electric organ on, thinking I would blow her out of it. I found the G key, but it wouldn't budge her fat ass. All it did was shudder and make her cheeks turn red, her face too. If she had false teeth it would have blown every one of them out of her mouth.

"Just as I finally pulled her out, the law came charging down the aisle again. I grabbed her and ran for the windows. The church was built on the side of a hill and it was three floors down to the bottom. Sherry pushed the window open and we flew down the back of the hill.

"I tumbled down and fell into the arms of the biggest policeman I have ever seen. I knocked him out and he fell right on top of me. At any other time I wouldn't have minded.

"Miss Sherry jumped up and ran down the street. I told her to come back and roll this guy off of me. She stopped and came back. She rolled him off of me, and then the bitch rolled him. We hailed the first cab just as the cop came to. He watched as we waved good bye, disappearing down Michigan Avenue."

What few out front knew was the identity of Miss Sherry from Ray's story. Sherry was a real impersonator from decades before, who had been Ray's partner for several years on the Vaudeville circuit. So often, he sprinkled reality into the fantastical stories he spun. As the years passed, the line between the truth and often-told tales blurred, so that even Ray began to believe his monologues.

Ray came offstage following his bows. As always after a performance, he sat at his dingy little dressing table, wiping away the layers of makeup. There was a soft knock at his door. It was the little red-headed waitress with a message from the manager, John Trujillo, asking Ray to stop by his office on his way out.

Pulling on his old trench coat, he wrapped a long wool scarf around his neck and descended the stairs from the dressing rooms. The bar had cleared out, with a few of the hardcore locals still nursing their drinks. They smiled at Ray as he passed.

When he opened the office door, he was greeted by four Kansas City policemen and two Texas Rangers. They informed him they had an arrest warrant for Ray Bourbon and Bobby Randall Crain.

Ray was read his rights as he was put in handcuffs. The charge was the murder of Mr. Blount from Big Springs, Texas. Everyone was stunned, as suddenly ancient-looking Ray was escorted for the last time through the red leather doors of the Jewel Box Lounge.

Following an unnerving all-night interrogation, Ray was placed in the Kansas City jail for a term of 90-days. Crain was already incarcerated when Ray was locked-up. The two were then extradited to Texas to stand trial.

Given Ray's incarceration in the male-only jail quarters, the issue of his alleged gender reassignment from years earlier was finally settled: the operation was a bogus hoax for publicity.

During his time in jail in Big Springs, Ray learned from Crain his account of the whole terrible tale, an account that would soon be seriously altered.

According to Crain, he and his current boyfriend, Bobby Eugene Chrisco, had concocted a scheme to extort a ransom from Ray. The duo went to Blount's Kennel and tried to force Blount, at gunpoint, to reveal the whereabouts of Ray's animals. They knew once they had the location of the dogs they would be paid handsomely for their return. Blount refused to reveal the location of the animals, and a fight broke out. In the scuffle, the gun fired and Blount was killed. Crain confessed to Ray that he had stolen the gun from Ray's apartment weeks before.

Ray was sure, given the frank nature of the confession Crain made, that he would tell the same to the authorities. Instead, the young hustler accused Ray of having hired him to rough-up the kennel owner. Neither Chrisco nor Crain would admit to having fired the gun.

The jury did not believe them. Chrisco was tried and convicted of Murder with Malice in Big Springs. He was given a life sentence.

Ray's trial was moved to the little town of Brownwood, Texas. With no funds available, he had to use the services of a court-appointed attorney. The jury was made up of ten men and two women. As the prosecutor spun a tale of the tired old drag queen who had seduced the unwitting young men into murdering Blount, Ray knew he was in serious trouble.

He had always been able to read an audience, and this audience was definitely not sympathetic to anything that queer.

During the trial, more details emerged the differed from the account given to Ray by Crain. Prosecutors learned that, in their escape, the two men had thrown the murder weapon off the road at an undisclosed location just outside of town. When police found the gun, they quickly traced it back to Ray.

Prosecutors Wayne Burns painted a convincing portrait of Ray as a deviant wanderer and a phony, an untrustworthy impersonator of women, who was incapable of caring for a person, much less animals.

Public Defender William Bell Burns countered with his depiction of Ray as a rural Texan with good intentions that went awry. "Rae Bourbon, he sits as a stranger in this courtroom . . . Rae's background is not like yours and mine. It is probably not like anyone we know, or anyone we have ever known."

Blount's widow said under oath that the pets they took in were in deplorable condition. "Just mixed breed dogs . . . not a purebred in the bunch. The cats were what we'd term alley cats . . . Some of them were in bad shape, ears chewed off, legs chewed off, big old inch sores on them, waste matter about an inch or an inch and a half thick on the floor. There were two or three dead carcasses where they'd eaten each other; some of them were there with their insides eaten out of them. It was just a bad scene."

Ray denied that they had been reduced to cannibalism, but he admitted to the unsanitary conditions and countered that they were better off with him than as castaways.

The jury deliberated for four hours.

When they returned with their verdict, Ray was found guilty on the charge of Accomplice to Murder with Malice. He received a life sentence. The only reason he did not receive the death penalty was because of his age.

Baby-faced Bobbie Randall Crain got-off with ten years.

When news got out that Ray was in a Texas prison, he received several offers of financial aid from friends. He managed to get a call through to Mae, who offered to help, but nothing came from her. His former record producer suggested re-releasing some of his old records to raise funds for a new defense. None of the former retail outlets expressed any interest in the project.

The record producer was told, "Rae had a wonderful talent. He's full of laughs. In today's market, he's just not dirty enough. It's no longer enough to be witty, and let's face it, being gay is old hat now."

Being old hat was something Ray could never have imagined applied to him. He had been a pioneer in the gay entertainment world. His journey from the music halls of London, to the Vaudeville stages of America, with stops along the way in silent movies and sound films, and more recordings than any gay performer, revealed an astonishing life. He had played Carnegie Hall, and a Royal residence, he had worked onstage for years next to the legendary Mae West. Few entertainers, gay or straight, could claim such an interesting history.

19
You've Gotta Hold on to Fame

Ray's incarceration in the depressing quarters that served as the Brownwood, Texas, jail seemed interminable to the still energized entertainer. When he first saw the imposing castle-like structure, he was amazed that such a building could house a jail. The four stories were made up of six-foot-long hand-carved sandstones. On the right side was an imposing turret, and on the left an even taller one.

After he got over the initial shock of prison life, he began to take in his surroundings.

The sheriff had a private apartment on the first floor, which was off limits to everyone except his family. There was a simple playground for his children in the back yard of the jail. Adjacent to the sheriff's quarters was a smaller apartment for the jailer, the man who would eventually befriend Ray.

The second floor, in addition to the cell that Ray shared with three other prisoners, contained the "bull pen," a cage where families could visit the inmates by standing around outside and conversing through the steel mesh.

Meals were basic, often consisting of beans, potatoes, and corn. Sunday was the one day when some form of meat was served. The only things that were provided in unlimited quantities were strong black coffee and endless piles of bread. Ray often took several slices of the latter back to his cell, a practice that nearly all the prisoners shared.

Ray was never content to be idle for any length of time, and the looming threat of a lengthy sentence began to unravel his mind. He had traveled the world from an early age, always involved in a new project. All he saw looming in his future were 18-inch-thick sandstone walls. The lack of privacy, four men to a cell, twelve to a block, with the toilet, bathtub, and sink all in the open only added to his gradual descent into an unstable state of mind.

An attempted suicide by a fellow prisoner seemed to push Ray to the brink. The unfortunate man was found unconscious, a rubber hose ripped from a gas heater jammed in his mouth.

Everyone in the cell block where Ray was housed thought they knew the story of his life and the reason for his incarceration. Like most second- and third-hand retellings, it had grown in detail and diminished in fact. An aged drag queen that now seemed to be out of touch with reality was not what hardened prisoners saw as a kindred spirit. Only one person displayed any kindness.

One evening, after everyone was in bed and on lockdown, Ray had been permitted to make some personal phone calls from the desk phone of his jailer, a sympathetic man who was sorry for this misfit.

Ray still carried the tattered little black book that contained so many names from his past. Most numbers were no longer in service, and those he did reach either hung up or made vague promises to get back to him. One name in the book was Bob Hope. Long a mega-star, Hope made an attempt to aid Ray after Ray had reached his secretary and left the sad story of his plight and a plea for help. Hope called Ray's attorney, William Bell, but was told there was little the comedian could do to reverse Ray's fate.

Returning that night to the second floor where he was housed, he remembered he had one more call to make. Mae often answered her own phone. He had spoken to her after his incarceration and she promised to explore some legal channels. He knew she was busy with her new film, but he decided to take a chance she would answer his call.

They never got a chance to talk.

Ray, writing from his cell in Brownwood, Texas, tried to reach everyone in show business with a cry for help. *Variety*, June 3, 1970, published a desperate letter from him:

"This is the town where they pulled *Midnight Cowboy* for being obscene. I am sure it must be obvious to you now what chance I had here for getting a fair trial. I'm hoping you will mention this as I seem to have been completely forgotten by everyone; especially ones I've done favors for. I'll be grateful for anything you can say to attract any kind of aid. I am now on an appeal. But I need help. The address of the jail where I'm in is 212 N. Broadway, Brownwood, Texas 76801."

No help arrived from the world of show business.

He descended the narrow staircase to the gloomy public space where visitors were detained until they were cleared. He called out to the jailer, knocking on the door of the adjacent quarters of the officer. He noticed an outside door was ajar. Stepping through, the fierce December wind suddenly slammed it closed and it locked behind him.

Frightened to leave the vicinity, he wandered in circles, clothed only in thin prison garb, the biting Texas gale pummeling his frail frame. He was found at dawn, asleep on the floor of a truck parked next to the jail. A recent heart attack and the onset of leukemia had made walking very difficult. As the guards lifted him from the icy floor of the vehicle, he was heard to say, "If they had just shot me and ended the whole thing I would have been so much better off."

During his interment, Ray was in contact with *The Advocate*, a popular gay publication with a worldwide circulation. He had written to them about his plight, and the magazine published a full-length article covering his situation. The piece resulted in a flood of sympathetic letters to the editor.

> "Bourbon said recent publicity has gotten him a few phone calls and letters, but nothing tangible yet in the way of help.
>
> "It's easy to think about it and make a phone call, but that's usually it... The only thing that is keeping me alive so far is the Sheriff here, Joe Townsend, and his Chief Deputy, Oral Evans, and people like that who, I think, understand and know in their hearts that I am guilty of nothing except ignorance. They've been so kind, exceptionally kind."

Ray sent a letter to the editor of *The Advocate*, thanking him for publishing his story:

> "I cannot tell you how grateful I am. I think you've done a wonderful job of letting people know what has hap-

pened to me and the complete lack of consideration of the people in the theatrical profession. Actually, I was tried and convicted because of my background and due to the branch of the profession I was in. I was illegally extradited from the state of Missouri. Texas has no jurisdiction over me ... Common sense would surely tell anyone that the killing of the man was not the answer to finding my pets ... Common sense would most certainly verify that if I'd known what was going on, I'd have stopped it ... I'd have called the police in Kansas City ... Big Springs ... the Governor of Texas ... President Lyndon Johnson ...! Is it a sin to love all pets and animals ... how do you go about telling people this, especially if the people you are talking to don't even know the meaning of the word LOVE, not the expression of love. I shall always be indebted to you and the ADVOCATE for your help."
Bless you muchly,
Rae Bourbon
Brownwood, Texas"

Responses poured in to *The Advocate*:

"To the Editor:
   "An SOS to our own consciences. Can we stop being divided enough to do something about Rae Bourbon? He was a contemporary of my beloved friend, Francis Renault, of whom I have written extensively in the article, 'Four Of A Kind,' in *Gayways Magazine*.

   "Rae Bourbon as a performing artist received excellent notices, and I would disagree with his album producer, James Gardiner, whom I once knew.

   "Bourbon's many clever songs might well go over as the highest of camp, especially in these days where there is so much permissiveness ... whatever form this (help) takes, a fund, publicity, or additional write-ups in the gay press, I appeal to the conscience of the gay world. You may knock drag, but let's not let them drag down Rae Bourbon any further 'til he gets another trial and fair treatment. We can do no less for our own kind."

Robert Liechtj
Bronx, N.Y.

Seven months later, Ray died on July 19, 1971. His death certificate authenticated his true sex. A combination of pulmonary problems exacerbated by influenza and poor medical care brought an end to his extraordinary journey. He had almost made it to his seventy-ninth birthday. With no living relatives, no partner, and no resources, Ray was one of those unfortunates who could end in a pauper's grave.

When word of Ray's passing reached his friend, Bob Wright, in New York the composer made hasty arrangements for Ray's cremation. The ashes were transported to the Woodlawn Park Cemetery in Miami, Florida. Most of his friends had died, so with only a handful of old friends to say farewell, Ray's unembellished urn was lowered into a simple grave.

It had been a long and eventful saga for one of the true pioneers of female impersonation, from the barren landscape of Sierra Blanca to the artificial glamour and illusion of theatre and film.

Mae continued to drift in and out of reality. She remained housebound for most of the 1970s, making a rare foray into the limelight. At times, she seemed as invigorated as ever.

In April 1973, the Masquer's Club honored Mae with the coveted "Spelvin" award. Hollywood mogul, Joe Pasternak, presented the ageless star with the golden statuette of a nude male figure. Suggestively running her gloved hand up and down the phallic object, indomitable Mae murmured, "Oh... another man in my life."

That night, the room was packed with industry giants and celebrities. Among those honoring the screen legend was George Raft, the man who had given Mae her start at Paramount. There were several musical numbers by her, all sung in that unique throaty voice. The most interesting moment of the evening came when Mae surprised everyone with a special number she had created that recalled the tumultuous trial that surrounded her scandalous play, *The Pleasure Man.*

It is interesting to hear her ambiguous nod of approval to a man who cross-dresses, but who is also sexually attractive to her. Mae's lifelong attitude toward gays was both complex and, at times, ill-informed. She was particularly confused when she found a handsome man attractive and then learned he was interested in his own gender. That may explain her obvious preference for drags and impersonators. The lyrics allow a little peek at her views on the subject:

"One summer's day, I wrote a play
It all began about a man
The kind of men all the girls fall for
Strictly a bedroom man
He wasn't cold, I made him bold
I made him bad, he could be had
And then I called him my pleasure man
And then for atmosphere I added in some big he-men
And called them merry Marys
But when the cops came in and saw the big he-men
They said, why these guys is fairies!
Cops don't understand him
They think he's off key
If they only knew what he meant to me
Call around some evening, they could plainly see
Why he's my pleasure man
They say he wore step-ins and ladies' brassieres
With his hands on his hips
And yelled, "oops my dears!"
They're breakin' my heart
When they say he's queer
My pleasure man
He's know from Haiti to the Barbary Coast
Each flapper and madam he's had 'em
And that's his boast
He's Solomon's ghost
I had to kill him, he got too gay

> And I had no gun to finish the play
> So I cut out his 'you know what'
> And he died that way
> My pleasure man."

Mae sang three songs that night and did an extended skit from her play, *Diamond Lil*. The next day, the *Hollywood Reporter* wrote:

"She shook the rafters with her shimmying. Sister Kate could take lessons."

In 1978, Mae made one of her last attempts to reinforce her image as the eternal sex goddess. Television interviewer, Dick Cavett, approached her about being a guest on his CBS special, *Back Lot*. She agreed only if he allowed her to include two live musical numbers from her past hits, "Frankie and Johnny" (1933), and "After You've Gone."

The producers of the show were highly skeptical that she could manage it. When it came time to tape the numbers, several problems arose, including Mae's memory. Her movements had to be carefully explained to her, and numerous takes were spliced together later to give the impression of a spontaneous performance.

The technicians were astounded at her physical ability to endure the repeated shots under the stress of hot lighting, heavy costumes, and repeated directions. She remained composed through the entire process, happy to be back in front of a camera.

The resulting program impressed both critics and audiences. For the moment, she seemed truly eternal.

The body is a resilient but delicate vessel. Mae's famous body, now mostly an illusion of undergarments and cleverly-constructed gowns, was growing increasingly delicate.

Heart problems, aggravated by diabetes, were taking a toll. Her live-in lover and caretaker since 1954, Paul Novak, monitored the intake of the sweet-toothed Mae on a 24-hour basis. Like a petulant child, Mae demanded from Novak that he allow her an ice cream or a slice of her favorite torte. She depended increasingly on his still powerful arm to guide her.

When Mae did appear in public, it required hours of preparation in the privacy of her Ravenswood apartment. First, there was a manicurist to maintain the famous hands. Then, a makeup artist would deftly layer her parchment-thin skin with a creamy theatrical makeup in shades of pale peach and pink to give the illusion of perfect smoothness. Her eyes were lifted at the corners with stiff extended false eyelashes. These propped up her drooping eye lids, much like a steel rod holds up an awning. A special device, created by the famous makeup artist, Mark Traynor, pulled-up the sagging jaw line and tightened the throat. It consisted of a pair of strong elastic bands that were attached at each side of the throat with industrial-strength glue and then tied tightly on top her head. The result was a jaw line mimicking the Mae of forty years ago. The clever contraption was hidden under a long and impossibly blonde wig. The result some producers saw, in the often illusionary world of Hollywood, was a still marketable icon.

The last years of Mae's life could only be described as "living in Mae Westland." She spent hours each day answering the fan letters that continued to arrive at Ravenswood. She opened her enormous mirrored closets and tried on outfits from her past, movie gowns, the enormous feathered picture hats, which had their own closet. A beautician visited her regularly, tending to the many long wigs, done in the sausage curls she favored, much like Baby Jane.

In 1976, America's First Lady, Mrs. Betty Ford, invited Mae to the White House for the Bicentennial State Dinner in honor of Queen Elizabeth. This was an enormous honor. Mae quickly penned her RSVP, accepting this momentous invitation. Just as quickly, she was filled with trepidation. She had developed an intense fear of flying in the last few years, and could no longer overcome it. A train trip was out of the question, so she followed up with a "Mae West regrets . . ." note. Her companion, Paul Novak, tried to persuade Mae to reconsider, offering to accompany her. She shot back, "It's a hell of a long way to go for dinner."

During this twilight of her life, Mae had employed Craig Russell, a gay household servant, who also worked as a drag queen. She was aware of his extracurricular activities, and even gave him tips on performing. After leaving her employ, he was approached by a Canadian filmmaker to star in a small-budget movie called *Out-*

rageous (1977). The resultant fifteen minutes of fame went to his head, and led him to make a startling accusation.

He claimed to have been raped by Mae's chauffer. He went as far as to say that Mae had watched the whole episode through a two-way mirror. He also claimed that Mae West was man, but here the story takes a bizarre turn.

He insisted that Mae had died in the mid-1950s. Since she was the sole support of her two siblings, they concocted a plot to deceive the public. The siblings released a statement that Mae's brother had passed away. Mae's brother then assumed Mae's identity, wearing all her costumes and wigs. The former employee said he had carefully examined photos from that time. What he found was a person with very large hands, strong facial structure, and rather masculine features. Celebrity certainly makes strange bedfellows.

November 22, 1980, saw Mae West's final exit. Her certificate of death from the State of California authenticated her true sex. She was born on August 17, 1893, in New York to John West of New York and Mathilda Doelger, of Germany. She was a divorced, self-employed entertainer residing at 570 N. Rossmore, Hollywood, California. Dr. John Mason indicated cause of death was cerebral thrombosis and diabetes mellitus.

The funeral was an invitation-only affair, conducted at the Old North Church in Forest Lawn, Hollywood Hills. Hundreds of mourners were present. At the head of the cortege was Paul Novak, Mae's longtime companion, and four of the muscle men from Mae's famous Las Vegas act.

The presiding minister read the service gazing down from the pulpit at a gold casket covered in 100s of white roses. He couldn't resist the chance to remember Mae with a play on her own words as he described Mae as a, "good woman, and goodness had everything to do with it." As the celebrities and fans began to file out, the church organist played a jazzy rendition of, "Frankie and Johnnie," Mae's famous song from *Diamond Lil*.

One of the ironies of the financial outcome of the Mae West's estate was the paltry sum of $10,000 that was settled on Mae's faithful companion, Paul Novak.

Three days later, Mae's remains were shipped to the Cypress Hills Abbey, 833 Jamaica Avenue, Brooklyn, New York. It was there that Mae joined her beloved Tillie.

The little blonde girl from Bushwick, who began as a child amateur in Vaudeville, had come home an icon. Perhaps her life was best summed up with her own words:

"You've gotta hold onto fame as long as you've got it. You can't let anything interfere. You've gotta live for your public. I don't regret it."

A verse from a song in one of Mae's most famous films, *I'm No Angel*, seems to ask the question, "Who was Mae West?"

"I walk and talk like a queen. Man that's just what I mean."

Just what did she mean?

Appendix A

Rae and Mae Comment on Longevity, Show Business, and Life

At the end of his life, Ray told an interviewer:

"Talent is the most requisite of all accoutrements one may possess. Your looks are nothing. Your background is nothing. Your experience is nothing. If you have talent, all else fades into oblivion. With me, it is not guesswork. I have been in show business for over fifty years. Never become overly familiar with people, else they may become so with you. As I have said many times, all aristocratic and artistic people are eccentric. That is because we are not afraid of the crowd, the audience. I am only eccentric because I do not suffer a fool gladly and I do not allow anyone to criticize my art, which I have practiced for over half a century."

When asked about the difference between his original name, Ray, and the current Rae:

"They are both simply names . . . Ray was my given name and one I used for many years . . . Rae is really my stage name. Do you mean the Rae character or the person Ray? It is complex, the Ray is the person you are interviewing now, the Rae is the name that makes my living. Rae doesn't really exist . . . if so I might be committed to a mental hospital . . . What I do onstage, to make people laugh, is not the person you would see in private life. My stage persona is a joke. So many critics cannot seem to get past the gowns, wigs, and makeup."

Mae wrote:

"I feel I am in a class by myself . . . I have only done what comes naturally. I never wanted children. I was too absorbed in myself . . . a woman becomes a different person when she is married. I wanted to live for myself. To be a star you have to be a little better than anyone else. I guess I wasn't conscious of being sexy . . . it was always natural for me, it was never a strain. I guess that is why it goes over so well. I make fun of vulgarity, I kid sex. My fans expect certain things of me. It's not what you do, but how you do it.

You have to be healthy on the inside or else it shows on the outside. I don't like to be made nervous or angry . . . it tears down your nervous system. My secret is positive thinking and no drinking. I've lived the same way ever since I can remember. Everything I do pertains to myself. I've always been two people . . . no one can write Mae West dialogue better than Mae West."

Appendix B

Films of Mae West

Night After Night (Paramount, 1932)

She Done Him Wrong (Paramount, 1933);
 based on Mae West's play, *Diamond Lil*)

I'm No Angel (Paramount, 1933)

Belle of the Nineties (Paramount, 1934;
 based on Mae West's original story, *It Ain't No Sin*)

Goin' To Town (Paramount, 1935)

Klondike Annie (Paramount, 1936)

Go West, Young Man (Paramount, 1936)

Every Day's a Holiday (Paramount, 1938)

My Little Chickadee (Universal, 1940)

The Heat's On (Columbia, 1943)

Myra Breckenridge (20th Century-Fox, 1970)

Sextette (Crown International, 1978)

PLAYS OF MAE WEST
(AS AUTHOR AND/OR PERFORMER)

Sex (1927; written under the pseudonym Jane Mast)

The Drag (1927; written under the pseudonym Jane Mast)
   [With Ray Bourbon, unattributed/credited]

The Wicked Age (1927)

Diamond 'Lil (1928; revival in England in 1947)
   [With Bourbon, as Bowery Rose]

Pleasure Man (1928; author only)

The Constant Sinner (1931; from the novel May West novel, *Babe Gordon*)

Clean Beds (1939; co-author)

Catherine Was Great (1944)
   [With Bourbon, as Florian]

Come On Up (1946; first known as *Ring Twice Tonight*)

Sextette (1961)

Appendix C
Films of Ray/Rae Bourbon

Tiger Love (1922)

Only a Shop Girl (1922) starring Estelle Taylor

Blood and Sand (1922) starring Rudolph Valentino

Manslaughter (1922) a Cecil B. DeMille Production
    starring Thomas Meighan

Beyond The Rocks (1922)
    starring Gloria Swanson and Rudolph Valentino

Bella Donna (1923) starring Pola Negri

Salome (1923) starring Alla Nazimova

The Alaskan (1924) starring Estelle Taylor

The Volga Boatman (1926) starring William Boyd (Hopalong Cassidy)

Where East Is East (1929) starring Lupe Velez, Estelle Taylor

Hip Zip Hooray (1933) (aka *Zip, Zip, Hooray*)
    a short starring Eugene Pallette

Gold Diggers of 1937 (1936) starring William Powell

Ever Since Eve (1937) starring Marion Davies

He Done His Duty (1937) a short

Little is known of the many other films in which Ray is said to have appeared either as an extra, bit player, or stunt double at Vitagraph Company of America, and the other silent film studios in New York, as well as California, because the films, along with the records associated with them, are considered to be lost.

He worked for a time at the relatively obscure Chesterfield Motion Picture Corp., and other poverty row lots, such as Monogram, but no records are known to remain.

Ray was a frequent stand-in for the actress, Estelle Taylor, during the 1920s. Late in life, Ray claimed to have been in Cecil B. DeMille's original version of *The Ten Commandments* (1923) as one of hundreds of other extras. As Ray told it, "Not with the original Moses, although I may look that old."

Aside from a myriad of clubs in the United States, Ray, as "Rae," appeared in such diverse and exotic locations as Buenos Aires, Cairo, Havana, Hong Kong, Istanbul, Juarez, Madrid, Mexico City, Paris, Rio de Janeiro, and Shanghai.

Appendix D

Sound Recordings of Ray/Rae Bourbon

What remains today of Ray/Rae Bourbon's unique voice is an amazingly large collection of recordings of him performing live, and in a studio. His recording career spanned more than thirty years.

He began in the days of 78 rpm recordings, where he is believed to have produced an estimated 40 cuts on various labels, some of which include:

I Want to Be Good (Brunswick Studios, 1931)

Trombone Trixie / First Swimming Lesson
   (Liberty Music Shop, New York, ca. 1935)

Bourbon to the Cleaners (Liberty Music Shop, New York, 1936)

In Other Words, aka *Fly Me to the Moon*
   (Western Record Company; Bourbana label; Hollywood, 1936)

Gigolo / Chiropractor's Wife
   (Western Record Company; Bourbana label; Hollywood, 1930s)

Navy Day for Tessie / Spanish (Western Record Company; Bourbana label; Bart Howard, piano; Hollywood, 1930s)

Russian Refugee / Tennis Champ (Western Record Company; Bourbana label; Bart Howard, piano; Hollywood, 1930s)

First Swimming Lesson / Love Child (Western Record Company; Bourbana label; Bart Howard, piano; Hollywood, 1930s.)

The Trial of Carrie P. Pots (Western Record Company; Bourbana label; Bart Howard, piano; Hollywood, 1930s.)

Cocktail Time / Forbidden Broadcast (Western Record Company; Bourbana label; Bart Howard, piano; Hollywood, 1930s.)

King Arthur's Knights / Strip Queen (Western Record Company; Bourbana label; Bart Howard, piano; Hollywood, 1930s.)

Country Ham / Forty-Five
(Imperial; Brenda Ughakki, piano; Hollywood, 1940s)

Hilarity from Hollywood (Hollywood, ca. 1940s)
Includes the tracks:
    "Strong, solid & sensational"
    "Bourbon to the cleaners"
    "The model"
    "Sahara"
    "Professor Yussell"
    "Family Tree"

Take a Lei / Chief Peanut Stand (Imperial; Four Stars Musical Group with Bart Howard; Hollywood, 1941)

Sunday Ride (Imperial; Bart Howard, piano; Hollywood, 1941)

My First Piece / My Last Piece (Imperial; Joey Melborn, piano; Hollywood, 1941)

Tessie / Fountain of Youth
(Imperial; Bart Howard, piano; Hollywood, 1941)

Her First Piece / Strip Tease Queen (ca. 1941-1949)

Later, single-acts by "Miss Rae Bourbon" were captured on 45-rpm records. Examples that survive at only one or two libraries in the U.S. include:

Barbary Coast (Lasses Record Company's "Celebrity Series," New Orleans, La., ca. 1950s)

Spanish / New Woman (Lasses, ca. 1950s)

Madam / Native (Lasses, ca. 1950s)

Dirty Fairy / Hollywood Drive-In (Lasses, 1957)

Finally, Rae's work was cut into long-playing (LP) 33 1/3 rpm vinyl discs, where many of his former 78 rpm work was re-issued. The most complete collection was produced on 10 discs in New York between 1954 and 1959 on the Under the Counter (UTC) label. Here are those known to survive, which have been re-released, as noted:

UTC-1: *An Evening in Copenhagen*

UTC-2: *You're Stepping on My Eyelashes* combined and re-released in 2002 as "The UTC Recordings, Volume 1," and includes:
"The Wedding"
"Mr. Wong"
"Erma's Weekend"
"The Raid"
"Mrs. Bevington Swope"
"A Gentleman's Gentleman"
"Sisters of Charity"
"Extended Play"
"Life Goes to a Party"
"Queen of the YMCA"
"Back in Drag Again"
"Queen of the Ballet"
"Tom Thumb"
"Peter Pan"
"The Family Tree"
"Queen of the Navy"
"I Must Have a Greek"
"Party Line"

UTC-3: *Don't Call Me Madam / The Family: A Trilogy*

UTC-4: *A Girl of the Golden West* combined and re-released in 2002 as "The UTC Recordings, Volume 2," and includes:
"The Neighbor's Party"
"Tennessee"
"The Family: Sunday Ride"
"The Family: The Cafeateria" (i.e., The Cafeteria)
"The Family: Bed-Time Story"
"Country Ham"
"To Hell with the Range"
"The Railroad's Comin' Thru"
"Horse Opera"
"Ugh!"
"Pocahontas"
"Where Does the Difference Come In"

UTC-5: *Bourbon 100 Proof*, and

UTC-6: *One on the Aisle: Claque-claque* combined and re-released in 2002 as "The UTC Recordings, Volume 3," and includes:
"An Oriental Opera"
"Sailor Boy"
"Hamlet's Soliloquy"
"The Carpenter"
"The New Neighbor"
"Tennis"
"Spots"
"Strong, Solid & Sensational"
"Toga Saga (A Greek fantasy)"
"Sahara"
"Brunhilde's Emulsion"
"Orchids to Alice"
"Carmen"

UTC-7: *Let Me Tell You about My Operation*, and

UTC-8: *Around the World in 80 Ways* combined and re-released in 2002 as "The UTC Recordings, Volume 4," and includes:
"Let Me Tell You about My Operation"
"Oh! Doctor"
"I'm in the Family Way"
"Mrs. Willoughby Will Definitely Object"
"When I Said 'NO' to Joe"
"I Don't Want To Be a Madam"
"Millie"
"The Piano Teacher"
"Telephone Girl at the Ritz"
"Russian Refugee"
"Cleopatra and Her Asp"
"The Stipend Must Rally 'Round Here"
"British Ways"
"Bourbon Goes Native"
"The Fortune Teller"
"Spanish"
"Nero"
"Mr. Wong"
"Ponce De Leon"
"One For The Road"

UTC-9: *Hollywood Expose*, and

UTC-10: *Ladies of Burlesque* combined and re-released in 2002 as "The UTC Recordings, Volume 5," and includes:
"Bourbon Has Been to the Cleaners"
"Percy"
"The Last of Bobby Soxers"
"When Yussel Gave Me Muscle in a Hustle"
"Dancers of Nature"
"My Petty-Gree"
"Constance Isn't Constant Anymore"
"She's Only a Link in a Daisy Chain"
"When Knighthood Was in Flower"
"Tessie, The Messy Extra"

"Strip Queen"
"Parade Girl"
"Cocktail Time"
"Anne, Fanny, Tessie, Bessie & Flo"
"Old Mrs. Richbit"
"Three Girls at a Matinee"
"Forty-Five"
"The Awkward Age"

In the 1960s, Ray Bourbon released, *A Trick Ain't Always a Treat*, on his own label, Jewel Records. This was a mix of studio and live material, the latter recorded from the stage of the Jewel Box Lounge, Kansas City, Missouri. Tracks include:
"The First Show"
"The Second Show"
"Spanish"
"New Woman"
"Barbary"
"The Party"

Just a few of the reviews of the above recordings include:
-"For the preferred list." Danton Walker, *New York Daily News*
-"The best night club star in the business." Earl Carroll
-"So real, and so funny, you think it is actually happening." Errol Flynn, film star

Testament to Ray Bourbon's legacy is the more recent re-issues of his work, some of which bring to light long-lost tracks. Notable are:

Doity Records, Volume 1 (Doity Records, 2000)
"Her First Piece"
"Swimming Lesson"

Her First Piece: The Best of the 78's (Cool Cat Daddy Productions, 2002)
"Sisters of charity"
"Her first piece"

"Three shop girls"
"Low brow Bourbon"
"Spanish passion"
"Cocktail time"
"Forbidden broadcast"
"Strip tease queen"
"Chiropractor's wife"
"Gigolo"
"Trombone Trixie"
"Bedtime store"
"Spanish opera"
"Oriental opera"
"Susie"
"Sarah from Sahara"

Gland Opera: Volume 2: Best of the 78's (Cool Cat Daddy Productions, 2002)
"Man's man"
"Take a lei"
"Sunday ride"
"Gland opera"
"To hell with the range"
"Hollywood appendicitis"
"Since Ivan started divin'"
"Hollywood drive-in storehouse"
"Boubon to the cleaners"
"The Bourbon motif"
"Strong, solid, sensational"
"The model"
"I had a piece"
"Vacation in Nevada"
"Air raid warden"

Yes! This is Ray Bourbon (Cool Cat Daddy Productions, 2002)
"The first show"
"The second show"
"Madam"

"Native"
"Dirty fairy"
"Hollywood drive-in"
"Untitled" (recorded at a private party in New Orleans, ca. 1965)

Appendix E

Cookin' With Mae and Rae

Mae, given the image she projected, probably never swathed that famous hourglass figure with an apron, yet her one of her recipes—Spiced Cheese Mould—was discovered in a 1936 booklet distributed by the Rosedale Theatre.

Ray, out of necessity for his gypsy existence, was a credible cook. Steve Puckett and Steve Harris, owners of Steves' Market and Deli in Brownwood, Texas, named a sandwich after him, the Ray Bourbon Club—appropriately stacked with ham. The Ray Bourbon Club consists of toasted focaccia, sliced ham, Swiss cheese, bacon, and a charred pineapple bourbon sauce.

Steves' Market and Deli in Brownwood, Texas.

Mae West's Spiced Cheese Mould Recipe

Mash 2, 3-ounce packages of cream cheese with 1/4 cup butter. Add 1 teaspoon paprika, 1 teaspoon capers, 2 minced anchovies, 1 tablespoon of chives (chopped), 1/2 teaspoon caraway seeds and 1/2 teaspoon salt. Blend all ingredients with cheese mixture very well. Place in mold, cover tightly, and set in refrigerator. Let this remain in refrigerator for several hours.

Mae West's photo accompanying her recipe.

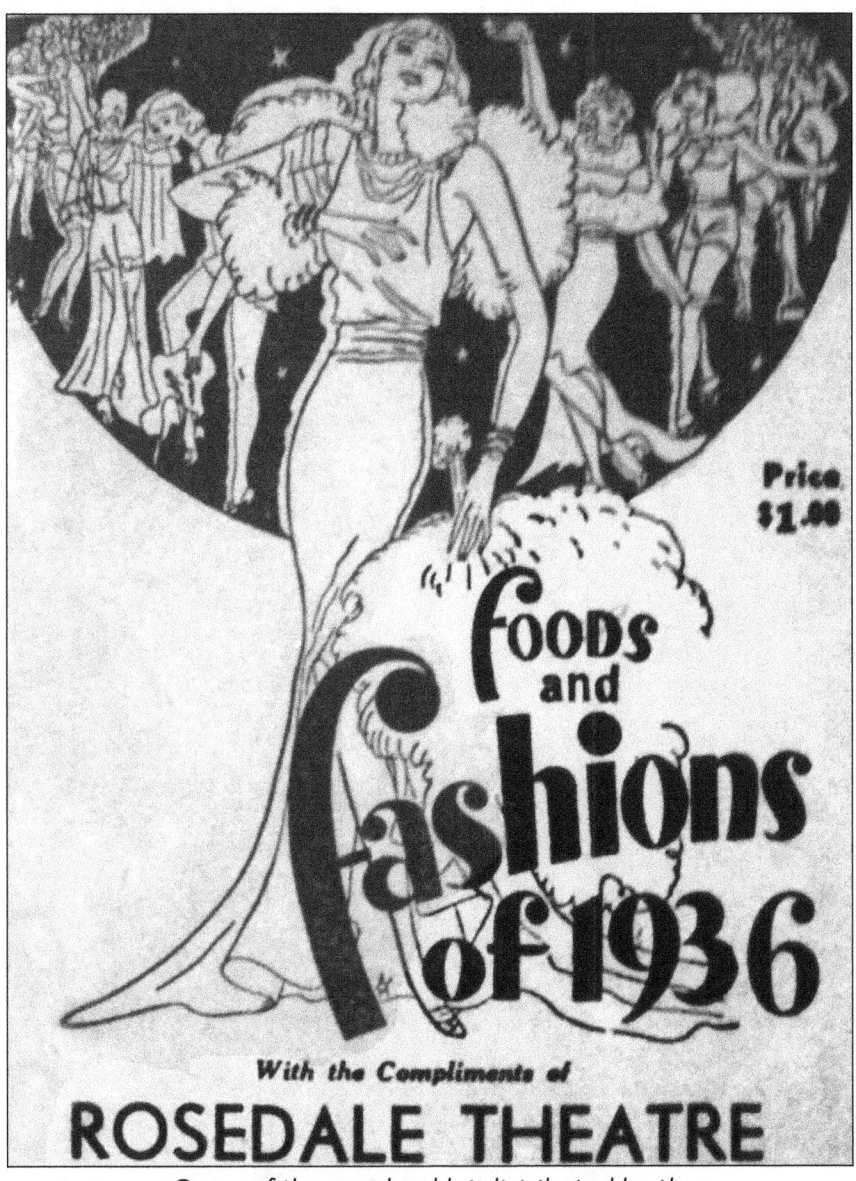

Cover of the 1936 booklet distributed by the Rosedale Theatre.

Bibliography

Basten, Fred E. *Max Factor's Hollywood*. (Santa Monica, Ca.: General Publishing Group, 1995.)

Bourbon, Rae. [See Mann, Richard F. below].

Conner, Floyd. *Lupe Velez and Her Lovers*. (New York: Barricade Books, 1993).

Drutman, Irving. *Good Company: A Memoir, Mostly Theatrical*. (Boston: Little, Brown and Company, 1976.)

Erdman, Andrew L. *Blue Vaudeville*. (London: McFarland & Co., Inc. 2004).

Freedom of Information Act Document CG 62-5703 State of Texas v. Ray Bourbon, 8067 Tex. 35d 555, 1971.

Gilbert, Douglas. *American Vaudeville*. (New York: Dover Publications, 1940).

Glyn, Elinor. *Beyond the Rocks*. (New York: The Macaulay Co., 1906.)

Harris, Warren G. *Cary Grant*. (New York: Zebra Books, 1987).

Jackson, David W. *Changing Times: Almanac and Digest of Kansas City's LGBTQIA History*. (Greenwood, Mo.: The Orderly Pack Rat, 2016).

"Juarez Actor Gets Fortune. Hal Waddell's Father Leaves 1,500,000 Estate." In the *El Paso Herald Post*, July 27, 1931.

Laurie, Joe. *Vaudeville: From the Honkey-Tonks to the Palace*. (New York: Henry Holt, 1953).

Leider, Emily Wartis. *Dark Lover*. (New York: Farrar, Straus and Giroux, 2003).

Mann, Richard F. [Alias of Rae Bourbon]. *Hookers*. (Philadelphia, Pa.: House of Bourbon, 1932)

Miller, Frank. *Censored Hollywood*. (Atlanta, Ga.: Turner Publishing, 1994.)

Mordden, Ethan. *The Hollywood Studios*. (New York: Simon & Schuster, Inc., 1989).

"Patronage Shows No Falling Off." *Motography*, November 17, 1917, page 1015.

Porter, Darwin. *The Secret Life of Humphrey Bogart*. (New York: The Georgia Literary Association, 2003.)

Puckett, Steve and Steve Harris. "Steve's Soapbox." Retrieved March 29, 2017, from the website: http://stevesmarketanddeli.com/2004/12/brownwood-bob-hope-mae-west-rae.htm

Rose, Phyllis. *Jazz Cleopatra*. (New York: Vintage Books, 1989).

Rosedale Theatre. *Food and Fashions of 1936*. "Mae West's Spice Cheese Mould."

Samuels, Charles and Louise. *Once Upon a Stage*. (New York: Dodd, Mead and Company, 1974).

Senelick, Laurence. *The Changing Room*. (London: Routledge, 2000.)

Sochen, June. *Mae West: She Who Laughs, Lasts*. (Arlington Heights, Il.: Harlan Davidson, 1992).

Variety, June 3, 1970, page 51. Letter to the editor from Rae Bourbon.

Wenden, D. J. *The Birth Of The Movies*. (New York: E.P. Dutton, 1974).

West, Mae, and Lillian Schlissel. *Three Plays by Mae West*. (New York: Routledge, 1997).

About the Author

Patrick Byrne, born to Irish immigrant parents, was educated at a private Jesuit boy's academy and Rockhurst University in Kansas City, Missouri. He describes his "peripatetic years" as spent whirling around town as a make-up artist, stylist, and wig master. This led to his fortuitous meeting with the subject of this book, Rae Bourbon. In his subsequent retrospective years, Byrne indulged his love of opera by creating a classical CD label, Ombra Records, devoted to Maria Callas. He also co-authored *The Colors of Callas, Reflections of an Icon* with Taylor Pero. Byrne is also the music critic for *The Belgian Opera Guide*.

About the Editor

David W. Jackson, author, historian, and historic preservationist, is founder and director of The Orderly Pack Rat which he founded in 1996 after graduating magna cum laude from Southeast Missouri State University with a BS in Historic Preservation—Archives Studies. His 20+year professional career included Archives and Education Director for the Jackson County (Mo.) Historical Society, and Archivist for Unity School of Christianity. In 2009, Jackson co-founded the Gay and Lesbian Archive of Mid-America (GLAMA). He is author of numerous books, periodical articles, and newspaper columns, including *The Phoenix Newsletter: Kansas City's LGBT Newsletter*. In 2016, Jackson published a second expanded edition of *Changing Times: Almanac and Digest of Kansas City's LGBTQIA History*. To learn more about Jackson and The Orderly Pack Rat, visit orderlypackrat.com.

INDEX

100 Club 316
Diamond 'Lil" (1928 355
20th Century-Fox 354
A La Broadway 45, 46
Abel, Betty and Milt xiii
Academy Awards xv, 262
Acker, Jean 112
Advocate magazine 344
After You've Gone 348
Alaskan, The (1924) 356
Albee, Edward F. 129, 130
Alex, Joe 253
All the Nice Girls Love a Sailor 20
Ameche, Don 242
An Old Man's Darling (1903) 22
Any Kind of Man 77
Arcade Hotel 89
Are You Listening? (1932) 196
Baby It's Cold Outside 302
Back Stage at Earl Carroll's 145
Baker, Josephine 251, 252, 253, 254, 255
Bankhead, Tallulah 190, 275, 277, 278, 280
Banton, Travis 207, 208
Barrie, Jean 135
Barrymore, John 118
Bayes, Nora 83
Beard, Phillip "Pansy" 329
Beardsley, Aubrey 113
Beck, Martin 130
Bella Donna (1923) 356
Belle of the Nineties (1934) 188, 210
Belle, Flower 248, 249
Bentley, Gladys 41, 42
Bergen, Edgar 242
Berkley, Busby 224
Berner, Doc 309
Best Boy, The 20, 31

Better Times (1922) 103
Beyond the Rocks (1906) 115
Beyond the Rocks (1922) 116, 125, 197, 286, 356
Big Boots (1889) 20
Billboard magazine 268
Biltmore Theatre 90
Blackwell, Mr. *See* Dick Ellis
Blair, Francis 143
Blanco, Benny 289
Blonde Venus (1932) 190
Blood and Sand (1922) 110, 356
Bob's Meat Market xv
Bogart, Humphrey 127
Botsford, A. M. 208
Bourbana label 358, 359
Bourbon's birth 3
Bourbon's death 346
Bowery Rose (Bourbon character) 283
Boys Will Be Girls 143
Brando, Marlon 275
Breen, Joseph 188, 208, 209, 210
Brennan, Jay 26
Britton, Jan 309
Brown and Berner 311
Brown of Harvard (1926) 196
Brown, Bothwell 122
Brown, Danny 309, 314, 315
Brownwood, Texas vii, 339, 342, 345
Bruno (female impersonator) 310
Burlesque 25, 26
Burnett, Carol 35
Bushwick, NY 1, 3, 8, 13, 192, 351
California 60, 64, 112, 131, 139, 144, 217, 241, 256, 265, 350
Camp 321
Candide 251
Cantor, Eddy 73

Captive, The (1926) 85, 89, 127
Carnegie Hall 257, 341
Carnival Lounge 203
Carradine, John 260
Carson, Daniel 143
Carson, Freda Josephine *See* Josephine Baker
Catherine Was Great (1944) 264, 266, 268, 269, 270, 323, 355
Catholic Legion of Decency 210
Cave, The 203
Cavett, Dick 348
Chaplin, Charlie 214, 237
Charlie's Aunt (1892) 31
Chase and Sanborn Hour 242, 244
Cheerio Club 203
Cherrill, Virginia 214
Chesterfield Motion Picture Corp 194, 357
Chez Boheme 204
Chrisco, Bobby Eugene 339
City Lights (1931) 214
Clayton, Herbert 35
Clean Beds (1939) 355
Cleopatra and Her Asp 81
Clover Club 204
Club Hollywood 205
Coconut Grove Theatre 308
Cohen, Emmanuel 209
Collingwood, Charles 305
Colony Club (Kansas City) 331
Columbia Pictures 196, 356
Columbia Records 278
Come On Up (1946) 280, 307, 355
Congo Room 304
Constant Sinner, The (1931) 92, 93, 126, 355
Cool Cat Daddy Productions 363, 364
Coon Chicken Inn 203
Cooper, Gary 190, 212, 213, 216
Coral, Tito 306
Cortez, Ricardo 260

Country Club Plaza 332
Crane, Bobby Randall 320, 332, 333, 338, 339, 340
Crawford, Joan 195
Crazy Gang 236, 237, 239
Crepe Paper Fashion Plate 54
Crescent 81
Crosland, Alan 116
Crown International 354
Cuddle Up And Cling To Me 52
Cunard, Lady 238
Daddy Was a Lady 318, 332
Daily Variety magazine 210
Dale, Lily 288
Dalton, Timothy 326
Dame, The v, 20, 21, 22, 30, 31, 32, 33, 34, 41, 60, 69, 85, 144, 146, 227, 229
Danse Sauvage 253
Davies, Marion 356
Davis, Carrie xvi, 310
Dean Martin Show 307
Deiro, Guido 74, 76, 77, 241
DeMille, Cecil B. 109, 356, 357
Deslys, Gaby 46
Destry Rides Again (1930) 246
Deuces Wild Club 289
Devil and the Deep (1932) 190
di Frasso, Countess Dorothy 212, 213, 214, 215, 217
Diamond Lil 93, 94, 95, 125, 133, 189, 191, 257, 280, 282, 283, 284, 285, 286, 289, 294, 348, 350, 354
Dietrich, Marlene 141, 190, 206, 207, 208, 245, 246
Dixie Steppers 253
Dogs (and Bourbon) 7, 13, 64, 113, 298, 315, 329, 330, 331, 332, 333, 339
Doity Records 363
Don't Call Me Madame 257
Dorney, Neil 143
Double entendres xii, 31, 38, 81, 278, 320

Drag queens *See* Female impersonators
Drag, The (1927) 86, 89, 96, 125, 198, 318, 355
Drift Inn 203
Eagle Has Two Heads, The (1947) 275
Ellington, Duke 209
Ellis, Butch xv
Ellis, Dick 266
Eltinge, Julian 53, 56, 102
England xvii, 12, 19, 20, 21, 22, 34, 35, 37, 38, 40, 42, 48, 57, 60, 81, 101, 103, 111, 112, 134, 227, 228, 229, 230, 235, 236, 239, 250, 276, 280, 281, 282, 299, 326, 341
Entratter, Jack 277
Errol, Bert 31
Ever Since Eve (1937) 145, 356
Every Day's a Holiday (1938) 242, 244, 245, 354
Factor, Max 111, 194, 195
Fag hag 195, 234
Farrell, Glenda 225
Fast Life (1932) 196
FBI (and Bourbon) 315, 316
Female impersonators ii, v, xix, 5, 20, 26, 27, 31, 32, 35, 39, 40, 41, 53, 56, 80, 86, 87, 88, 94, 96, 97, 99, 102, 103, 122, 134, 139, 140, 141, 143, 144, 207, 229, 250, 270, 271, 290, 291, 293, 296, 298, 309, 311, 320, 329, 347
Femme mimic 289
Fields, W.C. xi, 246, 247, 249, 250
Finnochio, Joseph 270, 271, 272, 276
Finnochio's 270
Fitzgerald, Theodora 116
Florian 265, 266, 268, 334
Flower Pot, The 97, 101
Follies (Juaraz, Mexico) 329
Follies Bergere 94, 251, 256

Fonzo, the Boy Wonder in Skirts *See* Lester Sweyd
Ford, Harrison 64
Forrest, Chet 97
Frank's Place 97
Frankie and Johnny (1933) 348
Gaff 309
Gaiety Theatre 203
Garbo, Greta 278, 280
Gardner, James 300
Gay xii, xiii, xvii, 27, 33, 37, 38, 39, 40, 41, 63, 86, 87, 88, 96, 97, 98, 99, 100, 101, 103, 105, 111, 114, 115, 116, 119, 121, 136, 139, 140, 144, 145, 146, 195, 196, 197, 200, 202, 203, 211, 212, 215, 225, 234, 250, 252, 255, 271, 290, 300, 316, 320, 321, 334, 340, 341, 344, 345, 346, 349
Gay Rights Movement 320
Gayways Magazine 345
Gender identity 71
Gender Identity Clinic *See* **Johns Hopkins Hospital**
Gender reassignment 292, 294, 298
Gilmore, Gita (female impersonator) 311
Glyn, Elinor 111, 115, 118, 119, 120, 197
Go West, Young Man (1936) 240, 354
Goin' to Town (1935) 210, 240, 354
Gold Diggers of 1933 (1933) 225
Gold Diggers of 1935 (1935) 224, 225
Gold Diggers of 1937 (1936) 224, 225, 356
Gold Diggers of Broadway (1929) 225
Golden Age of Motion Pictures 109
Golden Horseshoe xiii, xiv
Gone With the Wind (1939) 121
Gotham 81
Goulding, Edmund 211, 212, 213
Grant, Cary 104, 139, 140, 189, 191, 206, 213, 214, 240

Great Depression xi, xii, 128, 140, 145
Guglielmi, Rodolfo *See* Valentino, Rudloph
Guinan, Mary Louise Cecilia 127, 128, 288
Guinan, Texas 130
Guy What Takes His Time, A 190
Haines, William 195, 196, 197, 200, 201, 276, 280
Hamilton, George 326
Hamilton, Margaret 248
Hargitay, Mickey 305, 306
Harris, Steve vii
Hays Office 208, 209
Hays Society xii
Hays, Will B. 187, 210
Hayworth, Rita 286
He Done His Duty (1937) 356
Hearn, Edward 198, 200
Hearst, William Randolph 56
Heat's On, The (1943) xi, 263, 354
Hepburn, Katherine 141, 326
Herald Tribune 89, 211
Hip Zip Hooray (1933) 219
Holland Inn 145
Hookers 202
Horizontal Room 136, 137
Howard, Bart 145, 358, 359
Hudson, Rock 302, 303
Hudspeth County, Tx. 3, 4
Hughes, Howard 138
Hurst, William Randolph 111
Hussey, Jim 50
Hussy, The (1922) 125, 355
I Don't Care 47
I Want a Caveman 77
I Want to be Good (1931) 96
I'm No Angel (1933) 206, 262, 354
Imperial Records 359
Innuendos 16, 33, 45, 46, 209
It Ain't No Sin (1934) 188, 208, 210, 354

It's Not History, It's Her Story 302
Ivar Theatre 290
Jazz Singer (1927) 130
Jewel Box Lounge xiv, xv, xvii, xviii, 310, 311, 316, 328, 329, 330, 331, 333, 335, 338, 363
Jewel Box Revue 307, 309, 310, 314, 315, 316
Jimmy's Back Yard 141, 195
Johns Hopkins Hospital 292
Jolson, Al 46
Jory, Victor 260
Junkies xiii
Kansas City xii, xiii, xviii, 310, 316, 317, 328, 329, 330, 331, 332, 338, 339, 345
Kelly, John 101, 103, 104
Kelly, Orry 104
King brothers 260, 262
King Edward VIII 230
King, Frank 260
King, Morrie 260
Kinsey, Alfred 257
Klondike Annie (1936) 240, 354
Kozinsky *See* **King brothers**
Kratka, Irving 300
L.A. Examiner 298
La Boheme 140, 141
La Vie Parisienne 205
Lahr, Bert 73
LaMonte, Lestra 53
Las Vegas, Nevada 277, 297, 303, 304, 305, 310, 350
Lasses Record Co 359
Last of the Red Hot Mamas 270
Latin Quarter 306
Laughlin, Harry 51
Le Baron, William 45
Le Cage Aux Folles (1978) 265
Leach. Archibald *See* **Grant, Carry**
Lee, Eddie 143
Lee, Terry xvi

Lesbian 41, 89, 100, 127, 140
Levine, Nat 199
Liberty Music Shop 358
License to Kill (1989) 326
Lion in Winter (1968) 326
Little Tich 20
Living Daylights (1987) 326
Lloyd, Marie 34
Loew, Marcus 130
Look Magazine 77
Lowe, Edmund 260
Madden, Owney 94, 128
Mafia 101, 127, 140, 193
Male impersonators 20
Manders, Billie 31
Manhattan, NY 25, 128, 241, 252
Mann, Richard F. (pseudonym) *See* Bourbon, Ray
Mansfield, Jayne 305, 307
Manslaughter (1922) 109, 356
Marines Are Coming, The (1934) 200, 201
Martelle, Tommy 134, 143
Mascot Pictures 198, 199
Masked Model, The 64
Masquer's Club 346
Mast, Jane (pseudonym) *See* West, Mae
Max Sennet Studios 199
Mayer, L. B. 196, 197
McCarey, Leo 215
McCarey, Ray 215, 224
McCarthy, Charlie *See* Bergen, Edgar
Melborn, Joey 359
Memphis Blues 209
Menken, Helen 127
Merman, Ethel 309
Metro Goldwyn Mayer 123, 196, 197, 199, 200, 211, 212, 235
Miami, Florida 299, 308, 346
Midler, Bette xv

Midnight Cowboy 343
Midnight Express (1924) 196
Mike Todd Productions 265
Minter, Mary Miles 122
Mission Hills, Kansas 332
Monique Maphrodite 250
Monogram Pictures 261, 357
Motion Picture Producers and Distributors of America 187, 188, 208
Movie Classic Magazine 246
MPPDA *See* Motion Picture Producers and Distributors of America
Mr. Ed, The Talking Horse 307
Music halls v, xi, 19, 20, 21, 30, 31, 34, 35, 40, 137, 213, 227, 229, 253, 277, 321
My Little Chickadee (1940) 246, 248, 354
My Official Wife 62
My Old Flame 209
Myra Breckenridge (1970) 323, 324, 325, 326, 328, 331, 354
Nagel, Conrad 116
Nana (1944) 218
Nazimova, Alla 110, 111, 112, 114, 115, 356
New York Journal-American 292
New York, NY 1, 3, 26, 27, 37, 38, 40, 45, 53, 56, 58, 61, 63, 64, 73, 76, 77, 79, 80, 83, 85, 86, 88, 89, 90, 91, 93, 99, 100, 101, 103, 106, 111, 124, 125, 129, 131, 132, 139, 140, 188, 193, 197, 198, 203, 227, 241, 252, 264, 268, 283, 284, 307, 309, 320, 325, 327, 330, 346, 350, 351, 357, 358
Night After Night (1932) 131, 354
Norman, Karyl 140, 195
Notl, Fred 143
Novak, Paul 348, 349, 350
Novelty 81
O'Neill, Bobby 51

Old Howard 84
Old Mother Hubbard (1893) 21, 103
One Fine Day 35
Only a Shop Girl (1922) 356
Orpheum 81, 130
Orry-Kelly 214
Pallette, Eugene 356
Pangborn, Franklin 200
Pansy Craze 96, 136
Pantage's Theatre 302
Paper Creations 54
Paramount Studios xii, 94, 97, 105, 106, 109, 110, 113, 117, 120, 121, 122, 123, 131, 132, 133, 188, 189, 190, 191, 192, 205, 206, 207, 208, 209, 210, 211, 214, 240, 242, 245, 246, 250, 257, 261, 280, 303, 323, 330, 346, 354
Park Avenue 203
Parsons, Louella 111, 215
Pasternak, Joe 346
Pathe 262
Paul and Joe's 100
Pearce, George C. 115, 116
Peavey, Henry 121
Person to Person 305
Phelps, Charlie 102
Phelps, Lucien 278
Photoplay Magazine 104, 107, 133
Picturegoer Magazine 208, 246
Pimps xiii
Pioneer Trail Master 59
Playboy magazine 324
Pleasure Man (1928) 90, 91, 92, 94, 96, 126, 347, 355
Poli's Palace Theatre 51
Powell, William 356
Price, George 50
Pringle, Aileen 116
Prison (and Bourbon) 340, 342, 344
Prohibition 119, 136
Prospect Theatre 81

Prostitutes xiii, 38, 39, 331
Puckett, Steve vii
Queen of Camp 322
Queen of the Night Clubs (1929) 130
Quigley, Martin 188
Raft, George 94, 127, 130, 131, 133, 326, 346
Rambova, Natacha 110, 112, 114
Randall, Harry 21
Rape 11
Rasputin and the Empress (1932) 235
Ratoff, Gregory 262, 263
Ravenswood 192, 246, 348, 349
Red Skelton Show 307
Renault, Francis 103, 140, 345
Richman, Harry 83
Riddle, Randy vii
Rondezvous 203
Rose, The (1979) xv
Royal Theatre 14, 15, 16, 294
Russell, Jean 143
Sahara Hotel 304
Salome (1893) 113
Salome (1922) 110, 356
Salome, Mr. xvi, 48, 114
Sarne, David 323
Savoy, Bert 26
Schubert Brothers 92, 264
Scott, Malcolm 31, 32, 35, 48
Scott, Randolph 139, 213, 214, 240
Scrub woman 35, 41
Sennet, Max *See* Max Sennet Studios
Sex iii, 84, 86, 88, 89, 98, 125, 127, 188, 246, 318, 319
Sex (1927) 355
Sex-change *See* Gender reassignment
Sextette (1961) 308, 326, 349, 355
Sextette (1978) 326, 328, 349, 354
She Done Him Wrong (1933) 27, 133, 189, 190, 191, 206, 257, 354

She Is More to be Pitied 42
She Never Had Her Ticket Punched Before 20
Shea's Theatre 76
Shields, Jimmie 197
Ship Ahoy, 1909 20
Shubert Brothers 50
Sierra Blanca, Texas 3, 4, 7, 8, 346
Silvers, Sam 143
Simone Simone 260
Simpson, Wallis Warfield 230, 231
Sisters of Charity 335
Sitwell, Edith 281
Sitwell, Osbert 281
Sitwell, Sacheverell 281
Spangles, Charlie 102
Spices 50, 51
Spiritualism 287, 288
Sporting Widow, The (1911) 28
St. Louis, Missouri 252, 255, 268, 322
Starr, Ringo 326
Stonewall Inn 320
Straight xiii, xiv, xix, 13, 27, 28, 38, 39, 56, 63, 81, 87, 91, 99, 102, 107, 109, 123, 136, 139, 143, 211, 212, 213, 271, 299, 305, 310, 341
Street queens xiii
Street walkers xiii, 38, 54
Strippers xiii, 114
Studio of the Dance 14
Sugar Bowl 203
Sullivan, Ed 267
Sunset Boulevard (1950) 286
Swanson, Gloria 116, 117, 286, 356
Sweyd, Lester 103
Szekely, Emerick 292, 293
Tailor, Dorothy *See* di Frasso, Countess Dortothy
Tanguay, Eva 47, 48, 114
Taylor, Estelle 106, 123, 215, 218, 356, 357
Taylor, William Desmond 121

Temple, Shirley 244
Three Weeks (1907) 115
Tiger Love (1922) 356
Time magazine 269
Timony, James 29, 30, 131, 303
Todd, Michael 265
Todd, Mike 264, 267
Torch Club 289
Transgender 292, 316, 323
Transvestites xiii, 86, 136
Traverse, Madlaine 115
Tree, Dolly 93
Troost Avenue xiii, xiv, 331
Troubled Waters 209
True Confessions 188
Tucker, Lorenzo 92
Tucker, Sophie 270, 271
Tussaud, Madame 282
Twentieth Century 5, 323, 324
Twillie, Cuthbert J. (Fields) 248
Ubangi Club 42
Ughakki, Brenda 359
Under the Counter Records (UTC) 96, 278, 300, 360
Universal Studios 194, 246, 354
Valentino, Rudolph 63, 64, 110, 111, 112, 113, 114, 116, 117, 119, 120, 127, 128, 131, 198, 280, 288, 356
Vanishing Legion, The (1931) 200
Variety 26, 28, 49, 76, 129, 140, 143, 146, 192, 289, 306, 318, 343
Vaudeville ii, 13, 14, 15, 16, 19, 20, 25, 26, 27, 35, 38, 40, 41, 43, 47, 48, 50, 53, 54, 55, 60, 61, 63, 65, 67, 68, 70, 71, 73, 76, 77, 79, 80, 83, 84, 94, 96, 103, 128, 129, 130, 133, 135, 136, 187, 189, 190, 207, 246, 249, 252, 253, 257, 270, 273, 287, 303, 338, 341, 351
Vekroff, Perry N. 115
Velez, Lupe 215, 216, 217, 218, 219, 356
Vidal, Gore 323, 324

Vitagraph Film Co 58, 61, 62, 69, 101, 104, 106, 110, 111, 357
Volga Boatman, The (1926) 356
Waddell, Frank 4, 5, 7, 9
Waddell, Hal (adopted nickname) *See* **Bourbon, Ray**
Waddell, Richard (adopted name) *See* Bourbon, Ray
Walker, Jimmy 100
Wallace, Frank 28, 240, 241
Watch on the Rhine (1943) 262
Watts, Professor 14
Way Out West (1966) 322
Wayburn, Ned 189
Webster Hall 99
Welch, Raquel 323
West Quotes
  A thrill a day xi
  Come on up... xi
  Come over and see me 27
  Come up and see me 27, 269
  Good women are no fun. 302
  Goodness had nothing to do with it 132
  I said he was a good man, and I ought to know 247
  I see you're a man with ideals. I guess I better be going while you still got them. 250
  I walk and talk like a queen. Man that's just what I mean. 351
  I'd like to do all day what I do all night. 304
  I'm single, because I was born that way 74
  It's better to be looked over than overlooked 87
  When I am good, I am very good. But, when I am bad, I'm better xi
  You must come over 27
West, Beverly 304
West, Jack 2, 13
West, John 304
West, Matilda 'Tillie' 1, 2, 13, 14, 15, 17, 25, 29, 47, 85, 93, 126, 289, 351
Western Record Company 96, 358, 359
West's birth 1, 350
West's death 350
What Might Have Happened in the Garden of Eden (1937) 242
When I Take My Morning Promenade 34
Where East Is East (1929 356
Wicked Age, The (1927) 89, 125, 355
Wilde, Oscar 113, 334
Wilder, Billy 285
Willy of the Valley 247
Winchell, Walter 289
Wizard of Oz, The (1939) 248
Woman Accused, The (1933) 191
World War I 57
World War II 266
Worst Dressed List *See* **Dick Ellis**
Wright, Bob 97, 330, 346
Young and Beautiful (1934) 200
Youssoupov, Prince Felix 234
Ziegfeld Follies 256, 277
Zukor, Adolph 209

Double Entendre: The Parallel Lives of Mae West and Rae Bourbon

www.ingramcontent.com/pod-product-compliance
Lightning Source LLC
Chambersburg PA
CBHW060105170426
43198CB00010B/775